=Congressional Quarterly, inc.

ENERGY CRISIS
IN AMERICA

CONGRESSIONAL QUARTERLY

1735 K STREET, N. W., WASHINGTON, D. C.

Congressional Quarterly Inc.

Congressional Quarterly Inc., an editorial research service and publishing company, serves clients in the fields of news, education, business and government. It combines specific coverage of Congress, government and politics by Congressional Quarterly with the more general subject range of an affiliated service, Editorial Research Reports.

Congressional Quarterly was founded in 1945 by Nelson and Henrietta Poynter. Its basic periodical publication was and still is the CQ *Weekly Report,* mailed to clients every Saturday. A cumulative index is published quarterly.

The CQ *Almanac,* a compendium of legislation for one session of Congress, is published every spring. *Congress and the Nation* is published every four years as a record of government for one presidential term.

Congressional Quarterly also publishes paperback books on public affairs. These include the twice-yearly *Guide to Current American Government* and such recent titles as *Nixon: The Fourth Year of His Presidency* and *The U.S. Economy.*

CQ Direct Research is a consulting service which performs contract research and maintains a reference library and query desk for the convenience of clients.

Editorial Research Reports covers subjects beyond the specialized scope of Congressional Quarterly. It publishes reference material on foreign affairs, business, education, cultural affairs, national security, science and other topics of news interest. Service to clients includes a 6,000-word report four times a month bound and indexed semi-annually. Editorial Research Reports publishes paperback books in its fields of coverage. Founded in 1923, the service merged with Congressional Quarterly in 1956.

Book Service Editor: Robert A. Diamond

Contributors: Bonita Siverd, John Hamer, Robert A. Barnes, Ralph C. Deans, Richard C. Schroeder, Helen B. Shaffer, Elder Witt.
Cover: Earl Towery. Graphics: Art Director Howard Chapman.
Editorial Assistance: Janice L. Goldstein, Robert E. Healy.
Production Supervisor: Richard C. Young.

Library of Congress Catalog No 72-92522
International Standard Book No. 0-87187-038-X

Copyright 1973 by Congressional Quarterly Inc.
1735 K Street, N.W., Washington, D.C. 20006

U.S. Population Growth and Energy Consumption (1900-1980)

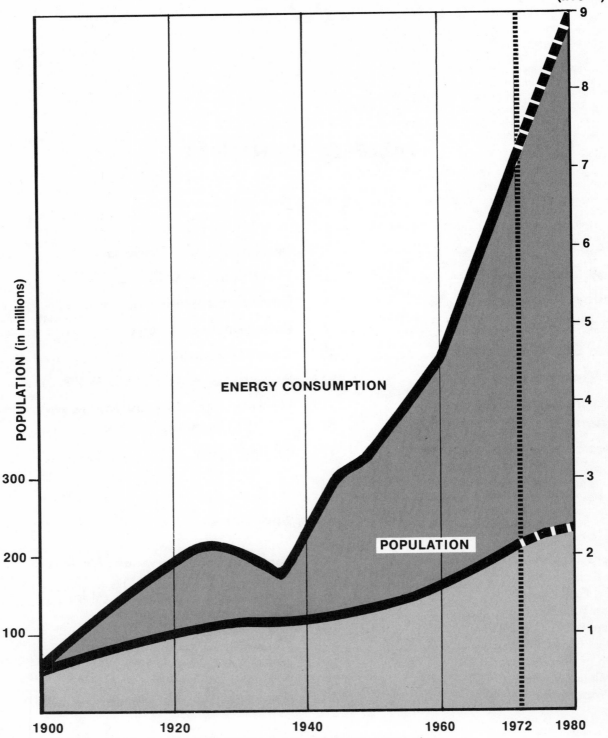

B.T.U.*
(x10¹⁶)

ENERGY CONSUMPTION

POPULATION

* British Thermal Unit: The quantity of heat required to raise the temperature of one pound of water one degree Fahrenheit.

Adapted from Earl Cook, "The Flow of Energy in an Industrial Society," © September 1971 by Scientific American Inc.

INTRODUCTION

American public attention rarely remains sharply focused upon any one domestic issue for very long—even if it involves a continuing problem of crucial importance to society. Instead, a systematic "issue-attention cycle" ...influence(s) public attitudes concerning most key domestic problems. Each of these problems suddenly leaps into prominence, remains there for a short time, and then—though still largely unresolved—gradually fades from the center of public attention. [1]

—Anthony Downs, 1972

Public opinion is currently focusing attention on the "energy crisis," as recollections of fuel shortages during the harsh 1972-73 winter remain fresh in mind, and the grim prospect of brownouts, rising gas and oil prices and possible rationing of gasoline are distinct possibilities in the near future.

A better perspective on the current "crisis" may be obtained by first examining how public opinion evolved during the "environmental crisis," an issue closely linked to the problem of energy. The "issue-attention cycle," according to Downs, has five stages:

(1) The pre-problem stage—an undesirable condition exists but has not yet captured public attention. (2) Alarmed discovery—a dramatic series of events focuses attention on a particular problem and is frequently accompanied by "euphoric enthusiasm" concerning an ability to solve the problem. (3) Realizing the cost of the solution. (4) Decline of intense interest—some people get discouraged, others feel threatened by solution of the problem, and still others become simply bored. (5) Post-problem stage—although the issue has passed into a "twilight realm of lesser attention," it bears a changed relation to that which prevailed in stage one. Now new institutions, private and public bureaucracies, programs and policies are in being and have been set in motion.

Downs conjectured that the environmental issue by 1972 was about "midway through the 'issue-attention cycle.'" An examination of development of that issue would appear to bear him out and offers some clues as to how the "energy crisis" displaced environmental concerns at the center of public attention.

Earth Day

Peak years for public attention on the environment were 1969-70. In December 1969, Congress cleared the National Environmental Policy Act (NEPA), which required federal agencies to issue environment impact statements before taking action or making recommendations having environmental consequences.

In a symbolic gesture, emphasizing the importance of the environment, President Nixon signed NEPA on Jan. 1, 1970, describing his action as the first official act of the new "decade." In February, he sent Congress a major environmental message outlining a 37-point program of legislative and administrative actions. What was needed, he stressed, was "total mobilization" to clean up the environment.

"Earth Day," originally suggested by Sen. Gaylord Nelson (D Wis.), marked the highpoint of harmony on the issue of environmental protection. Celebrated April 22, 1970, Earth Day was observed by millions of Americans engaged in environmental teach-ins, anti-pollution protests and various clean-up projects. Congress adjourned for the day as members addressed rallies throughout the nation.

In July the President sent Congress a Reorganization plan, approved by the House in September and the Senate in October, establishing an independent Environmental Protection Agency. EPA consolidated major anti-pollution programs previously separated among existing government agencies.

In December, Congress cleared the Clean Air Act, the most comprehensive air pollution bill in U.S. history. Nixon described the bill as a "cooperative effort" of both parties, signing it at a White House ceremony attended by newsmen and 40 sponsors of the measure.

Counter-Ecology. In 1971-72, the 92nd Congress continued to churn out a bumper crop of environmental legislation, but there were clear indications that the public was beginning to lose some of its ardor for the environmental issue. Although the President officially proclaimed "Earth Week" in both years, the event turned out each year to be a somewhat more tepid affair than it had been in 1970. *The New York Times* reported in April 1972 that "Earth Week was observed in a low-key atmosphere amid indications of the movement's coming of age."

The President, alert to shifting public opinion, issued his "clean energy" message in June 1971 (*text p. 88*), stressing the importance of developing a fast-breeder-nuclear reactor by 1980. He maintained that it was possible to "balance environmental and energy needs." In September, addressing the Economic Club of Detroit, he said: "We are not going to allow the environmental issue...to destroy the industrial system that made this the great country it is."

By 1972, it was apparent that the ecological honeymoon was over; a counter-ecology movement had set in as the public, spurred by industrial spokesmen, began to assess the costs of cleaning up the environment. Organized labor became disenchanted with ecology when EPA issued estimates that some 50,000 to 125,000 jobs would be lost in plants that could not meet the new anti-pollution standards.

Veto and Impoundment. Throughout 1972 and in his Feb. 15, 1973 message on natural resources (*excerpt p. 91*) the President continued to call for congressional action on environmental proposals from his 1970 message on which Congress had yet to complete action.

But for Democratic critics of his environmental policies, his most significant action was the veto in October of the $24.7 billion water pollution bill. Following the

---

1 "Up and Down with Ecology," *The Public Interest*, Summer 1972, p. 38.

veto override, the administration announced that it would impound $6-billion fiscal 1973-74 funds authorized in the bill. This was a clear indication that the environment was taking a second place to budgetary considerations in the White House's set of priorities. It also suggested that the environmental priority was no longer prominent in the public's mind. As *Forbes* magazine commented in its October 1, 1972 issue, "Energy is about to replace ecology as the pet of Washington politics."

Energy Crisis

Publication of *Energy Crisis in America* reflects Congressional Quarterly's judgment that the energy problem has moved from the pre-problem stage of Downs' cycle to stage two—intense public interest. Indeed, the environmental crisis itself helped focus the public's attention on energy in two important ways:

• First, the continued theme of the environmentalists has been that the earth's resources are finite; that the air we breathe and the water we drink can not be taken for granted. This theme prepared the public for the analogous argument that the earth's energy resources—particularly fossil fuels—could be exhausted.

• Second, the public has increasingly understood that one of the primary costs in solving the environmental problem is to place severe limits on the use of available sources of energy. Blocking construction of the Alaska pipeline may increase the costs of petroleum products in the Pacific Northwest and retard the economic development of Alaska.

(Each chapter of this book originally appeared in the Congressional Quarterly Weekly Report or Editorial Research Reports and retains the original date of publication on the first page.)

Eschatology of Doom. To plot the energy crisis at stage two of Downs' model does not mean that there is any "euphoric enthusiasm" for easy solutions to the problem. Indeed, most of the writing on the subject projects various scenarios of doom. According to some estimates, at currently accelerating rates of consumption, the nation will exhaust domestic supplies of petroleum (which supplies 45 percent of the nation's energy needs) in 10 years—before the more advanced nuclear technology can take up the slack. Hence, so the scenario continues, the United States must import more oil from abroad—primarily from the Middle East where unstable governments headed by Arab sheiks control 75 percent of the world's proven petroleum reserves along the Persian Gulf.

Dependence on these sources of petroleum, it is argued, would place the United States at the mercy of anti-Israeli governments who would "blackmail" Washington into reducing its traditional commitment to the Jewish state. Alternatively, the oil producing states can use their growing dollar revenues to wreak havoc on the international monetary markets, thereby threatening a world monetary crisis whenever it suits their fancy.

Energy Politics. The energy crisis, like the environmental crisis before it, has fueled an upsurge of political activity. In late February and early March, these were major developments:

• On Capitol Hill, Sen. Henry M. Jackson (D Wash.), chairman of the Interior Committee, and a likely candidate for the Democratic presidential nomination in 1976, has renewed hearings on the energy crisis which he describes as "the most critical problem—domestic or international facing the nation today."

• The White House announced in late February President Nixon's appointment of a special assistant on energy policy and has ordered a National Security Council study of the impact of increasing reliance on imported fuel by the United States. It was also announced that the President would deliver a comprehensive message on energy within three to six weeks.

• The White House disclosed that former Treasury Secretary John B. Connally, a Texas Democrat who may soon become a Republican to challenge Vice President Agnew for the Republican nomination in 1976, is on a semi-official world tour to discuss energy problems with world leaders.

Budget Priorities. As crises go, the energy crisis is only modestly represented in federal spending. Outlays for research and development of energy sources have risen from $537-million in fiscal 1972 to an estimated $772-million in fiscal 1974—or about one quarter of one percent of the total federal $288-billion fiscal 1974 budget. During the mid-1960s, when placing a man on the moon was considered a top national priority, the federal government was spending over $5-billion annually on space programs.

'Energy Day'

The environmental crisis has had its "Earth Days" and "Earth Weeks"; but no one has yet to proclaim an energy day. Indeed, it is somewhat difficult to imagine what kind of behavior would be appropriate for the occasion.

But perhaps one version of "energy day" was involuntarily celebrated on the night of Nov. 9, 1965, when 25 million people living in an 80,000-square mile area of the northeastern United States and two provinces of Canada suffered a sudden massive power failure and "blackout." The incident was attributed to a malfunction at an Ontario generating plant and the failure of safety devices to isolate other interlocking power systems.

Somewhat less dramatic but more frequent examples of involuntary energy conservation have occurred in recent years in the form of brownouts and heating fuel shortages.

Planned Conservation. Involuntary conservation of energy—either with a bang, such as during the 1965 blackout, or with a whimper, during a brownout—is one way the energy crisis could solve itself. But more careful planning of consumption of existing fuels, better insulation and reduction in the size of automobiles could invalidate the current exponential projections of U.S. energy consumption and thus buy more time for the development of more advanced techniques of energy production. *(p. 6, 28, 59-61)*

Whichever choice is taken—be it increased reliance on foreign energy sources, accelerated development of advanced technology or conservation of energy sources—one thing is clear: long after the "energy crisis" has entered the "post-problem" stage, the problem of energy will remain.

Robert A. Diamond
Book Service Editor
March, 1973

POWER SUPPLIES: GROWING PROBLEM FOR MILLIONS IN 1970s

For millions of Americans, the energy crisis became real during the winter of 1972-73. After decades of dependence on cheap and plentiful energy, the United States suddenly seemed unable to muster enough fuel to heat its homes and power its factories. Following bitter January temperatures, schools shut down in Denver, idled factories forced thousands of workers off their jobs in Alabama and Louisiana and a major oil supplier announced Jan. 26 that it would ration heating oil in four eastern states.

"We've come to a turning point—we've reached the end of the road on cheap energy," Hank Lippek, a Senate Commerce Committee aide, told Congressional Quarterly. Former Commerce Secretary Peter G. Peterson was more blunt. "Popeye is running out of cheap spinach," he declared Nov. 14.

Demand Up, Reserves Short. With less than 6 percent of the world's population, the United States guzzled one third of the globe's energy production in 1972. And its appetite was growing—energy demand was projected to more than double by the year 2000. But dwindling supplies of fossil fuels—petroleum, natural gas, coal—and distribution problems threatened to curb this exponential growth abruptly.

To many observers, the "energy crisis" was caused by several complex and interacting factors:

• Skyrocketing, apparently unquenchable national demand for all kinds of energy, and lifestyles which squandered it. *(Box, p. 5)*

• Leveling off in output of domestic fuels—particularly oil and gas—and a decline in coal production. For the past five years, the demand for oil and gas outstripped annual production while known reserves dropped.

• Increased environmental consciousness, which forced cutbacks in the use of certain polluting fuels and stymied efforts to construct a number of nuclear power plants.

• Federal policies which held down the price of natural gas and restricted oil imports while scrimping on funding for research on a series of new energy sources.

The mid-winter fuel shortages embodied those factors as well as others. Stringent federal laws limiting the use of high-sulphur coal and oil forced many industries to switch to clean-burning natural gas, which brought about shortages in gas supply. Denied that fuel, many customers moved to low-sulphur oil—heating oil—already in limited supply because the summer 1971 wage-price freeze and subsequent controls locked heating oil prices into their seasonal low prices while gasoline rates were high.

Some reports speculated that efforts to step up production of heating oil at the expense of gasoline refining would result in gasoline shortages—and rationing—by early spring. *(Gasoline prices, p. 9)*

Coming to Grips. The "energy crisis," to many experts, was no more complicated than a recognition that the United States was approaching the end of its supply

White House Study

Confirming the administration's increasing concern over energy problems, President Nixon Feb. 23 appointed Charles J. DiBona, 41, as his special consultant on energy. He will work with a special White House committee investigating the energy situation. *(National Security Council Study p. 7)*

In announcing the appointment, presidential press secretary Ronald L. Ziegler revealed that Nixon would deliver a comprehensive message on the "complex subject" of energy within three to six weeks.

In a message Feb. 15 dealing with primarily environmental questions, Nixon had termed concern for adequate supplies of energy "one of the highest priorities" of his administration. *(p. 91)*

of cheap fossil fuel reserves, with little prospect of new power sources for the next 15 years. After 1985, they argued, technological advances would provide the nation with abundant energy from nuclear power plants. The problem was to heat, cool and move the country in the interim.

"It's a massive problem of management," John Andelin, an aide to Rep. Mike McCormack (D Wash.), told Congressional Quarterly.

The nation which devoured one third of the world's energy resources lacked a single authority to coordinate that massive consumption and plan for future energy use. Federal authority over energy policy was scattered among 64 departments and agencies, and that proliferation led to similar jurisdictional squabbles among competing congressional committees.

"The Senate is prepared to move, to take on significant changes in public policy as they relate to energy," Richard Grundy, executive secretary of a Senate fuel study, said. "But in the House...the committees with serious roles in energy policy—Commerce and Interior—are faced with holdover legislation from last year which may not let them take on any new legislation."

In the White House, President Nixon was preparing a message to Congress on energy policy that was expected to propose sweeping measures to spur exploration and production of domestic fuel reserves and research into new sources of energy. *(Box, this page)*

Fossil Fuels

In 1972, petroleum filled 44 percent of the nation's energy needs, while natural gas supplied 32 percent and coal provided 18 percent, according to an Interior Department study. Nuclear and hydropower together accounted for less than 5 percent of the nation's energy requirements although reliance on nuclear power was expected to increase tenfold by 1985. The first federal study to assume perfection of the technique of producing gas from coal, the report projected heavy consumption of coal through 1985. *(Box p. 5)*

Petroleum—the "Swing" Fuel. Petroleum, the world's key energy resource, supplied the United States with nearly 45 percent of its fuel in 1972—and demand was projected to remain steady through the year 2000. While 200 million Americans jammed streets and highways in their 100 million automobiles in 1972, more than 300 million persons were expected to be driving 300 million cars in 2000.

Under existing national policies, petroleum served as the nation's "swing" fuel, according to the National Petroleum Council, because oil was the only fuel source available in sufficient quantities to fill the gaps between supply and demand of other fuels.

But the United States will be hard pressed to find sufficient domestic oil preserves to slake projected requirements. Of the estimated 2.9 trillion barrels of petroleum liquids in the United States, only 52 billion barrels were identified and recoverable, according to the U.S. Geological Survey—less than a 10 years' supply at existing consumption rates. Most of the oil that was relatively easy to find—clearly indicated, close to the surface, readily produced—was already discovered, leaving oil producers to drill deeper and more costly wells in their search for petroleum. In the last 20 years, exploratory wells drilled decreased 44 percent while over-all drilling activity dropped 63 percent.

In 1971, the United States imported nearly 28 percent of its oil needs, and dependency on foreign imports was projected to jump to anywhere from 50 percent to 65 percent by 1980. Three-quarters of the western world's proven oil reserves lay in the oil-rich but politically unstable nations of the Middle East. Saudi Arabia's proven reserves alone were nearly four times those of the United States. While only 10 percent of the oil imported by the United States in 1971 was imported from the Middle East, those countries were projected to supply more than 61 percent of total imports in 1980 if the United States continued its existing import and exploration policies.

The prospect of such reliance on foreign fuels stirred increasing dissatisfaction among members of Congress and the administration in late 1972. Opponents feared that the United States was opening itself to "political blackmail" as Middle Eastern nations became increasingly self-assertive and sought to raise prices or restrict supply of their countries' oil production.

Equally threatening to the nation's economic growth was the prospect of mushrooming balance-of-payments deficits. Foreign oil purchases—totaling $2.1-billion in 1970—were estimated to jump to $13-billion in 1975 and $31-billion in 1985 under continuation of existing policies.

Conservationists feared that burgeoning shipments of oil by tankers would drastically increase the potential for environmentally disastrous oil spills. Oil shipments over water in 1972 resulted in more than 10,000 spills. Environmentalists were equally opposed to shipment of Alaskan oil overland through the proposed trans-Alaskan pipeline. *(Pipeline controversy p. 16)*

Under existing law, the level of oil imports was restricted on the basis of estimated domestic production and national security interests. Established in March 1959 by President Eisenhower, the quota system was the subject of a year-long study in 1969 by a seven-member Cabinet task force, which recommended replacement of the quota system with a variable, gradually reduced tariff on oil imports. President Nixon rejected the study's recommendations pending full consultations with foreign governments. *(1970 Almanac p. 895, 1969 Almanac p. 951)*

Critics of the quota system argued that it was failing to achieve its goal of ensuring an adequate supply of oil. Responding to this criticism, President Nixon Jan. 8 and again Jan. 17 took steps to relieve the heating and industrial oil shortage. His second announcement suspended quotas through April 30 and set higher limits for imports of crude oil through 1973.

Natural Gas—Regulated and Cheap. More than a third of the nation's total energy requirements were met by natural gas in 1972. Forty-three percent of industry and 150 million Americans relied on gas to power generators or heat and cool their homes.

In the last two decades, the increased demand for gas far outdistanced the growth in consumption of petroleum, coal or nuclear power. Consumption of gas increased by an average rate of 6.6 percent a year—representing nearly two-thirds of the growth in the country's energy production.

But scarce supplies of natural gas threatened to curtail this growth rate abruptly. In 1972, new gas customers could not be taken on in 21 states. Proven and recoverable gas reserves totaled about 290 trillion cubic feet in 1972 —less than 11 years' supply—although estimated total reserves, including those inaccessible under existing technology, were 6,600 trillion cubic feet.

Proven reserves declined because gas production dropped. In 1968, for the first time—and each year since —the United States marketed more gas than it found in new reserves. Total drilling dropped 38 percent since 1959, while exploratory drilling declined by 43 percent.

The accelerating popularity of gas and its accompanying scarcity stemmed from seemingly contradictory economic facts. Although gas was highly prized for its clean-burning qualities, tight regulation by the Federal Power Commission (FPC) held prices down well below those of competing fuels such as coal and oil. Its low price and a zealous marketing campaign ("Gas Heats Best") brought a flock of industrial as well as private customers and, according to the industry, discouraged exploration for new reserves.

Many experts argued that because gas was relatively cheap and clean burning, it was best suited for heating homes, schools and hospitals. Yet factories and power plants consumed more than 70 percent of 1972 gas production, and purchased this power through interruptible contracts at rates lower than those offered to private users. The contracts specified that when gas supplies tightened those customers were the first to be denied, as many were in the unusually cold winter of 1972-73. Many of the large industrial customers, however, were equipped to switch to more readily available oil supplies under those circumstances.

FPC control over natural gas prices stemmed from the Natural Gas Act of 1938, which authorized the commission to regulate the rates charged for the wholesale

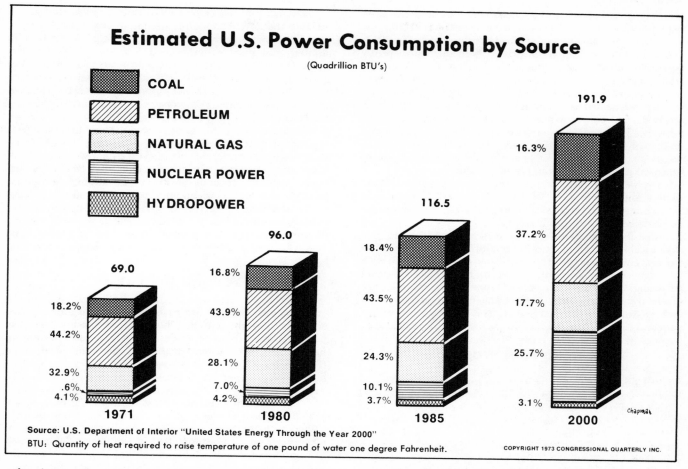

Estimated U.S. Power Consumption by Source

(Quadrillion BTU's)

- COAL
- PETROLEUM
- NATURAL GAS
- NUCLEAR POWER
- HYDROPOWER

1971 — 69.0
18.2%
44.2%
32.9%
.6%
4.1%

1980 — 96.0
16.8%
43.9%
28.1%
7.0%
4.2%

1985 — 116.5
18.4%
43.5%
24.3%
10.1%
3.7%

2000 — 191.9
16.3%
37.2%
17.7%
25.7%
3.1%

Chapman

Source: U.S. Department of Interior "United States Energy Through the Year 2000"

BTU: Quantity of heat required to raise temperature of one pound of water one degree Fahrenheit.

COPYRIGHT 1973 CONGRESSIONAL QUARTERLY INC.

sale of natural gas in interstate commerce. But whether the FPC was empowered to regulate the prices charged for natural gas by independent producers selling to interstate pipeline companies was the subject of an ongoing congressional and legal struggle culminating in 1954. That year, the Supreme Court in the *Phillips Petroleum* case ruled that the 1938 act gave the commission jurisdiction over rates charged to interstate pipelines. Repeated attempts to pass legislation freeing independent natural gas producers from federal regulation failed in the ensuing years. In 1950, President Truman vetoed a bill cleared by Congress exempting independent producers from FPC regulation. In 1956, a partial-exemption bill passed Congress but was vetoed by President Eisenhower—who favored the measure—because a lobbyist for the bill had offered a senator a campaign contribution in connection with its passage. No deregulation measure has cleared Congress since that time. *(Congress and the Nation Vol. I, p. 980, Vol. II, p. 502)*

The price of gas sold in the intrastate market, which was not regulated by the FPC, was nearly double interstate rates. Natural gas sold within the state in which it was drilled sold for about 42 cents per thousand cubic feet, compared with approximately 22 cents per thousand cubic feet of gas sold outside the state in which it was found.

Recent FPC rulings, however, seemed to indicate that the commission planned to allow market forces to drive up the price of natural gas sold on the interstate market.

In August 1972, the FPC approved a new pricing method— "optional pricing"—which permitted producers to negotiate with the commission to sell newly discovered gas to interstate pipelines at rates above the area ceilings previously set by the FPC. The ruling was intended to spur gas exploration and encourage producers to make more gas available to the interstate market.

Many observers argued that the nature of the natural gas market required some federal control to prevent excessive profit-taking. Noting that the six largest gas producers supplied about half the nation's gas demand while exceptionally high costs of equipment and gas tract leasing curbed competition, opponents contended that major gas producers would enjoy windfall profits if the price of natural gas were not regulated.

Supporters of legislation to decontrol natural gas prices argued that such action was the only way to spark increased domestic exploration and that companies operating under long-term contracts would not be free to boost their prices immediately.

Coal—Dirty but Promising. Coal, the nation's most abundant fossil fuel, represented 75 percent of U.S. fossil fuel reserves but supplied only 18 percent of its requirements in 1972. The major drawbacks to expanded mining of and reliance on coal were environmental and technological. When mined, it scarred the land and when burned it polluted the air. Nearly 3.2 trillion tons of coal were estimated to exist, with up to 390 billion tons recoverable

—a supply to last from 300 to 800 years if the technology to extract it and burn it cleanly were developed.

The coal industry was fighting a downswing in 1972. Coal production dropped nearly 5 percent below 1970's record 603 million tons. Since that year nearly 850 underground mines have closed down.

Part of the explanation for the industry's decline was its own scaled-down projections of coal demand which resulted from earlier expectations that nuclear fuel would power an increased number of coal-fired generating plants in the 1970s. Other factors were the strict legal requirements in two pieces of legislation that simultaneously squeezed mine operators and their customers.

In 1969, the first of these measures, the Coal Mine Health and Safety Act (PL 91-173), set safety standards for mining operations which upped costs for operators and lowered worker productivity. *(1969 Almanac p. 735)*

The following year, the Clean Air Act of 1970 (PL 91-604) established air pollution standards which eliminated the market for much of the mine's output. Most coal, with its high sulphur content, failed to meet sulphur oxide emission standards when burned. As a result, the majority of electric power plants east of the Mississippi switched from coal to oil as their boiler fuel. *(1970 Almanac p. 472)*

Curbing Fuel Waste

Cheap and seemingly abundant supplies of fuel have encouraged Americans to use more and care less about energy resources levels of consumption.

The United States wastes one-half of the energy gained from the fuel it burns, according to one estimate. Automobiles, for example, waste more than 80 percent of their energy. The pilot light on a gas stove consumes one third of the fuel used by the appliance.

An October 1972 study by the Office of Emergency Preparedness (OEP) suggested that the United States could reduce energy demand by 1980 by as much as the equivalent of 7.3 million barrels of oil a day—at an estimated annual savings of $10.7-billion. That amount of oil represented nearly two-thirds of the oil imports projected by OEP for 1980.

Conserving energy would pay off in three ways—reducing U.S. dependency on foreign fuels, providing breathing time for development of alternate sources of fuel and limiting certain adverse environmental effects threatened by stepped-up use of energy.

To save more energy would require basic changes in the national lifestyle. The OEP report zeroed in on transportation—which consumed 20 percent of all the energy used in 1968—as one area where significant energy savings might be made. Shifting people and freight from energy-extravagant car and jet transportation to mass transit and rail facilities would effect major reductions in the amount of energy used. Better insulation of homes and buildings, more efficient air conditioning systems and increased use of flourescent instead of incandescent lighting would significantly trim energy consumption on the home front.

If these and other energy conservation measures were implemented, OEP concluded, attainment of the projected rate of petroleum consumption for 1980 could be delayed for as much as 10 years.

Surface mining surpassed underground mining in 1971 as the nation's leading method of coal production for the first time. Industry spokesmen argued that strip mining was more efficient and less costly than underground mining, while environmentalists contended the method destroyed the land and polluted surrounding bodies of water. It was not apparent whether strip coal mining was necessary to ensure an adequate supply of the fuel. *(Strip mining p. 27)*

But a solution to the second environmental problem associated with the use of coal—sulphur dioxide emissions—seemed apparent in late 1972. A federal study of U.S. and Japanese experience concluded that commercially feasible technology to curb sulphur emissions existed. But if the technology were adopted on a large scale, the study cautioned, still another environmental roadblock would be encountered. About 42 million tons of sulphur-containing sludge would be produced each year, raising mammoth waste disposal problems.

Fuel for the Future

Nuclear Power. Shrinking domestic supplies of fossil fuels and the nation's booming demand for electric power produced great pressures in the last decade to harness nuclear power. In 1972, Americans used twice the electrical energy they consumed 19 years earlier; demand was expected to jump five to seven times by the year 2000.

The 29 nuclear plants operating in 1972 produced less that 1 percent of the nation's power—less than was obtained from burning wood. But the 55 plants under construction and firm orders for an additional 76 revealed the industry's hopes that nuclear power as early as 1985 would substantially ease the burden of heating and cooling the nation. *(Map p. 43)*

Although properly operated nuclear power plants produced less air pollution than conventional plants, they presented unique safety and waste disposal problems. Haunting environmentalists and scientists who opposed continued construction of nuclear plants was the fear of an accidental break in the nuclear reactor's cooling system. The reactor would be automatically shut down in such a case, but the heat contained within the reactor, it was theorized, would melt the protective core and release deadly radioactive material up to 75 miles downwind from a plant. *(Nuclear options p. 47)*

Backup cooling systems were mandatory in all nuclear power plants under Atomic Energy Commission (AEC) regulations, but the adequacy of the systems had not been fully tested. Outgoing AEC Chairman James R. Schlesinger told the congressional Joint Committee on Atomic Energy Jan. 23: "The reactors are very safe. That does not mean they are without risk. We do not have a riskless society." *(Chapter on AEC, p. 42)*

Byproducts of nuclear plants presented additional problems. The water used to cool reactors—released into surrounding rivers or streams at temperatures as much as 12 degrees higher than normal—endangered plant and aquatic life. Environmentalists feared that human life as well as wildlife was threatened by the highly toxic radioactive waste products of nuclear plants which must be isolated for 1,000 years or more before being rendered harmless. Existing practices of underground storage required surveillance for centuries to ensure that unwary future generations did not unearth the poisons.

Although a chief attraction of nuclear fuel was its low cost, an increase in the price of the uranium needed to fuel reactors may raise the price of nuclear-generated energy to a prohibitive level. By one estimate, the United States had less than one million tons of ore available at competitive prices—enough to last 10 years.

Fast Breeder Reactor. New technology may beat this race with the clock. Hailed by Nixon in 1971 as "our best hope for meeting the nation's growing demand for economical clean energy," the fast-breeder nuclear reactor over the long term creates as much fissionable material as it uses to generate heat—thereby solving the problems of declining ore reserves and limited enrichment capacity. Completion of the nation's first large-scale breeder plant, to be located at Oak Ridge, Tenn., was set for 1980. *(New energy sources p. 54)*

Administration Initiatives

President Nixon's efforts to hammer out a cohesive national energy policy were expected to culminate with a message on energy. *(Box p.3)*

Previous attempts to consolidate energy authority—fragmented under existing practice among 64 federal departments and agencies—have met with little success. In his 1971 state of the union message, Nixon proposed to reorganize the federal government to create four cabinet departments out of seven existing ones. He suggested that a Department of Natural Resources—responsible for energy and mineral resources as well as land, recreation, water and marine resources—absorb the Interior Department, parts of the Departments of Commerce, Agriculture and Transportation and portions of the Atomic Energy Commission and the Army Corps of Engineers, thereby assimilating many but not all of the federal agencies which influenced energy policy. That proposal was largely ignored by Congress for two years. *(1971 Almanac p. 764, 1972 Almanac p. 374)*

In an effort to sidestep congressional opposition to the Department of Natural Resources, Nixon Jan. 5, 1972, named Agriculture Secretary Earl L. Butz one of three presidential counselors with broad authority over areas of domestic concern. Butz was given responsibility for natural resources—including energy policy—and in effect was handed control over at least the Interior Department's actions in that area.

Another administration effort to formulate energy policy was visible in the cabinet-level task force on energy established in August 1970. Several of its recommendations were highlighted in Nixon's June 1971 message on energy—the first such message by an American president.

Nixon recommended additional federal support for successful demonstration of a fast breeder nuclear reactor by 1980 and increased sales of oil and gas leases on the Outer Continental Shelf. *(Text p. 88)*

President Nixon has ordered an exhaustive National Security Council (NSC) study of the impact of increasing reliance on imported fuel on U.S. foreign policy, according to press reports. A team of administration officials—national security adviser Henry A. Kissinger, domestic policy chief John D. Ehrlichman and Treasury Secretary George P. Shultz—will oversee the investigation. The

---

Aviation Fuel Shortage

Scheduled airlines hope to use the shortage of aviation fuel as a means of convincing the Civil Aeronautics Board (CAB) to permit fewer flights over the same routes. George A. Spater, chairman of American Airlines, called for "the extension of existing capacity control agreements" among airlines in an address Jan. 23 to the Aero Club of Washington.

"Aviation fuel has become a scarce resource," he said. "The shortages of jet fuel that occurred this month are a foretaste of a much more serious long-term problem. On an annual basis, capacity control on the four trans-continental routes and the New York-San Juan route have saved 170 million gallons of fuel."

Flight reductions sufficient to achieve a 55 percent load factor, a stated objective of the CAB, would produce an annual fuel saving of more than 480 million gallons, Spater stated.

---

study will focus on the existing oil import quota system and the national security implications of extensive reliance on the Soviet Union and Middle Eastern nations for oil and natural gas supplies.

The energy message being prepared for Congress was expected to focus on the need to increase domestic fuel supplies and avoid excessive reliance on foreign sources of oil and gas. Among the proposals expected from the administration were:

● The end or modification of the Federal Power Commission's control over natural gas prices.

● Measures to cut dependence on oil and gas imports by accelerating development of domestic reserves. Through increased leasing of oil and gas reserves located on federal lands and the Outer Continental Shelf, the government was expected to make available hundreds of potentially energy-rich tracts, possibly leading to the first oil and gas drilling off the shores of the Atlantic coast.

● Conversion of a large segment of the nation's electric power producing plants to coal-fired from oil-fired generating units—to take advantage of the nation's abundant supply of coal. The President was expected to call for incentives to attract investment to two major but faltering industries—coal mining and railroads—but an administration spokesman in mid-January denied reports that it would request relaxation of federal air quality standards to facilitate a shift to the high-sulphur fuels.

● Stepped-up funding for research and development of new fuel sources, particularly the fast breeder reactor and coal gasification.

● Further consolidation of federal authority over energy policy, perhaps with the appointment of one individual responsible for energy resources.

● Voluntary public and industrial cooperation with energy conservation programs—but no measures to force a reduction in energy consumption which might impede economic growth.

Senate Gearing Up

"The 93rd Congress must do more than worry about electric swizzle sticks," urged a Senate Interior Committee study on energy conservation. Committees concerned with energy policy were gearing up for action on a wide range of measures to develop a national energy policy.

Interior. Speaking in Pittsburgh before the Coal Mining Institute of America, Sen. Henry M. Jackson (D Wash.), Interior Committee chairman, declared Dec. 8: "I am convinced that development of a national energy policy is the most critical problem—domestic or international—facing the nation today."

Two major bills considered but not enacted in 1972 will serve as the keystone of the committee's efforts to formulate such a policy, according to a committee aide. Hearings began Feb. 6 and 7 on a bill (S 268) to assist states in land use planning which considered all land use requirements—including energy production and transmission as well as recreation needs.

"Increased reliance on coal to meet the growing shortage of electric power requires strong and realistic regulations to avoid irreparable environmental damage," Jackson said Jan. 18. Hearings were scheduled to begin late in the spring of 1973 on a bill (S 425) to regulate strip coal mining.

Commerce. Two major energy bills before the Senate Commerce Committee in 1973 would coordinate federal energy policy and boost funding for research and development of new energy sources. A bill (S 70) to establish a three-man energy council to review and coordinate energy consumption and formulate energy-use recommendations was the subject of hearings Feb. 7 and 8."

Testimony on another measure (S 357) to increase funding for research and development of new fuel sources—to be financed by a 1 percent surcharge on energy consumption—was heard by the committee March 1.

Although the committee held jurisdiction over the FPC, a committee staff member indicated that he did not expect early action on a bill to deregulate the price of natural gas. More likely, he said, was consideration of measures to streamline FPC regulatory procedures and confirm the commission's authority to set a single national gas rate by rulemaking.

Public Works. Addressing his colleagues on the Senate floor Jan. 16, Jennings Randolph (D W. Va.), Public Works Committee chairman, emphasized his concern that the United States was embarking on a "gigantic gamble" that adequate supplies of fossil fuels or substitute sources will be available in the future. Among the 26 proposals he outlined as elements of a national energy policy were several to be considered by the committee in 1973.

Chief among those, according to a committee spokesman, was a bill to establish a national deep-water port policy requiring that development of such ports recognize the need for reliance on domestic energy supplies. Hearings on bills (S 180, S 836) requiring state or congressional approval of such ports were held Feb. 26.

Randolph indicated Jan. 16 that the Buildings and Grounds Subcommittee would study proposed guidelines to incorporate energy conservation practices in new construction, including mandatory standards for federal and federally insured homes and buildings.

Joint Committee on Atomic Energy. A new permanent Subcommittee on Energy was established Feb. 8 by the Joint Committee on Atomic Energy. The subcommittee—to be chaired by Jackson—planned a broad-based study of nuclear energy as it related to other energy sources.

And the Study Goes On

After 35 days of hearings on 19 different energy-related topics, the National Fuels and Energy Policy Study in late January had not yet called it quits on its effort to comprehend the nation's energy situation. The most exhaustive congressional investigation of energy policy in recent years, the study group held hearings on a broad range of energy issues—from deep-water ports and supertankers to federal policy on oil and gas leases. *(1972 Almanac p. 374)*

"The problem has grown in magnitude since we took the lid off the can," Richard Grundy, executive secretary of the study, told Congressional Quarterly. Launched in May 1971 under S Res 45, the task force included representatives of the Interior, Commerce, Public Works and Atomic Energy Committees. Its final report—scheduled for September or October—was to lay out the components of a national energy policy, forming the basis for legislation to implement its recommendations.

"But Congress will have to act in several areas before we get the final report out," Grundy said. To that end, the group planned a series of interim reports on such items as government reorganization, federal energy research priorities, natural gas pricing policy and energy conservation.

House Hiatus

Staff members of key House committees concerned with energy policy reported that few hearings on energy-oriented bills had been scheduled, although several were expected to be considered early in the session.

Interior. Rep. James A. Haley (D Fla.), Interior Committee chairman, told Congressional Quarterly that "we must face up to" the nation's energy problems and "thoroughly study" the situation, although no specific plans had been made to continue the energy study group which met in 1972. Haley set as top committee priorities legislation to establish national land use policy and to regulate the surface mining of coal and other minerals.

Interstate and Foreign Commerce. A bill (HR 1258) to establish within the White House a three-man Council on Energy Policy to advise the President and formulate recommendations on long-term energy use likely will be considered early in the session. The Federal Power Commission's authority was expected to be the subject of at least two committee hearings—one concerning the FPC's new "optional pricing" policy for natural gas, and another on several pending measures (HR 2553, HR 2866) to modify FPC control over natural gas prices.

Public Works. Heading the list of legislation to be considered by the committee was a multi-billion highway bill which failed to clear the 92nd Congress—and the question of whether to open up the Highway Trust Fund, reserved exclusively for highway construction under existing law, for construction of mass transit facilities. This would reduce the demand for petroleum products. The committee Feb. 2 formed a new Subcommittee on Energy to continue its 1972 study of energy as it affected the economic development of the country.

SHORTAGES AND HIGHER PRICES PREDICTED FOR FUTURE

Motorists might dispute it, but gasoline, a business which involves six of the country's largest corporations, 220,000 retail outlets, 3.7 cents of every consumer dollar and more than one-fifth of all the energy used in the nation, has been a relatively good buy. According to *Platt's Oilgram*, a McGraw-Hill daily oil price-reporting service, the average cost of regular-grade gasoline in the 55 key U.S. markets surveyed was 37.29 cents a gallon—25.43 cents for the gasoline and 11.86 cents for federal and state taxes—in October. The average pump price in 1961 was 30.76 cents a gallon. In just over 10 years, the cost of gasoline went up 18 percent. In contrast, the Consumer Price Index recorded a 38 percent rise in the over-all cost of living during that time. *(p. 10)*

But gasoline may not be a good buy much longer. From industry officials, trade journals and congressional committees have come dire warnings of higher prices and shortages in the months and years ahead. Some authorities predict that gasoline prices may increase by 50 percent or more in the next few years—making driving a luxury that not all Americans can afford. The reasons for these bleak forecasts include increased consumption, growing dependence on foreign petroleum, and over-burdened refining capacity at home. Refineries transform almost half of every barrel (32½ gallons) of crude oil into gasoline.

After holding hearings Sept. 27-28 on "Inadequacy of Petroleum Supplies," a House Small Business subcommittee reported that domestic producers of crude oil currently provide some 12 million barrels a day whereas demand is running at 16 million barrels. Neither domestic producers nor refiners are able to meet this demand and import restrictions have not been loosened enough to avert shortages, the subcommittee reported.[1] Rep. Neal Smith (D Iowa), the subcommittee chairman, spoke of "numerous reports of supply shortages" already and said these should alert the various agencies of government "to the possibility of critical shortages occurring in the near future." *(Footnote sources, p. 15)*

Oil and gasoline demand in the United States is increasing much faster than the country's current supply. Wilson M. Laird, director of the Committee on Exploration of the American Petroleum Institute told the Utah Petroleum Council in Salt Lake City on Sept. 13, 1972: "As petroleum gets harder to find, costs go up, for we must go deeper into the ground or under the sea or drill in difficult terrain like Alaska. The average cost of drilling an exploratory well in 1960 was $55,000. Today the average cost is almost $100,000." Exploratory drilling in the continental United States during the past 15 years has declined by more than 50 percent despite a doubling of demand for oil.

In addition to crude oil shortages, lack of refining capacity has also contributed to the gasoline scarcity. The National Petroleum Council estimates that by 1985 at

least 50 new refineries must be added to the 250 now operating in order to meet consumer demands for gasoline. But high construction costs and environmental opposition have dissuaded oil companies from planning new plants. Robert H. Multhaup, vice president of planning for the M.W. Kellogg Co., a major refinery contractor, told *Business Week* in August 1972: "If we don't clear up the obstacles to refineries, rising prices will solve our problems. When they go over 60 cents a gallon, there will be more people riding to work in car pools, pushing for mass transit and buying smaller cars."

At the present time, only one new refinery is under construction[2] and none is planned. The lead time, or interval from the decision to build a new refinery until it is in operation, is considered to be a minimum of three years and may be as long as seven years. Recounting these facts, the House subcommittee surmised: "The demand for additional petroleum products,...estimated at 5 percent a year, must be met by increasing imports."

Consumption-Production Gap

On an average day, Americans use four million barrels of imported oil in their cars, homes, offices and factories—about 25 per cent of all that is used in this country. Many authorities believe that oil imports will account for 50 percent or more within a decade. The Department of the Interior said in January 1972, in a report titled *United States Energy:* "Even if it were possible to maintain domestic production near its present rate with the help of Alaska North Slope oil, foreign petroleum may need to be imported into the United States at a rate of eight million barrels a day in 1980." The House Subcommittee on the Near East, in a report to the parent Committee on Foreign Affairs, Sept. 29, 1972, indicated that the consumer-production gap will be even wider by 1980, as shown in the following table.

	1971
Consumption	15.6 million barrels a day
Production	12.0 million barrels a day
	1980
Consumption	24.0 million barrels a day
Production	13.0 million barrels a day

The expected need for more oil will require a change in the Mandatory Oil Import Program which sets limits on how much oil may be imported. It came into being by executive order of President Eisenhower, March 10, 1959, which stated: "The new program is designed to insure a stable healthy industry in the United States capable of exploring for and developing new hemisphere reserves to replace those being depleted. The basis of the new program...is the certified requirements of our national security which make it necessary that we preserve to the greatest extent possible a vigorous, healthy petroleum industry in the United States."

Rising Prices of Imported Oil. Oil import quotas have become the target of increasing criticism in recent years. President Nixon appointed a cabinet-level Task Force on Oil Import Control, headed by the then-Secretary of Labor George P. Shultz, in March 1969. The group's final report, made public Feb. 20, 1970, concluded that the import program was not adequately responsive to "present and future security considerations," and five of the seven members recommended that quotas be phased out. They saw removal of quotas as a way to reduce gasoline prices. *(Later developments p.4)*

Americans pay at least $5 billion in higher prices each year because of the oil import quotas, according to a report issued Nov. 3, 1971, by the staff of the congressional Joint Economic Committee. Limitations on cheaper foreign oil, it is argued, have not only resulted in higher prices for consumers but have not worked particularly well in spurring oil exploration in this country. Since 1970, President Nixon has raised oil import quotas five times because of domestic shortages. He acted in 1972 to authorize refiners to import 25,000 barrels a day from a contingent reserve and an additional 12,500 a day from Canada. Moreover, refiners were permitted to borrow against their 1973 allocation up to 10 percent of their 1972 quotas.

But even if quotas were abolished, Americans might find that fuel oil and gasoline would not become substantially cheaper. Future oil imports will, of necessity, come primarily from the Persian Gulf and North Africa. These areas provided only about 15 percent of this country's petroleum imports in 1971; most of the oil came from other countries in the western hemisphere, primarily Canada and Venezuela. But it is in the Persian Gulf and North Africa where 75 percent of the world's known petroleum reserves lie. While it is claimed that Persian Gulf oil "is 30 times cheaper to produce than Texas or Alaskan oil,"[3] the oil-exporting countries are demanding that they, rather than the foreign oil companies, be the principal beneficiaries of the oil revenues.

In 1960, a number of oil producing nations formed the Organization of Petroleum Exporting Countries (OPEC), a group which now includes Abu Dhabi, Algeria, Indonesia, Iran, Iraq, Kuwait, Libya, Nigeria, Qatar, Saudi Arabia and Venezuela. With the recent oil shortages, the OPEC countries have been able to increase their prices. *U.S. News & World Report* noted that in 1970 the price of Middle Eastern oil delivered to the East Coast averaged $1.30 a barrel less than the price of that produced in the United States, the magazine reported March 27, 1972.

Higher prices are not all the OPEC countries want. As an alternative to nationalization, their minimum terms are a 20 percent share in the ownership of the companies, rising eventually to 51 percent. In March 1972, seven major international oil companies—Standard Oil of New Jersey, Standard Oil of California, Texaco, Mobil, Royal Dutch Shell, British Petroleum and the French Compagnie Francaise des Petroles (CFP)—and five of the six Persian Gulf states[4] reached an agreement "in principle" on these demands. After six months of negotiations over compensation to the companies and the timetable for the transfer to national control, an accord, which is believed to meet almost all of the pro-

Gasoline Prices

Period	Service Station Price (excl. Taxes)	State and Federal Taxes	Service Station Price (incl. taxes)	All Consumer Items (index pts.)
1962	20.36	10.28	30.64	90.6
1963	20.11	10.31	30.42	91.7
1964	19.98	10.37	30.35	92.9
1965	20.70	10.45	31.15	94.5
1966	21.57	10.51	32.08	97.2
1967	22.55	10.61	33.16	100.0
1968	22.93	10.78	33.71	104.2
1969	23.85	10.99	34.84	109.8
1970	24.55	11.14	35.69	116.3
1971	25.20	11.23	36.43	121.3
1972 (est.)	24.46	11.67	36.13	125.3
Increase 1962-1972:	20.1%	13.5%	17.9%	38.3%
1972				
January	25.12¢	11.41¢	36.53¢	123.2
February	25.53	11.52	37.05	123.8
March	23.33	11.46	34.79	124.0
April	23.85	11.49	35.34	124.3
May	22.85	11.56	34.41	124.7
June	23.61	11.60	35.20	125.0
July	24.04	11.78	35.82	125.5
August	23.51	11.78	35.29	125.7
September	26.12	11.83	37.95	126.2
October	25.43	11.86	37.29	126.6
November	25.01	11.85	36.87	126.9
December	25.17	11.85	37.02	127.3
Increase 1972	0.2%	3.7%	1.3%	3.2%

SOURCES: *Platt's Oilgram, U.S. Bureau of Labor Statistics*

ducing countries' demands, was finally reached on Oct. 5. Details of the agreement will not be released until it is formally approved by the Arab governments.

The House Foreign Affairs Subcommittee on the Near East has urged the United States to minimize its future dependence on oil from the Middle East. In its report of Sept. 29, 1972, the subcommittee said: "The oil-exporting countries hold the trump cards...and if they do not spend more of their large and increasing revenues in the next several years on social and economic development, most of them will have enough currency reserves to withstand any loss of income through a cutoff of oil." Similarly, Stewart L. Udall, Secretary of the Interior from 1961 to 1969, warned in the October 1972 issue of *Atlantic:* "I am convinced that reliance on 'cheap imports' is the riskiest course for the United States to follow. In all likelihood, such a policy would produce chronic fuel shortages that would lead to gas rationing and/or strict control of gasoline prices."

However, oil import problems might be lessened under terms of a proposal made by Sheik Ahmed Zaki Yamani, Saudi Arabia's Minister of Oil and Minerals. Speaking before the Middle East Institute in Washington, D.C., on Sept. 30, 1972, the sheik suggested a commercial oil agreement between the United States and his country that would give Saudi Arabian oil a "special place" in America. The agreement he proposed would exempt Saudi Arabian oil from U.S. restrictions and duties and "encourage the increasing investment of Saudi capital in marketing the oil" in the United States. "This would practically guarantee its flow to these markets," he said. The State Department called the informal proposal an "interesting suggestion" and agreed to study it.

Environmental Regulations on Motorists. If the United States is to avoid increasing dependence on foreign oil, it must develop its domestic reserves more fully or reduce its consumption of gasoline. The National Petroleum Council estimates that about 55 percent of the country's oil is still in the ground, primarily under the waters off the Continental Shelf and in Alaska. It is difficult and expensive to uncover and transport this oil. Drilling for undersea and Alaskan oil has been further hindered in recent years by court challenges from environmental groups.

A major oil discovery was made at Prudhoe Bay on the North Slope of Alaska in February 1968, but this oil still awaits transportation to the continental United States. A proposed pipeline extending 789 miles from Prudhoe Bay to the ice-free port of Valdez in southern Alaska has encountered stiff opposition from conservationists who argue that oil spills caused by breaks in the pipeline could permanently damage the Arctic environment. The Department of the Interior on March 20, 1972, released a six-volume study, *Final Environmental Statement on the Proposed Trans Alaska Pipeline,* which concluded that although the pipeline posed a potential threat to the environment, Alaskan oil was necessary for national security—to lessen dependence on foreign oil. *(Later developments p. 16-22)*

The 1972 Annual Report of the Council of Economic Advisors, submitted to President Nixon on Jan. 24, gave another reason for construction of the pipeline. "The development of the...field and transportation of the oil to the West Coast would save the nation $15 billion to $17 billion during the expected 20-year life of the field." The following May 11, Secretary of the Interior Rogers C. B. Morton announced that construction of the Alaska Pipeline was in the national interest. However, no building permit has yet been issued. Legal battles have developed between the seven oil companies that want to build the pipeline and the state of Alaska over royalty payments to the state. Moreover, litigation filed by environmentalist groups is pending in federal appeals court.

Environmentalists also oppose offshore leasing and drilling. Since 1969, there have been three major offshore drilling accidents—the disastrous leak from a well in the Santa Barbara channel in January 1969, the blowout of a well off the Louisiana coast in March 1970 and another blowout south of New Orleans the following December. The Santa Barbara incident was a factor in passage of the National Environmental Act of 1969, which requires federal agencies to assess the environmental impact of their decisions.

Richard J. Gonzalez, a consultant to the American Petroleum Institute, criticized environmental hindrances to the search for oil in testimony before the Joint Economic Committee's Subcommittee on Priorities and Eco-

---

Definition of Terms

Branded gasoline. Well known, or "brand name," gasolines of the major oil companies, such as Texaco, Shell, Mobil.

Unbranded gasoline. Brands of smaller companies like Martin, Hudson, Amerada Hess.

Integrated companies. Gigantic corporations involved in most steps from production and refining to marketing.

Major marketers. Distributors of gasoline for integrated companies.

Independent marketers. Usually small, new or unintegrated retailers who buy gasoline from others.

Jobbers. Wholesalers who buy from refineries and sell to service stations.

---

nomy in Government. Testifying Jan. 12, 1972, he said: "Delays in Alaska, restrictions on the development of oil off the coast of California, delays in offshore leasing by the federal government, and opposition to offshore leasing along the East Coast all serve to limit future supplies and to increase future prices to consumers.... The best chance for limiting future cost and price increases on domestic oil and gas is for several giant fields to be found and developed promptly in new areas."

A more immediate threat of increased gasoline prices is posed by regulations to control automobile pollution. The administrator of the Environmental Protection Agency (EPA), William D. Ruckelshaus, announced Feb. 22, 1972, that the agency was proposing to require large-volume gasoline stations to carry fuel that would be virtually lead-free by July 1, 1974. According to Ruckelshaus, if the proposed regulations are put into effect they would reduce lead emissions by about 66 percent by 1977.

More crude oil is needed to yield a gallon of lead-free fuel than a gallon of leaded gasoline. EPA estimates that unleaded gasoline will cost 1.65 cents a gallon more than the leaded variety. Unleaded fuel is also expected to cut mileage by 3 to 15 percent, further increasing the cost to motorists. Philip E. Robinson, vice president of Lead Industries Association, testified at EPA hearings, in Washington on April 12, 1972, that studies had shown that customers using unleaded gasoline would face a 5.5 to 7 cents a gallon rise in price.

Besides the gasoline regulations on lead additives, emission standards written into the Clean Air Act of 1970 require a 90 percent reduction in major automobile pollutants—hydrocarbons and carbon monoxide—by Jan. 1, 1975. If an automobile maker can demonstrate that it tried but was unable to meet those standards, the company will receive a year's extension. The new anti-pollution engines will burn considerably more gasoline than older models.

Price Factors. The price of gasoline is also affected by the structure of the petroleum industry. According to the *1972 National Petroleum News Factbook Issue,* an annual publication of McGraw-Hill, there are 220,000 gasoline service stations in the United States and they will do more than $30 billion worth of business in 1972. Annon M. Card, a vice president of

Texaco, Inc., told the Senate Subcommittee on Anti-trust and Monopoly on Feb. 8, 1972: "Gasoline today represents 75 to 80 percent of the service station dollar sales volume, and is the major contributor to the gross income and net profits of most retail operations." About 70 per cent of the stations are major marketers *(Definitions p. 11)*. *Business Week* reported in May 1972:

Today, about half of the more than 150,000 or so stations operated by the top oil companies are either owned by the oil companies or leased by the company from another party. All of these stations are then leased or subleased, usually on a yearly basis, to individual dealers to buy and sell the oil company's products at a commission. The rest of the major stations are owned by people who may either operate them or lease them to a dealer...."

The majors, which in the mid-1940s did more than 95 percent of the country's gasoline business have been losing ground to the independents since the early 1960s. In 1963, the independents accounted for 25 percent of the total sales; by 1972 they had captured almost one-third of the country's retail gasoline market. The chief reason is the lower price offered at independent stations—usually two to five cents a gallon less than for name brands.

A number of independents also introduced self-service pumps, further lowering the cost of the gasoline. In the last few years, some of the majors have opened their own outlets—under other names—to sell gasoline a few cents below brandname prices. Phillips established Buy Right and Jackpot, Shell opened Ride, and Humble created Alert stations to attract price-conscious motorists. Major brand dealers have also followed the independents in providing self-service pumps for customers.

Independent dealers purchase their gasoline from jobbers, who may get the gasoline from either independent or major oil company refineries. Major-brand jobbers frequently sell surplus gasoline to independent stations for less than what the branded dealers pay. This policy has angered major marketers who claim that the independents are being given an unfair price advantages at their expense. But with the growing fuel shortage the independents are beginning to suffer. Major refineries are barely able to supply their own branded stations. Independents must pay higher prices for fuel. Paul Castenuay of the Minnesota Independent Retailers' Association (MIRA) told the Senate Banking and Currency Subcommittee on Small Business, Sept. 20, 1972, that independents in his state were buying "black market" gasoline at prices up to eight cents a gallon higher than usual. He predicted that many of them would be forced out of business and that the loss of this competition would enable major dealers to raise prices.

Gasoline shortages, if they continue, may also bring an end to the fierce and widespread gasoline wars that have flared up during the last 15 years. One authority explains that "price wars are for the most part the spectacular outcome of sharp competition in a high-volume industry.... Price wars are started by sellers—little, intermediate or big—who...have one purpose in common. They are trying to reach profit through volume."[5]

Gasoline price wars may be started by majors who lower prices to compete with area independents, or by independents who seek to widen the price differential. Both,

but especially the independents, are hurt by these wars. Major dealers are usually given subsidies by the oil companies whose brands they market. These subsidies cover about 70 percent of the price cut; the dealer pays the rest. Independents generally suffer the entire price-cutting loss. During a long gasoline price war, many do not survive.

It is sometimes assumed that the only winner in a price war is the motorist who often saves 10 cents or more on every gallon of gasoline. However, it is asserted that the consumer is really the victim. Fred C. Allvine and James M. Patterson, in their book *Competition, Ltd.: The Marketing of Gasoline* (1972), contend that when the major oil companies encourage lower prices in a competitive area, they raise the price of gasoline to "artificially high levels" in other areas. Moreover, gasoline prices are generally higher than ever after the war is over.

Petroleum Industry Economics

For fifty years after the first commercially successful oil well was drilled in the United States, in 1859 at Titusville the major refined product of crude oil was kerosene for lighting. In the early 1900s, Richard O'Connor wrote in *The Oil Barons* (1971), "The electric light was beginning to supplant the gas mantle and the kerosene lamp, and the oil industry might have foundered if a new demand for gasoline and lubricants had not suddenly developed." The gasoline-fueled automobile had come on the scene and was beginning to revolutionize the petroleum industry.

Origins Of U.S. Oil Imports

(thousands of barrels daily)

WESTERN HEMISPHERE

Year	Canada	Venezuela	Other
1971	835	1,065	1,210
1970	766	990	1,102
1969	608	875	999
1968	507	886	871
1967	450	937	757
1966	384	1,018	674
1961	193	815	491
1951	1	364	362

EASTERN HEMISPHERE

Year	Middle East	Africa	Other
1971	330	160	250
1970	184	127	250
1969	193	229	262
1968	219	159	198
1967	209	59	125
1966	318	87	92
1961	344	7	67
1951	108	——	9

SOURCE: *1972 National Petroleum News Factbook Issue*

In 1929 the production of crude oil reached one billion barrels, in contrast to 53 million barrels in 1895, and gasoline represented 44 per cent of all petroleum products. A thermal cracking process patented by William M. Burton in 1913 made it possible to extract more and better gasoline from crude oil. By applying intense heat and pressure to the crude oil, the larger petroleum molecules could be broken into smaller molecules of lighter fuels, including gasoline. Other improvements followed. It was discovered that small amounts of tetraethyl lead added to gasoline reduced engine knock and that catalytic cracking was more effective and efficient than thermal cracking. "If no improvements had been made in gasoline refining techniques since 1920, refiners would have to process over three billion barrels of additional crude oil per year to meet our gasoline requirements today. [6]

Changes in Exports and Imports. The United States became the world's leading producer of petroleum in the last century and maintained that leadership until well into the second half of this century. Between the start of commercial oil production in 1859 and 1950, there were only six years—1897 through 1902—in which the American output of crude oil did not exceed that of the rest of the world combined. The United States was also the leading exporter of oil during that time, accounting for as much as 72 percent of the world's petroleum exports in 1924. This figure fell to 48 percent in 1930 and declined further in the late 1940s as foreign production, particularly in the Middle East, rose at a fast rate. By 1948, the United States no longer exported more crude oil and refined products than it imported.

Despite high levels of production, warnings of oil shortages have persisted since the very outset. In 1861, two years after the first successful drilling, there were predictions that the new bonanza would not last much longer. Various authorities in the 1920s warned that the end of the petroleum era in the United States would come in 1926, 1928, 1931 or 1933. And in 1948, James V. Forrestal, the Secretary of Defense, cautioned that "Unless we have access to Middle Eastern oil, American motorcar companies will have to design a four-cylinder motorcar sometime within the next five years." [7]

Fears of domestic shortages and especially the lure of profits led a number of American oil concerns to invest in foreign fields. Until the Depression Thirties, federal policy was to encourage American companies to exploit foreign petroleum deposits and so reduce the drain on domestic resources. The policy was changed by the discovery of extensive new fields in California, Oklahoma and Texas. The Revenue Act of 1932 imposed a tax of 21 cents a barrel on imported foreign crude and fuel oils. The restrictive effects of the import tax on oil were diluted after 1939 when concessions granted under the reciprocal trade agreements program cut the tax in half—at first on only a portion but eventually on all oil imports. Complaints over those concessions were held to a minimum by heavy wartime demands for oil, but strong pressure for import restrictions developed by the end of the war.

The Truman administration, convinced of the need to encourage imports to help foreign countries close the then-prevailing dollar gap, resisted the pressure. But the demand for import limitations intensified after the Korean War and the easing of the dollar shortage abroad. Congress, after long debate, gave the President authority in 1955 to impose controls on oil imports. Despite this grant of power, the Eisenhower administration sought to accomplish a reduction through voluntary means. In July 1957, Eisenhower asked major oil importing companies to make what would amount to a cut of nearly 20 percent in scheduled imports. Although crude imports were cut back, the reduction was offset to some extent by increased imports of petroleum products and residual fuel oil. Finally, on March 10, 1959, Eisenhower issued his executive order imposing compulsory controls on all incoming petroleum in an effort to keep imports down to about 10 percent of domestic consumption.

Integrated Concerns. Large American-owned international oil companies such as Standard Oil of New Jersey, Standard Oil of California, Socony-Vacuum (Mobil), Gulf and Texas (Texaco) [8] were critical of the 1959 import restrictions. Nevertheless, these restrictions were by no means a total liability to the oil giants; quotas helped keep the price of oil and its refined products high. This was particularly important during the period of world oil surpluses in the early 1960s when unrestricted imports would have served to flood the American market with oil and substantially lower the price.

Quotas, which were intended to stimulate domestic oil exploration, did not discourage the large concerns from foreign investment. Dartmouth economist William Barrett, in a study presented at the Joint Economic Committee's hearings in January 1972 on "Oil Prices and Phase II," found that between 1959 and 1969 the U.S. petroleum industry spent almost six times as much in foreign countries as it did at home. While the giant oil companies complained about import restrictions, another factor was threatening their profits far more than quotas. This was the demand by foreign governments for a larger share in the oil revenues. Until 1950, oil companies generally paid the host government a fixed royalty of 20 to 25 cents a barrel. In return, they were exempt from all taxes and given complete freedom in setting production and pricing policy. A sharp rise in oil prices after World War II brought forth demands for new agreements.

Iran nationalized the British-owned Anglo Iranian Oil Company in 1951, an action that persuaded most other international oil companies to grant concessions to the petroleum-producing countries. By 1952 agreements calling for a 50-50 split of profits were common. "The companies' share (of revenues) was almost halved, falling from an average of about $1.52 per barrel in 1948 to about $.87 in 1960. But thanks to the very low costs of production and the great expansion of output, company profits remained very high." Oil company payments to Middle Eastern states were almost three times higher in 1970 than they were in 1960. Yet the companies still managed to reap substantial profits.

These profits are, in large part, due to U.S. tax policies. In a Senate speech on Sept. 21, 1972, Sen. Frank S. Moss (D Utah) said that the income tax rate for most corporations is 48 percent but "the major petroleum companies pay an effective income tax of less than 7 percent." One of the most publicized of the industry's tax advantages is the oil depletion allowance. The allowance permits companies and individuals to deduct 22 percent—reduced from 27.5 percent in 1969—of the gross income from oil and gas production from their taxable income. The petroleum industry has argued over the years that such tax treatment is necessary to encourage exploration and enable producers to offset the depletion of their source of income. Opponents of the oil depletion allowance have argued that exploration has lagged despite the tax provision. President Truman in 1950 called it the most inequitable provision of the tax law.

President Nixon defended the allowance in remarks made May 6, 1972, at the Texas ranch of John B. Connally, who was then Secretary of the Treasury. "All the evidence shows that we are going to have a major energy crisis in this country in the Eighties," Nixon said. "To avoid that energy crisis, we have to provide incentive rather than disincentive for people to go out and explore for oil. That is why you have depletion." *Forbes* magazine, in its issue of Oct. 1, 1972, offered another argument for the depletion allowance: "No one ever describes the depletion allowance as a subsidy that holds down the retail price of a gallon of gas—which in a sense it is. Without that subsidy, gasoline at U.S. pumps might reach the $1 a gallon it costs in Europe."

Separation of Large-Company Functions. A different view was presented by Beverly C. Moore, Jr., a lawyer for Ralph Nader's Corporate Accountability Research Group, at the "Oil Prices and Phase II" hearings. "The oil depletion allowance promotes vertical integration of refining and production, as integrated companies post high prices on the crude oil that they sell to themselves in order to shift their profits to the production level and maximize their depletion benefits," Moore said. "The relatively independent refiners, who have no depletion allowance, see their profit margins squeezed and their options reduced to bankruptcy or vertical merger." *(Energy ownership p. 38)*

The Federal Trade Commission (FTC) has been investigating oil company control over the production, refining, transportation and marketing of gasoline. Allvine and Patterson strongly recommend that integrated oil companies be required to divorce their crude oil operations from their marketing activities. The major oil companies are unanimous in their opposition. Card, the Texaco vice president, said in his congressional testimony that consumers would pay more as a result of the "loss of today's efficient national distribution network." The major further argue that divorcement would discourage them from undertaking the research needed to improve the quality of branded gasoline. This research, they contend, is what makes one brand of gasoline different from another and is responsible for the high quality of their own products. However, the assumption that there is any significant difference in gasolines is being challenged by a number of authorities who insist that gasoline is a fungible commodity.

The report of the Office of Emergency Preparedness in April 1971 suggested that gasoline brands might be more alike than oil companies admit. "When a customer purchases branded gasoline, it is by no means to be concluded that the gasoline he purchases was refined in a refinery of the company owning the brand name. Those companies maintaining or approaching a nationwide marketing effort often must either purchase or exchange products in order to market in some of the areas in which they are active."

Complete divorcement of producing and marketing functions is not likely to occur in the near future. For one

thing, the petroleum industry has immense influence in both the legislative and executive branches of government. For another, large numbers of motorists have grown accustomed to using a particular brand of gasoline and developed some loyalty to it. Until there is conclusive proof that all gasoline is the same, and that it is to the motorist's advantage to have oil companies removed from marketing, the majors will continue to advertise and sell their own brands.

Alternatives to Gasoline Consumption

There is little doubt that current oil shortages will mean a substantial rise in gasoline prices. The extent of these projected rises and their effect on consumers is a subject of growing concern to the auto and oil industries. If motorists are obliged to pay two dollars every time they drive six or seven miles, as some persons predict, automobile use and automobile ownership may again become the rich man's luxury it was in the early 1900s.

Stewart L. Udall is convinced that the public could ultimately benefit from exorbitant gasoline prices. He wrote in the *Atlantic:* "A limit on the automobile population of the United States would be the best of news for our cities.... Less horsepower, smaller cars and fewer autos mean more safety, healthier urban environments, more constraints on suburban sprawl, more efficient use of fuel. Less oil consumption for fuel means more oil to share with our children and theirs, more energy self-sufficiency, more oil for use in basic industrial processes. Less investment in highways means more money for efficient public transportation, more open space, more investment in cheap, fast intercity trains."

However, the American public, wedded to the private automobile is unlikely to share Udall's enthusiasm for mass transit or for future environmental or energy benefits when these advantages mean surrendering the mobility and convenience to which they are now accustomed. If gasoline becomes too scarce or too expensive, they are far more likely to demand other sources to fuel their automobiles.

Modification of Gasoline Engine. When the electric broughams and Stanley Steamers of the early 20th century tooled off into apparent oblivion, they were mourned by few and in time scarcely remembered. The gasoline-fueled internal combustion engine, more powerful than electric and less cumbersome than steam, forced all competitors off the streets and highways. However, concern about pollution and more recently about diminishing gasoline supplies has revived interest in steam and electricity as substitutes for the gasoline engine. Electric cars emit virtually no pollutants and steam cars relatively few. Electric automobiles are powered by batteries and steam cars by kerosene or other petroleum byproducts that require less crude oil. But steam and electric autos present problems that may be insurmountable.

Still another possible replacement for the gasoline engine is the gas turbine. Ford and General Motors are expected soon to install gas turbines on some of their large trucks. Like the steam engine, fuel for the turbine engine—unleaded gasoline, kerosene or diesel fuel can be used—is burned continuously and thus spews out few pollutants. The major problem with these engines is the high cost of the materials needed to form the turbine wheels. At the present time, "alloys which resist the heat are expensive. Such expense is acceptable for planes and large trucks, but prohibitive for mass production of cars."[9]

The auto industry seems far more interested in modifying the internal combustion engine than in converting to steam or electricity or turbines. Detroit has seized upon the Wankel rotary engine, which has been used in a few German and Japanese cars, as its best hope for meeting higher pollution-control standards which will be applied in 1974. The Wankel is a simpler, smaller and lighter piece of machinery than the reciprocating internal combustion engine and would thus be able to accommodate the bulky pollution-control devices soon to be required on all American cars. While the Wankel has been plagued by a number of problems, it has one overriding advantage: "It is the only engine known that can meet future federal emission standards without prohibitive cost or special gasolines."[10]

Gaseous Fuel or Hydrogen as Gasoline Substitute.
Auto makers are understandably more interested in the development of alternative sources of fuel than in the replacement of the internal combustion engine. The idea of gasoline substitutes is by no means a new one. In January 1947, the Senate's Special Committee Investigating Petroleum Resources issued a report pointing out that production of liquid fuels from natural gas, oil shale and coal could provide a means of meeting the threatened petroleum shortage without resort to large-scale imports. The recent interest in gaseous fuels—compressed or liquified natural gas and liquified petroleum gas or propane—is more the result of concern about auto pollution than about gasoline shortages.

There are estimated to be 300,000 motor vehicles using liquid petroleum gas and 2,000 using natural gas in the country. But use of gaseous fuels, especially for private automobiles, is not without problems. A heavy and bulky tank of compressed gas will keep an automobile running for only about 80 miles, compared with 200 to 300 miles for a tankful of gasoline. While fleet operators have been able to open their own refilling stations, there has, until very recently, been no such service for the individual motorist. The dearth of service stations offering natural gas could be easily overcome; a far more serious problem is a developing shortage of natural gas. If this shortage continues, as is anticipated, motorists may see little benefit in conversion.

Projected shortages of oil, gasoline and natural gas have spurred efforts to find an inexpensive, abundant and nonpolluting automobile fuel. One contender which

seems almost too good to be true is hydrogen. Hydrogen is available in immense quantities in every body of water in the world—water is two party hydrogen and one part oxygen. When hydrogen is ignited, it reverts to water, without discharging air-fouling pollutants, and can be used again. The major problem with hydrogen is how to remove it cheaply and easily for use in automobiles.

Most hydrogen now comes from natural gas, but approaching shortages make natural gas an impractical source. The simplest way to produce hydrogen is by electrolysis—passing an electric current through water—but this process is prohibitively expensive. "As an interim measure, reasonably inexpensive hydrogen for auto fuel and other direct applications might be made from coal, which is far more abundant than natural gas. But ultimately, it will be necessary either to reduce electrolysis costs sharply or to devise an economical way to 'crack' water thermally."[11] Some researchers working with hydrogen feel that if enough money and expertise is put into effort, a way could be found to make hydrogen competitive with gasoline as an automobile fuel in about 10 years.

Few observers, however, seem to feel that there will be a major alternative to gasoline for at least several decades. But if shortages continue and prices skyrocket, and the American public remains dependent on the automobile, the alternatives will be examined much more closely in the next few years. The fact that new and different methods of automotive fuel are being given an increasing amount of publicity in the popular press could indicate that change is much closer than generally expected.

[1] A report of the Subcommittee on Special Small Business Problems to the House Select Committee on Small Business, Oct. 18, 1972.

[2] A new Mobil Oil Corporation refinery being built at Joiet, Ill., is expected to become operational late in 1972 or early in 1973. At full capacity, it will be able to process 164,000 barrels a day.

[3] Fred Halliday, "The Americanization of the Persian Gulf," Ramparts, October 1972, p. 20

[4] They are Abu Dhabi, Iraq, Kuwait, Qatar and Saudi Arabia. Iran is working out a separate deal with the oil companies.

[5] Harold M. Fleming, Gasoline Prices and Competition (1966), pp. 67-68.

[6] American Petroleum Institute, Facts About Oil (1971), pp. 4-5, 25.

[7] The Forrestal Diaries (1951), p. 357.

[8] These five companies, according to the Office of Emergency Preparedness in its Report on Crude Oil and Gasoline Price Increases of November 1970, "produced over half of the production and almost half of the refinery runs in the Free World outside of the United States."

[9] "Radical New Engines for Cars," U.S. News & World Report, May 1, 1972, p. 46.

[10] Charles G. Burck, "A Car That May Reshape the Industry's Future," Fortune, July 1972, pp. 74-75.

[11] When Hydrogen Becomes the World's Chief Fuel," Business Week, Sept. 23, 1972, p. 101.

ALASKAN OIL: POWERFUL INTERESTS IN PIPELINE BATTLE

Two powerful coalitions of organized interests are grappling over an issue affecting the last great wilderness in the United States—Alaska. One of the richest oil strikes in American history touched off the controversy.

The battle lines are smudged but with exceptions shape up something like this: On one side are important elements of the oil industry and their allies in government and industry; on the other are environmental groups and their allies. *(1973 developments, p. 22)*

The division is complicated by costly company efforts to solve environmental objections, spurred by the virtual certainty of unprecedented government controls resulting from ceaseless prodding by environmental pressure groups.

Despite overlappings that obscure the line between the forces—such as financing of some environmentalists by their nominal opponents—a basic gap exists in this as in many other environmental disputes: Between those who give higher priority, on one side, to an energy crisis and, on the other, to an ecology crisis.

Both sides say their stance serves the public interest. Both possess strong political connections. Figures in both broad factions express hopes of reconciling differences, in spite of strong words exchanged in the recent past. Though working arrangements may emerge, political, economic and philosophical differences going beyond environmental topics render complete accord unlikely.

Immediately at stake is what industry sources say is the costliest private construction project ever—a proposed 48-inch pipeline to haul oil 789 miles south across Alaska. Estimated construction costs have swollen to well above $2-billion in three years of struggle.

Proponents say the oil is badly needed by the nation and cite benefits from development of Alaska's natural resources. They say the benefits far outweigh ecological risks which they pledge will be held to a minimum under close government supervision.

Opponents express unresolved fears of damage to the environment from construction of a pipeline carrying 170-degree oil across tundra and permafrost. They cite the possibility of pipeline breaks from earth settling or tremors, speak of potential oil spills from supertankers and have challenged in the past whether native rights were adequately protected. They also question whether alternatives have been sufficiently considered.

Broader Issues

Some liken the situation to that prevailing in the early American West. Upon resolution of the pipeline dispute hinge at least in part broad questions of public policy. Some of these pertain to:

• Development of huge new oil resources on Alaska's icelocked North Slope at a time when the United States is relying increasingly on foreign oil, particularly from the turbulent Middle East during the next decade. Officials warn that U.S. national security is jeopardized by over-dependence on foreign sources.

• The opening to development or widespread use for business or recreation of the largely virgin lands of Alaska, one-fifth the area of the other 49 states put together and more than twice as big as Texas. Alaskan state officials make it plain they look to mineral income to develop and operate the nation's 49th state.

• A test of the growing activism among lawyer groups that have sprung into existence to convert lobbying into a sophisticated triple threat operating in the judicial, executive and legislative arenas at federal, state and local levels.

This has carried over into a general election year which finds national and international environmentalists with strong support from tax-exempt foundations bucking heavily financed oil, shipping and financial interests. The dispute is inextricably bound up in politics.

David R. Brower, former Sierra Club executive whose three-year-old organization, Friends of the Earth, has been a prime foe of the pipeline to date, indicates he is ready to postpone Alaskan oil development for at least several years longer. "We must cut down on the use of fossil fuels," Brower said in January 1972. "We need a cooling of this drive for more energy."

A tax-exempt companion group formed by Brower when he founded the politically oriented Friends of the Earth is called the John Muir Institute for Environmental Studies. It was made possible by an $80,000 gift from Robert O. Anderson, chairman of Atlantic Richfield, one of the main oil companies seeking to develop Alaskan oil.

E. L. Patton, president of Alyeska Pipeline Service Company, the consortium proposing to build the pipeline, termed some charges by Brower and other environmentalists "balderdash" and another—that the Alaskan oil was destined for Japan—"plain foolishness" when Patton and Brower spoke on the same platform before the Pipe Line Contractors Association.

The Sierra Club, veteran of wilderness fights from the Redwoods to the Everglades and now shifted onto an international footing, says the story of Alaska "and of the pressures to extract the black gold that lies beneath it reflects nothing less than a test case of what the struggle to save this planet is all about."

Dispute Over New Law. In the middle of the Alaska oil controversy is the National Environmental Policy Act of 1969 (42 U.S.C. 4321). Largely the outgrowth of legislation proposed by Rep. John D. Dingell (D Mich.) and by Senators Henry M. Jackson (D Wash.) and Edmund S. Muskie (D Maine), both candidates for the 1972 Democratic nomination for President, it was virtually unopposed when enacted by Congress late in 1969 and was promptly signed by President Nixon—symbolically, as his first official act of the 1970s.

The law declares as national policy the safeguarding of the environment and requires that environmental impact must figure in government decision making. The law has been a primary tool of opponents to the Alaska pipeline as originally conceived.

As the formerly non-controversial law becomes more and more the legal basis for bitter environmental struggles over large stakes, attorneys on both sides say the legislation may have been a sleeper subject to court interpretation as granting powers which few members of Congress realized when they voted for it. One writer on environmental law likened the act's use in the Alaska pipeline case to the role once reserved for the Colt revolver: "the great equalizer."

Court rulings in the Alaska pipeline or others of the approximately 160 cases pending under the law may ultimately determine the extent to which the 1969 law established, as some suggest, a new judicial veto power over the executive branch based on an open-ended definition of environment.

"Life under the National Environmental Policy Act has approached chaos," the *Oil & Gas Journal* said editorially in 1972. Noting the proliferation of court suits filed under the act and resultant delays in major decisions from executive departments and agencies, the publication for the domestic oil industry said:

"Under this hopeless confusion, the environment is running the government."

Alaska Pipeline

An Atlantic Richfield Company well struck oil commercially on Alaska's North Slope in the summer of 1968. The major obstacle to large-scale development of the field was the difficulty of transporting the oil at economical cost from the frozen north to markets far to the south.

In October 1968, eight companies based in the United States, Canada and Great Britain set up the Trans-Alaska Pipeline System (TAPS) as a joint enterprise. The major participants, directly or through subsidiaries, were Atlantic Richfield, Humble Oil & Refining Company and British Petroleum. Humble is a subsidiary of Standard Oil Company (New Jersey), world's largest oil company.

The state of Alaska, which included 2 million acres of North Slope land in its selections for state ownership in compliance with the Alaska Statehood Act of 1959, auctioned leases Sept. 11, 1969, netting $900-million from oil companies.

By January 1972, about 15 billion barrels of proven reserves had been located on the Beaufort Sea, site of the Atlantic discovery. Of these, Atlantic Richfield's proven reserves were about 1.9 billion barrels. Some estimates are that Alaskan oil reserves may exceed 100 billion barrels, far beyond known U.S. reserves.

The oil companies applied for permits to build an access road and a four-foot pipeline to Valdez in south Alaska. Tankers would carry the oil from that point.

Opposition to the proposed pipeline soon crystalized. Opponents attacked on several fronts in the courts, Congress and administrative agencies. They opposed the building of a road—first step toward actual pipeline construction and toward opening up the Alaska interior—and pressed Alaskan native land ownership claims.

Various groups said the heated oil could melt the terrain along the pipeline, causing changes in a delicately balanced environment lacking the capability of regenerating itself because of climate. They said caribou migrations might be interfered with by fear of crossing the pipe where it was above ground. Ecologists have cited dangers of pollution from oil spills in Alaskan waters and in Washington's Puget Sound to which oil would be hauled. Some have challenged the need for the oil and suggested Japan would become the major recipient.

In a move which has held up the pipeline until at least 1972, three plaintiffs on April 13, 1970, won a preliminary injunction from U.S. District Court Judge George A. Hart Jr. in Washington, D.C.

The judge barred the secretary of the interior, who was then former Alaska Gov. Walter J. Hickel, from issuing a pipeline construction permit. Plaintiffs obtained the order on grounds that the Interior Department had not complied with the National Environmental Policy Act of 1969 by filing a detailed statement on environmental impact of the pipeline proposal and of possible alternatives.

The injunction obtained by the Wilderness Society, Friends of the Earth and the Environmental Defense Fund Inc. of New York continues in effect until Hickel's successor, Secretary of Interior Rogers C. B. Morton, publishes a final environmental impact statement. The statement has been postponed several times. *(1973 developments, p. 21, 22)*

Alyeska Formation. Trans-Alaska Pipeline System was succeeded by the Alyeska Pipeline Service Company, the formation of which was announced Aug. 28, 1970, at Houston, where Humble Oil has its home office. The group was set up to build and operate the pipeline, with original owners retaining their interests. It was headed by Edward L. Patton, former manager of a new oil refinery complex opened by Humble near San Francisco Bay.

It was Humble that conducted a multi-million-dollar exploration of possible tanker routes from the Arctic in 1969, during which the icebreaker *S.S. Manhattan* became the first commercial ship to make a round trip through the Northwest Passage. Humble also has studied the feasibility of building a new pipeline across the United States from Puget Sound to the East Coast.

Alyeska has sought in various ways to. counter the claims of its foes. For example, it published a full-page advertisement in *The New York Times* Jan. 19, 1971, giving assurances concerning the pipeline and the environment. "Geology and engineering are our areas of basic competence," the ad said. After discussing some of the questions involved, Alyeska said:

"On this you have our pledge: The environmental disturbances will be avoided where possible, held to a minimum where unavoidable and restored to the fullest practicable extent. And we can assure you that the pipeline will be the most carefully engineered and constructed crude oil pipeline in the world."

Pipeline Interests

Major proponents of an Alaska pipeline and the opening of the Alaskan frontier to development include:

- Oil and gas interests.
- The state of Alaska, admitted to the Union in 1959.

• Shipping, and lumber and other natural resources interests.

In addition to business and financial interests, there also are those motivated by considerations of national security and the desire to develop domestic oil as insurance against excessive reliance on foreign oil. Without referring to Alaskan oil, Adm. Elmo R. Zumwalt, chief of naval operations, told the Senate Armed Services Committee Feb. 22, 1972, that "the potential for coercion of the U.S." when the United States imports about half its petroleum perhaps by 1985 "is ominous when one considers the measures the Soviets are taking to improve their navy."

Oil Companies. The original oil consortium that formed Trans-Alaska Pipeline System consisted of:

Amerada Hess Corporation; Atlantic Pipe Line Company, a subsidiary of Atlantic Richfield Company; B. P. Pipe Line Company, a subsidiary of B. P. Alaska Inc.; Home Pipe Line Company, a subsidiary of Home Oil Company of Canada which later sold its interest; Humble Pipe Line Company, a subsidiary of Humble Oil & Refining Company, which in turn is a subsidiary of Standard Oil Company (New Jersey); Mobil Pipe Line Company, a subsidiary of Mobil Oil Company; Phillips Petroleum Company, and Union Oil Company of California.

Corporate officials, with some of the directorships or other positions they have held—within the period 1970-72 unless specified—included:

• Amerada Hess Corporation.

Chairman and chief executive officer: H. W. McCollum, director, American Petroleum Institute (API).

Chairman, executive committee: Leon Hess.

President: A. T. Jacobson, director, API.

• Atlantic Richfield Company.

Chairman and chief executive officer: Robert O. Anderson, director, Chase Manhattan Bank; director, Chase Manhattan Corporation, a one-bank holding company; director, Pan American World Airways Inc.; director, Columbia Broadcasting System Inc.; director, Smith Kline & French Laboratories; chairman, Diamond A Cattle Company; director, API; chairman, Aspen Institute for Humanistic Studies; director, Resources for the Future; vice chairman, John F. Kennedy Center for the Performing Arts; member, finance committee, Nixon for President, 1967-68; Republican national committeeman, New Mexico, 1968—.

Vice chairman: Rollin Eckis, director, API.

President: Thornton F. Bradshaw, director, Atlas Chemical Industries Inc.; director, National Industrial Conference Board; director, Foreign Policy Association; director, API.

Directors include:

Courtlandt S. Gross, president, 1956-61, and chairman of board, 1961-67, Lockheed Aircraft Corporation, now chairman of Lockheed finance committee and director; director, Smith Kline & French Laboratories; director, Girard Company.

Robert S. Ingersoll, chairman and director, Borg-Warner Corporation; trustee, Aspen Institute for Humanistic Studies; confirmed Feb. 25, 1972, as U.S. Ambassador to Japan.

Ellmore C. Patterson, chairman and chief executive officer, Morgan Guaranty Trust Company of New York; chairman and chief executive officer, J. P. Morgan & Company Inc., a holding company; director, Atchison, Topeka & Santa Fe (AT&SF) Railway; trustee, Carnegie Endowment for International Peace; trustee, Alfred P. Sloan Foundation.

Kendrick R. Wilson Jr., chairman of board, Avco Corporation, a conglomerate.

• Humble Oil & Refining Company, subsidiary of Standard Oil Company (New Jersey).

Chairman and chief executive officer: M. A. Wright, various posts with Standard Oil (New Jersey) culminating in executive vice president, 1960-66, when he took the top post with Humble; president, 1966-67, and chairman of board, 1967-68, U.S. Chamber of Commerce; director, National Wildlife Federation.

Vice chairman: Charles F. Jones, director, National Science Foundation.

President: T. D. Barrow

• Standard Oil Company (New Jersey)

Chairman of board, chairman of executive committee and chief executive officer: John K. Jamieson. Canadian-born, moved to United States in 1958, naturalized in 1964; executive vice president and director, Humble Oil & Refining Company, 1962-63; president, Humble, 1963-64; executive vice president, Standard Oil (New Jersey), 1964-65; president, Standard Oil (New Jersey), 1965-69; chairman, 1969—; director, Chase Manhattan Bank; director, Chase Manhattan Corporation.

President: Milo M. Brisco, director, First National City Bank, New York City; director, First National City Corporation; member, New York Urban Coalition, 1967—.

Directors include:

Bert S. Cross, chairman of finance committee and director, Minnesota Mining & Manufacturing Company; chairman, National Industrial Pollution Control Council.

W. H. Franklin, president and director, Caterpillar Tractor Company.

T. Vincent Learson, chairman and chief executive officer, International Business Machines Corporation (IBM); director, Carborundum Company.

Donald S. MacNaughton, chairman and chief executive officer, Prudential Insurance Company of America; on policy council, Common Cause.

• Mobil Oil Corporation.

Chairman and chief executive officer: Rawleigh Warner Jr., director, API; director, Time Inc.; director, Caterpillar Tractor Company; director, Bedford Stuyvesant Development & Service Corporation.

Directors include:

Grayson L. Kirk, president emeritus, Columbia University; finance committee and director, IBM Corporation; director, Council on Foreign Relations.

Lewis A. Lapham, vice chairman and director, Bankers Trust Company; president and director, Bankers Trust New York Corporation; director, H. J. Heinz Company; director, Tri-Continental Corporation; president of Grace Lines Inc., 1953-59.

George C. McGhee, various ambassadorial posts with State Department plus assistant secretary for Near Eastern, South Asian and African affairs, 1949-51; chairman, policy planning council and counselor, State Department, 1961; under secretary of state for political affairs, 1961-63; special assistant to chairman of Urban Coalition, 1969-70; director, Aspen Institute for Humanistic Studies.

Albert L. Williams, chairman of finance committee, member of executive committee and director, IBM Corp.; director, First National City Bank; director, General Foods Corporation; director, Eli Lilly & Company; director, GM Corporation; trustee, Alfred P. Sloan Foundation.

• Phillips Petroleum Company.

Chairman of board and chief executive officer: W. W. Keeler, head of at least 10 Phillips enterprises in various countries; special consultant to secretary of interior, 1961; chairman, National Petroleum Council, advisory group to Interior Department, 1971.

Chairman, executive committee: William C. Douce.

Deputy chairman: John M. Houchin, vice president, American Independent Oil Company; director, API.

President: William F. Martin, director, American Independent Oil Company.

Directors include:

Clark M. Clifford, secretary of defense, 1968-69, whose firm Clifford, Warnke, Glass, McIlwain & Finney registered in 1970 to lobby for Avco Corporation "in support of adequate appropriations for mineral resources research."

A. F. Mayne, president and director, A. F. Mayne & Associates Ltd., Montreal; director, Kennecott Copper Corporation.

William Piel Jr., partner, Sullivan & Cromwell, New York City.

William I. Spencer, president and director, First National City Bank; president and director, First National City Corporation; director, United Aircraft Corporation; president and director, First National City Foundation; director, Sears, Roebuck & Company; director, Bedford Stuyvesant Development and Service Corporation.

W. Clarke Wescoe, executive vice president (for medical affairs) and director, Sterling Drug Inc.; president and chief executive officer, Winthrop Laboratories, a division of Sterling Drug Inc.; director, Hallmark Cards Inc.

● Union Oil Company of California.

President and chief executive officer: Fred L. Hartley, director, North American Rockwell Corporation; chairman, Union Oil Company of Canada Ltd.; vice president and director, California State Chamber of Commerce; director, DiGiorgio Corporation.

Directors include:

Robert DiGiorgio, chairman and chief executive officer, DiGiorgio Corporation, San Francisco, dealing in lumber, food, wholesale groceries, drugs, recreational vehicles, etc.; director, Bankamerica Corporation; member of executive committee, Bank of America N.T. & S.A.; director, Foremost-McKesson Inc.; director, AT&SF Railway.

Prentis C. Hale, chairman, Broadway-Hale Stores Inc.; director, Bank of America N.T. & S.A.; director, Foremost-McKesson Inc.; director, AT&SF Railway.

R. O. Hunt, director, Crown Zellerbach Corporation (formerly its chairman and chief executive officer).

Henry T. Mudd, chairman and chief executive officer, Cyprus Mines Corporation; vice chairman, Marcona Corporation; director, United California Bank; director, Southern Pacific Company; chairman, Pima Mining Company; director, North American Rockwell Corporation.

Charles B. Thornton, chairman and chief executive officer, Litton Industries Inc.; director, MCA Inc.; director, United California Bank; member of executive committee and director, Cyprus Mines Corporation; member of finance committee and director, Trans World Airlines Inc.

State of Alaska. State officials have pushed for approval of the pipeline project. Four days after Earth Day 1970, which focused national attention on environmental issues, more than 100 Alaskan businessmen accompanied Gov. Keith Miller to Washington to lobby for prompt approval of the pipeline and road permits.

Eric E. Wohlforth, revenue commissioner for the state, said in a speech Feb. 4, 1972, that the state's pipeline position stems partly from the view "that Alaska's economic future is deeply wedded to the public conveyance of petroleum throughout the state....

"Any final assessment of the economic potential of the state must start with a realization of one basic fact. To an extent greater than any other state, Alaska owns its sub-surface resources. With development of those resources we can and will share in the monetary gain which their ultimate sale will represent. Thus, unlike other oil and gas states, our state revenues need not be derived only from taxation of the resources but also from the participation in their development."

Wohlforth said passage of the native claims legislation in 1971 was "a giant step" toward developing Alaska's resources, adding:

"The battles which will be faced over the issue of 'lock up Alaska forever' as proposed by some environmentalists versus the state's desire for 'sound development' are similar to those which Alaskans faced during the natural disaster of the earthquake of 1964 and the Fairbanks flood of 1967."

Maritime. Secretary of Commerce Maurice H. Stans, just before resigning in mid-February 1972 to head President Nixon's election campaign funds drive as he had in 1968, addressed a dinner sponsored by the National Maritime Council.

Stans, who was budget director when Alaska became a state, said the proposed Alaska pipeline "offers perhaps the greatest single opportunity for new cargoes and new jobs that the American fleet has ever had."

"A fleet of some 30 new supertankers would be needed to carry North Slope oil from southern Alaska to the West Coast, and constructing them would pump an estimated $1-billion through the shipbuilding industry into the economy," Stans said.

He said the environmental dangers were recognized, but that "when the minimized risks are weighed against the great need for the pipeline and its potential benefits, I am certain that it must be built."

Pipeline Opponents

Opposition to the Alaska pipeline draws recruits from pre-pipeline battles over the Alaska wilderness. Many participants are active to varying degrees on environmental fronts elsewhere, involving such issues as offshore oil drilling, the supersonic transport, auto exhaust fumes, tanker or refinery pollution, power plants and thermal pollution, nuclear testing, waste disposal, auto safety and consumer affairs.

Groups gravitating around environment as their focus include those operating largely as pressure and public opinion organizations and lawyer task force groups. Supporting these are foundations, some former government officials and miscellaneous elements from among student, antiwar, civil rights and consumer activists. Other allies have included members of Congress and federal officials, as well as Alaskan native factions. Ties are sometimes tenuous but real.

Among groups whose activities have tended to hold up the pipeline development on one basis or another, with some of the participants' associations, are:

Sierra Club. Long a pressure group in the environmental field, the club underwent a change in management and expanded its membership in the 1970s. Executive Director Michael McCloskey said the group's membership doubled in 2½ years to 140,000 at the start of 1972.

"Our size gives us a powerful voice in the halls of Congress and in dealing with government agencies across the country," McCloskey wrote in the club's *Bulletin*. "Our chance of prevailing is proportional to the strength we can amass."

The club in 1971 fought the supersonic transport, the Amchitka nuclear test, timber cutting in national forests and what it contended was lack of adequate environmental protection in the Alaska Native Claims Act.

The Sierra Club engages in grassroots pressure campaigns which have relied heavily on book publication. Book editor John G. Mitchell has said several books "had a profound influence on the outcome of crucial issues." One, called *Oil on Ice*, dealt with the Alaska oil situation and was sent to members of Congress as the club's first "Battlebook."

President Raymond Sherwin says growing numbers of legislators have become sensitive to environmental problems through club efforts but adds: "However, to be effective we must be in their offices and committee rooms when crucial decisions are being made."

The Sierra Club Foundation supports the non-legislative activities of the Sierra Club, including legal action conducted by the Sierra Club Legal Defense Fund which had about 60 court suits in progress in mid-1971.

Two of the Sierra Club's attorneys are James Watt Moorman, director of the Sierra Club Legal Defense Fund, and David Sive. Moorman is secretary of the Center for Law and Social Policy. Sive, who was executive director of the Committee on Natural Resources, New York State Constitutional Convention, in 1967, is a partner in Winer, Neuberger & Sive, New York City. He is secretary of the John Muir Institute for Environmental Affairs and is on the executive committee of Friends of the Earth. Sive was an attorney for the Committee for Nuclear Responsibility, which with other groups unsuccessfully sought to prevent the Amchitka underground test off Alaska Nov. 6, 1971.

Center for Law and Social Policy. Three of the six attorneys who brought the injunction suit which blocked the Alaska pipeline pending a final environmental impact study were connected with the Center for Law and Social Policy. It was incorporated Nov. 14, 1968, and has received extensive foundation funding including grants from the Ford Foundation, Stern Fund, Meyer Fund and Rockefeller Brothers Fund, whose chairman, Laurance S. Rockefeller, was a director of the Natural Resources Defense Council founded at Princeton in March 1970 to fight conservation cases.

Initial directors of the center were Arthur J. Goldberg, chairman, Charles R. Halpern, Richard B. Sobol and Bruce J. Terris. Leadership as of the annual report filed April 6, 1971, included:

Chairman of board: Goldberg, secretary of labor, 1961-62; associate justice of the Supreme Court, 1962-65; U.S. ambassador to the United Nations, 1965-68.

Vice chairman: David F. Cavers, president of the Council on Law Related Studies at Cambridge, Mass.; Mitchell Rogovin of Arnold & Porter, assistant attorney general (tax division), 1966-69. Rogovin also was treasurer for the center.

Secretary: James W. Moorman, who with Halpern and Dennis M. Flannery of the center participated in the injunction suit filed by Wilderness Society, Friends of the Earth and the Environmental Defense Fund.

Trustees include Stewart L. Udall, secretary of the interior (D Ariz.), 1961-69; J. Lee Rankin, Office of Corporation Counsel, New York City, U.S. solicitor general, 1956-61, chief counsel, Warren Commission, 1963-64; Ramsey Clark, attorney general, 1967-68, chairman of national advisory council to American Civil Liberties Union, 1969—; and Mrs. Marian W. Edelman, Washington Research Project.

Goldberg, Clark and their New York law firm Paul, Weiss, Goldberg, Rifkind, Wharton & Garrison registered July 18, 1969, to lobby for the Alaska Federation of Natives on land claims legislation. They testified on the group's behalf Aug. 7, 1969, before the Senate Interior and Insular Affairs Committee.

Congress cleared the Alaska Native Claims Settlement Act (HR 10367—PL 92-203) Dec. 14, 1971, granting Alaska's estimated 53,000 natives $462.5-million in grants, $500-million from state and federal mineral revenues and ownership claims to 40 million of Alaska's 365 million acres.

Another lobbyist for the Alaska Federation of Natives was Claude J. Desautels Associates, which registered April 28, 1971. Desautels was executive assistant to Rep. Wayne N. Aspinall (D Colo.), 1949-61; congressional liaison for Presidents Kennedy and Johnson, 1961-65; executive assistant to the postmaster general, 1965-68. Aspinall, chairman of the House Interior and Insular Affairs Committee, was a sponsor of the Alaska Native Claims Settlement Act and urged passage in the final form, noting he had worked on native claims since 1951. Rep. John P. Saylor (R Pa.), ranking Republican on the Interior Committee, told the House Dec. 14, 1971, that if the same formula had been applied for all Indian tribes in the United States, "there has never been enough money in the U.S. Treasury to pay their claims."

Of Alaska's 365 million acres, about 95 percent were under federal control in March 1972. When pending land selections authorized by Congress are completed, about 60 percent of Alaska will be under some form of federal control.

The right-of-way for the proposed Alaska pipeline from the North Slope to Valdez has been reserved under Interior Department supervision. All Alaska public lands are frozen under department authority until March 17, 1972.

Udall is one of the three directors of both the Overview Foundation Inc., a non-profit environmental consulting group, and the Overview Corporation, environmental consultants. The president and treasurer of both organizations, headquartered across from the Executive Office Building, is Henry L. Kimelman, in 1972 the national finance chairman for Sen. George McGovern's (D S.D.) campaign for the Democratic presidential nomination. Kimelman ranked third ($24,306.50) among McGovern's contributors as made public Feb. 28, 1972. Reports filed Sept. 10, 1972, showed Kimelman loaning the McGovern campaign $50,000.

Friends of the Earth. The Friends of the Earth was among plaintiffs in the pipeline-blocking case filed in April 1970 against Alyeska. David R. Brower, longtime chief officer of the Sierra Club forced out in a leadership fight, in September 1969 announced formation of the Friends of the Earth, its subsidiary League of Conservation Voters and the John Muir Institute for Environmental Studies. The Friends of the Earth and the institute are internationally based.

Brower is president of the Friends of the Earth and vice president of the institute, founded with financial help from Atlantic Richfield Chairman Robert O. Anderson. The institute's president is Max Linn of Albuquerque, N.M., public relations director for Sandia Laboratories, a key nuclear installation. Linn also was named a vice *(Continued on p. 22)*

Pipeline Dispute May Reach Supreme Court

Construction of the controversial trans-Alaska oil pipeline will ultimately be approved or rejected by the United States Supreme Court.

When U.S. District Court Judge George L. Hart on Aug. 15, 1972, lifted the injunction blocking construction which he had imposed in 1970, Hart said he anticipated that appeals almost certainly would take the case to the high court.

Environmental organizations—led by the Wilderness Society, Environmental Defense Fund and Friends of the Earth—vowed to take their flight against construction to the nation's highest judicial forum, if necessary.

Interior Secretary Rogers C. B. Morton Feb. 27 said the administration would appeal to the Supreme Court a decision handed down Feb. 9 by a federal appeals court halting pipeline construction. *(p. 22)*

Appeals. But the judicial appeals process must be exhausted first. On Aug. 22, the three environmental groups filed an appeal to the U.S. Court of Appeals. Parties in the contoversy were told to be ready to argue the case by early October.

The latest court development was precipitated by Interior Secretary Rogers C. B. Morton's May 11 announcement that he would issue a permit for pipeline construction. The announcement actually was the two-week notice which Morton was required by court to give so that opponents could prepare their legal response.

"We will use the coming days to seek out every legal strategy that might work," said President David R. Brower of Friends of the Earth May 11. "We hope that the public will join with us in calling for a halt to this destructive, totally unnecessary project."

Lloyd Tupling of the Sierrra Club told Congressional Quarterly: "There are still several hurdles that have to be crossed before bulldozers begin to move in Alaska—legally, anyway."

The Interior Department March 20, 1972, released a nine-volume environmental impact statement which said that some environmental damage was inevitable but that the trans-Alaska route was the most feasible economically. The report included three volumes analyzing the economic and national security implications of the pipeline.

The public was allowed 45 days to file comments on the impact statement with the President's Council on Environmental Quality. However, the price of the massive study was $42.50 and only a few copies were available for public scrutiny. Lawyers for the environmental groups which won a delay of the pipeline construction said it took them 28 days to obtain copies of the statement.

A bipartisan group of 23 senators, more than 80 members of the House and many environmentalists called for further public hearings on the impact statement after it was issued.

However, Interior Under Secretary William T. Pecora ruled out further hearings, saying that Morton felt additional hearings would be "a circus." Pecora said that there had been "ample opportunity for substantive comment" prior to issuance of the impact statement.

Other Opposition. Rep. Les Aspin (D Wis.), long a critic of the Alaska pipeline, said May 11 that he was "saddened and disappointed" by Morton's approval: "This decision is a blatant example of the interests of the oil industry superseding the public interest," Aspin said. "Apparently, contributions from the oil companies to the Nixon campaign are simply more important to the administration than the good will of environmentalists and Midwest and East Coast consumers."

George Alderson, legislative director for Friends of the Earth, called the decision "capricious in the extreme."

Dr. Edgar Wayburn, past president of the Sierra Club, said the Morton decision was "inconsistent with the (Interior) Department's own environmental impact statement.... Why, if the pipeline must be constructed through some of the most difficult terrain in the world, through permafrost, through rugged mountains and gorges and 350 streams and rivers, should we deliberately run it through two of the most earthquake prone areas in the world—areas where recently earthquakes registered 8.5 on the Richter scale?"

Canadian Route. Opponents of the trans-Alaska pipeline have recommended an alternate route through Canada to the midwestern United States. They have argued that a Canadian pipeline would be cheaper, less costly to operate and maintain, more secure from earthquakes, less harmful to the environment and safer for national security. A combined group of Canadian and American petroleum companies already plans to build a natural gas pipeline from Alaska's north slope to the Midwest, and environmentalists contend that a parallel oil pipeline could be built at the same time.

On April 20, Senate Minority Whip Robert P. Griffin (R Mich.) and nearly a dozen other Republican senators sent a letter to Morton urging serious consideration of the Canadian route and further hearings.

"The only public hearings to date on the proposed pipeline were held by the (Interior) Department over a year ago," the Griffin letter stated. "They are clearly inadequate. Since then the Canadian alternative has become more attractive, several changes have been proposed in the Alaska pipeline and some detailed data have been presented for the first time on the environmental impact of the pipeline."

Administration Views. Administration spokesmen have said that prompt construction of the trans-Alaska pipeline would increase domestic oil production and lessen U.S. dependence on foreign oil.

In addition, completion of the pipeline would require spending at least $1-billion to build new oil tankers, which would benefit the U.S. shipbuilding industry and decrease the country's dependence on foreign-owned tankers.

president of Friends of the Earth, along with Stewart M. Ogilvy of Yonkers, N.Y. Attorney David Sive, on the Friends of the Earth executive committee, was appointed secretary of the John Muir Institute.

The Friends of the Earth registered in 1970 as a congressional lobby organization "to promote legislation to preserve, restore and encourage rational use of the ecosphere." Executive director Gary A. Soucie, also formerly with the Sierra Club, is a registered lobbyist for Friends of the Earth.

In 1970, the Friends of the Earth won 11 of the 12 House races and one of the three Senate contests in which it took part. Among those it successfully backed was Sen. Philip A. Hart (D Mich.), chairman of the Senate Commerce Energy, Natural Resources and Environment Subcommittee.

Other Environmental Groups

Among the many other environment-oriented groups that have shown varying degrees and types of involvement in Alaskan issues are:

• Conservation Foundation. Incorporated in 1948 in New York, the foundation moved to Washington in 1965. Not a membership group, it is financed by grants and gifts from foundations, organizations and individuals and is a non-profit organization to which contributions are deductible for income tax purposes. Donors have included the Ford Foundation.

Sydney Howe, the foundation's president, and two members of Congress—Sen. Gaylord Nelson (D Wis.) and Rep. Paul N. McCloskey Jr. (R Calif.), in 1972 opposing Richard M. Nixon for the Republican presidential nomination—incorporated Environmental Teach-In Inc., which was the guiding force behind Earth Day which focused attention on the environment April 22, 1970. Staff members of the Conservation Foundation helped plan the program and set up the Teach-In office.

Russell E. Train, past president of the Conservation Foundation, held the number two post in the Interior Department as under secretary during preliminary moves in 1969 on the Alaska pipeline permit and now is chairman of the Council on Environmental Quality established by the National Environmental Policy Act of 1969.

An annual report filed with the Foundation Center in August 1971 showed among trustees as of Dec. 31, 1970:

Chairman: Samuel H. Ordway Jr., a lawyer, vice president of the Conservation Foundation, 1948-61; president, 1961-65; chairman, 1969—. He served on the U.S. Civil Service Commission, 1937-39.

Vice chairman: William H. Whyte, a writer who was assistant managing editor of *Fortune* magazine, 1951-59.

Eugene R. Black, president and chairman, International Bank for Reconstruction and Development, 1949-62; director, International Telephone & Telegraph Corporation; director, *New York Times;* director, Chase International Investment Corporation; chairman of John F. Kennedy Library; director,

Boise Cascade Corporation; chairman, Overseas Development Council; chairman, Council of Economic Advisers of state of New York.

Ernest Brooks Jr., president of Old Dominion Foundation, New York City.

Mrs. Edgar M. Cullman, whose husband is president of General Cigar Company.

Gilbert M. Grosvenor, associate editor, *National Geographic.*

S. Dillon Ripley, secretary, Smithsonian Institution.

The foundation's consulting council included Donald E. Nicoll, aide to Sen. Edmund S. Muskie (D Maine); Dr. Michael F. Brewer, vice president of Resources for the Future, and Joseph L. Sax of the University of Michigan, chairman of the American Bar Association's Committee on Public Lands and Waters and a trustee of the Center for Law and Social Policy.

The Conservation Foundation opposed granting of the pipeline authority on the basis of the Interior Department's first impact statement, contending it did not ensure environmental protection. Howe said the foundation in 1972 considered it important that alternative routes across Canada be fully considered, with Canadian participation.

Outlook

Calling construction of the trans-Alaskan pipeline a "matter of urgency," the Nixon administration Feb. 27 revealed it would ask both the Supreme Court and Congress for a final go-ahead signal.

Interior Secretary Morton announced that day the Justice Department will appeal to the Supreme Court a decision handed down Feb. 9 by the U.S. Court of Appeals for the District of Columbia. The appeals court barred the interior secretary from granting Alaska a permit to begin construction of the pipeline, holding that the right-of-way across public lands requested by the oil consortium was wider than the Mineral Leasing Act of 1920 would allow. The court did not address the environmental questions raised by the suit.

Morton also said he would ask Congress to amend the 1920 act "to remove any doubt about my authority to issue permits necessary for construction" of the pipeline. He discounted the Canadian route: "A pipeline across Canada would involve great delay in delivery of oil to oil markets," he said.

A bill (S 970) divesting federal courts of jurisdiction over the pipeline was introduced Feb. 21, 1973, by Alaskan Senators Mike Gravel (D) and Ted Stevens (R). The measure would declare that the Interior Department's environmental impact statement met NEPA requirements. Other bills (S 993, HR 4707) authorizing construction of a trans-Canadian pipeline following a study of its environmental effects were submitted Feb. 26.

A final decision on the controversial pipeline, however, was not expected until the fall of 1973, when the Supreme Court was expected to rule on the Justice Department appeal. Any attempt to push legislation through Congress authorizing construction of the trans-Alaskan route would likely be met with prolonged debate.

EL PASO PIPELINE: COURT DECISION ENDS 16-YEAR STRUGGLE

A 16-year struggle by El Paso Natural Gas Company to retain control of a huge natural gas market in the West ended March 5, 1973, when the Supreme Court directed El Paso to sell $290-million in assets of the old Pacific Northwest Pipeline Corporation.

In a 6-0 decision, the court unanimously affirmed a lower court ruling awarding Pacific Northwest to a combine of four companies known as the Apco group. The holdings ensure Apco access to the lucrative natural gas markets of the Northwest and California and provide major incentives to develop new gas supplies in Canada. (*Details, p. 26*)

The court's decision severely undercut El Paso's drive to induce Congress to legalize its 1957 merger with Pacific Northwest, held illegal by the Supreme Court in 1964. Spokesmen for the chief proponents of bills to preserve the merger told Congressional Quarterly that further efforts to overturn the court's directive were unlikely. Bills to permit El Paso to retain the pipeline by holding the merger immune from antitrust requirements had been considered by the 92nd Congress but were bottled up in committee at the session's end.

Although the Supreme Court had ordered El Paso to sell Pacific Northwest in 1964, divestiture was delayed for nine years as the court in 1967 and again in 1969 rejected divestiture proposals.

In the third divestiture plan approved by the lower courts, the Colorado Interstate Gas Co. in June 1972 was awarded the contested pipeline for the second time. The same day, however, the Colorado States Gas Producing Company gained control of Colorado Interstate Gas Co. in an action that had been in the making for several months.

This touched off new legal fighting, with the Justice Department and a group of competing companies opposing the award to Colorado Interstate on grounds that it no longer existed as an independent company.

On Aug. 30, 1972, U.S. District Judge Hatfield Chilson awarded the Pacific Northwest system instead to the Apco group—Apco Oil Corp., Alaska Interstate Co., Gulf Interstate Co. and Tipperary Land and Exploration Corp.

El Paso appealed that decision to the Supreme Court in November 1972, contending that a "drastic change has occurred in gas supplies and gas reserves of natural gas pipelines" in recent years. The Justice Department had argued that "the energy crisis cannot be solved by recision of remedies to correct violations of the antitrust laws."

Background

El Paso, the major supplier of natural gas to the northwestern states and California, initiated its merger with Pacific Northwest in 1957. At the time, gas was widely produced as a byproduct of oil production and was being flared (burned) on a massive scale. Since then, gas has come into its own as a valuable resource in itself.

The stakes, involving many millions of dollars from the beginning, have soared higher with western population and industrial growth and with the increasing focus on reconciling competing demands from energy needs and environmental considerations. Neither a shortage of energy fuels nor a national priority on environmental problems was in the foreground when the battle began. (*Concentration of energy ownership p. 38*)

Natural gas, as the cleanest energy fuel yet available for large-scale use, has been injected squarely into the tug-of-war over energy and environment. Like other energy fuels, gas is reported in short supply within the United States by government and industry officials. Major companies are turning to foreign sources to meet U.S. demand. El Paso plans to import large quantities of liquefied natural gas from Algeria to the East Coast after it builds a planned fleet of giant supertankers.

A Federal Power Commission staff report on energy requirements cited at 1972 hearings said: "It is estimated that between 1971 and 1990 the United States will require 186.4 trillion cubic feet more gas than will be available even after making liberal allowances for pipeline imports, liquefied natural gas imports, coal gas, Alaskan gas and reformed gas."

The shortage is in produced gas, President F. Donald Hart of the American Gas Association points out. He says "there is no shortage of natural gas under the ground. The key...is to make it worthwhile for producers...to invest the tremendous sums...and take the significant risks involved in drilling for new supplies of natural gas."

After El Paso acquired nearly all of Pacific Northwest's common stock, the Justice Department in July 1957 filed an antitrust action under Section 7 of the Clayton Act—an action which El Paso officials said came as a surprise, since they had discussed the merger with Attorney General Herbert Brownell earlier. A month later, El Paso applied for FPC approval of an assets merger under Section 7 of the Natural Gas Act.

The FPC approved the merger in 1959, and it was completed eight days later. In 1962, the Supreme Court nullified the FPC order, ruling that court antitrust questions should have been settled before the FPC acted on the general issues of broad public interest. Justices John M. Harlan and Potter Stewart dissented from the court's decision by Justice William O. Douglas, stating it created "a wholly artificial imbalance between antitrust law enforcement and administrative regulation...."

The Supreme Court in 1964 held the merger a violation of the Clayton Act and ordered El Paso's divestiture of the pipeline assets. Justice Douglas wrote: "If El Paso can absorb Pacific Northwest without violating Section 7 of the Clayton Act, that section has no meaning in the natural gas field." Justice Harlan in a partial dissent concurred with the finding but said it was time for Congress to re-examine the "anachronistic system of dual regulation" and opposed the "peremptory ordering of divestiture." In all, the Supreme Court has acted five times, leaving its 1964 ruling intact.

The company contends that the Supreme Court has never passed on the broad question of whether the merger serves the public interest, confining itself to the narrower question of whether the merger produced some limiting of competition within the affected area. The controversy has hit all three branches of the federal government and the executives of many western states as well.

Scores of lawyers have taken part, including members of nationally prominent law firms. From time to time, there have been unsubstantiated charges of improper pressures, lobbying and involvement in political campaigns. One accusation resulted in a special inquiry.

Howard Boyd, board chairman of El Paso, told a 1972 House hearing the case then involved about 31 different parties. He said that when he last testified in court, 54 lawyers waited in the courtroom to cross-examine him.

"I can assure you that with the conflicting interests that were there, there is no hope that Solomon in his greatest wisdom could come forth with a decree that would be acceptable to more than just a small majority of that group," Boyd said.

The complexity of Congress' involvement in the controversy, in 1971-72 centering on El Paso's attempt to win congressional exemption from the Clayton Act antitrust provision, was pointed up by Sen. John V. Tunney (D Calif.), whose state originated the fight.

"We are very confused," he said at an Oct. 22, 1971, hearing. "None of us up here are experts on this problem. We hear absolutely contradictory testimony, and we are trying to cut through the maze."

Legislative Battle

At the same time teams of lawyers argued in the courts over the El Paso merger, a decade-long struggle directly affecting the issue was waged off and on in Congress.

As early as 1962, after the Supreme Court's first ruling in the dispute, the FPC proposed legislation giving it sole jurisdiction over natural gas pipeline mergers and exempting FPC-approved mergers from antitrust laws.

Bills (S 2290, HR 6483) incorporating the proposal were first introduced in the 89th Congress (1965-66) at the FPC's request. In 1966, El Paso sought western governors' support for a bill enabling it to avoid divestiture, switching to back the FPC-sponsored legislation but with a proposed amendment to cover mergers then in litigation.

Attorney General Ramsey Clark opposed the antitrust exemption provision as unnecessary and "because competition...continues to play an important and necessary role in assuring the public an adequate supply of natural gas at reasonable prices."

A similar bill (S 1687) was the subject of 1967 hearings by the Senate Commerce Committee after its introduction by Chairman Warren G. Magnuson (D Wash.) at the FPC's request. Deputy Attorney General Warren Christopher told Congress the Justice Department "would be strongly opposed to any amendment of S 1687 which would 'forgive' the El Paso-Pacific Northwest merger, or

which would give the commission the authority to approve such a past merger which has been held unlawful by the courts."

El Paso noted that Arthur H. Dean of the New York law firm Sullivan and Cromwell and El Paso's chief executive officer discussed the intended merger beforehand with Attorney General Brownell, who then offered no objection. The company cited the FPC trial examiner's 1959 decision after exhaustive hearings which said, "There are other factors of greater importance showing this merger to be required by the public convenience and necessity which indeed far outweigh this single factor of the elimination of Pacific as a competitor...." The FPC's approval was unanimous. The earlier bills did not get out of committee.

1972 Bills. Identical bills (S 2404, HR 10331) in the Senate and House proposed in 1971-72 to permit El Paso to retain the pipeline by holding the merger immune from antitrust requirements.

Proponents contend that conditions have changed since 1957 and the public interest would be best served by upholding the merger. By the nature of the judicial system, they say, only Congress is in a position to consider the over-all picture, weighing all factors.

The company has much support, from governors and utilities commissions of most of the states involved, from the FPC and from some members of Congress, including Magnuson and many of the members from affected states.

In the intervening years since the merger, many former opponents have switched positions, largely on grounds of re-examination or that conditions have changed. Among them is Edmund G. Brown, who as California's attorney general personally telephoned Attorney General Brownell in 1957 to initiate the antitrust action.

Brown testified in June 1972 that his position changed in 1964 while he was governor of California, on the basis of new studies by state experts. He said that when the action was originally touched off, "it appeared to us that there were virtually unlimited supplies of natural gas available and that it would be in California's interest to have as many suppliers as possible competing to deliver this gas to our consumers."

In 1957, El Paso was the only out-of-state supplier of natural gas to California. In 1972, there were two others, gas was in short supply and pollution awareness had increased the demand for clean fuel, Brown said.

"At a time when enormous financial resources are going to be needed to help develop new gas supplies, it seems to me to be sheer folly to weaken the major supplier to our state that is capable, if it remains a unified company, to expend the vast amounts of money and effort that will be needed to help alleviate the gas shortage crisis," Brown testified.

El Paso Chairman Boyd testified: "What the Department of Justice hoped to achieve was that it would provide two companies, both seeking the same market and thereby prompted to put together the most attractive package so that the purchaser would select one or the other. By virtue of the facts existing today this is just unattainable because the market is insatiable and however many sellers tender their gas to whatever markets, I can assure you it will be all purchased."

Former Assistant Attorney General Richard W. McLaren in 1971 called the El Paso case "one of the department's most important enforcement actions" since 1950.

Leading Participants in El Paso Case

Among leading corporate parties in the El Paso merger dispute in 1972, with a partial list of corporate positions indicated in 1972 directories for selected individuals were the following:

El Paso Natural Gas Company. Formed in 1928 to deliver natural gas from wells in southeast New Mexico to nearby El Paso, Texas, the company by 1972 served 11 western states. Its 22,735 miles of pipelines were the largest mileage of any gas company in the United States. Its total assets were placed at $1,975,768,000 by a company spokesman during House hearings in June 1972. The *Oil & Gas Journal* listed El Paso's 1971 net income at $73,868,000.

El Paso sold its gas mainly to distributing companies, including those serving all major population centers in its area. The company also sold directly to a small number of industrial customers and to electric utilities for generator fuel.

Chairman and chief executive officer: Howard Boyd. He was personal secretary to Attorney General Homer Cummings in 1934; special attorney, Justice Department, 1935; assistant U.S. attorney for the District of Columbia, 1935-39; a partner in the Hogan and Hartson law firm at Washington, D.C., 1939-52; with El Paso from 1952 on, including service as company president, 1960-65.

President: Hugh F. Steen, who worked up from the position of laborer in El Paso from 1932 on.

G. Scott Cuming, vice president and general counsel, attorney with the Pacific Northwest Pipeline Corporation, 1955-59, with El Paso thereafter.

Willard F. Rockwell Jr., board chairman, North American Rockwell Corporation; director, Mellon National Bank & Trust Company.

Franz Schneider, financial writer; director, Continental Oil Company, director, Phelps Dodge Corporation; director, Transcontinental Gas Pipe Line.

Arthur H. Dean, partner in the New York law firm, Sullivan and Cromwell; general counsel and director, American Metal Climax Inc.; director, Bank of New York International Corporation; trustee, Bank of New York; director, Crown Zellerbach Corporation; director, Campbell Soup Company; member, Council on Foreign Relations; held government diplomatic posts.

Alfred C. Glassell Jr., president of Glassell Drilling Company and of Glassell Producing Company Inc.; director, First City National Bank; director, Transcontinental Gas Pipe Line Corporation.

Leon M. Payne, partner, general counsel and secretary of Florida Gas Transmission Company and Florida Gas Company.

Sam D. Young, chairman of board, El Paso National Bank; director, Hilton Hotels Corporation; director, *El Paso Times*. Frank L. King, chairman of board, United California Bank International. Paul Kayser, president of El Paso, 1929-60; chairman and chief executive officer of El Paso, 1960-65.

Lobbyists. Among those who have represented El Paso in lobbying of Congress are the law firm Sharon, Pierson, Semmes, Crolius and Finley and the public relations firm Hill & Knowlton. A chief lobbyist on the bill has been John H. Sharon, former legislative and executive aide. Another member of the firm registered to lobby on the bill is Michael Monroney, son of former Sen. A.S. Mike Monroney (D Okla. House 1939-51, Senate 1951-69). Andrew T. Hatcher, former press aide to President John F. Kennedy, has lobbied for El Paso as a representative of Hill and Knowlton.

Colorado Interstate Gas Company. A division of the Colorado Interstate Corporation. The company operates 4,184 miles of gas pipeline and had a 1971 net income of $10,003,000, the *Oil & Gas Journal* said.

Directors of the corporation include William Bellano, president of Island Creek Coal Company and executive vice president of Occidental Petroleum Corporation; Russell T. Tutt, president of El Pomar Investment Company and chairman of the executive committee, Holly Sugar Corporation; and Albert K. Mitchell, former Republican national committeeman in New Mexico.

Among board members of the Coastal States Gas Producing Company was Leon Jaworski, president of the American Bar Association; special assistant U.S. attorney general, 1962-65; a member of the President's Law Enforcement and Violence commissions.

Apco Group. A combination of applicants for the Pacific Northwest properties made up of Alaska Interstate Company, 37.5 percent; Apco Oil Corporation, 37.5 percent; Gulf Interstate Company, 15 percent, and Tipperrary Land & Exploration Corporation, 10 percent. Several former attorneys with the Federal Power Commission are in law firms registered to lobby for various companies in the group.

He said the Justice Department considered the need for and the appropriateness of the court-ordered divestiture as clear in 1971 as it was in 1964.

McLaren told Senate hearings that enactment of a "forgiveness" bill would have a "very detrimental effect on antitrust enforcement.... If obtaining forgiveness legislation is a realistically available alternative to divestiture, defendants may very well conclude that they are obliged to their shareholders to pursue the legislative route as far as they can. In these circumstances, it would be in their interests to delay judicial proceedings on relief questions and compliance with court-ordered divestiture in every possible way."

Justice spokesmen made it clear their position continued unchanged in 1972. One official told Congressional Quarterly that in the race between court action and legislative action, "It is to El Paso's interest to string out the case as long as it can, and it is doing this."

An El Paso spokesman called it "false to assert that El Paso has been responsible for delay..." He wrote Congressional Quarterly that the company "has *never* initiated a motion of any kind requesting delay" and has never initiated any of the many appeals.

The wide gulf between opposing positions has been **reflected** in views set before Congress and in the public press.

The *St. Louis Post Dispatch,* for example, likened the El Paso case to that of the International Telephone & Telegraph Co., which entered the news after an out-of-court antitrust settlement.

Noting that 12 senators led by Magnuson sponsored the El Paso exemption bill, the newspaper on July 1, 1972, said: "The moral of this case, as in the ITT case, seems to be that if a litigant has the economic resources to stay in the battle and take its plea to the highest levels of government, it has a good chance of winning, no matter what the law says."

Robert E. Maloney, chairman of the executive committee of the Western Sunset Transmission Company, an unsuccessful applicant for the divested property, outlined a frequently-expressed opposition position: "It should be generally conceded that it is unwise to make the Congress of the United States a court of last resort for those having the resources of El Paso to mount large-scale lobbying and publicity campaigns."

The *Wall Street Journal* published a different view in an editorial page column July 26, 1971. Written by Roger W. Benedict, it carried the headline: "U.S. vs. El Paso: Antitrust Gone Mad." Benedict said that from the beginning, the case "has hinged on whether relatively narrow and largely theoretical interpretations of antitrust law should take precedence over a much broader evaluation of what best serves the public."

Mrs. Virginia Knauer, the President's consumer adviser, testified that any weakening of antitrust enforcement would be against consumers' long-range interests and expressed doubts that it had been shown that benefits of the forgiveness bill outweighed disadvantages.

Beverly C. Moore Jr., associate of Ralph Nader's Corporate Accountability Research Group, strongly opposed the measure, saying "the integrity of antitrust enforcement and the encouragement of powerful economic interests to flex their political muscles is at stake." Questioning reasons for "the gradual but steady change from opposition to advocacy of this legislation" by many officials and members of Congress, Moore told the Senate Commerce Committee Oct. 22, 1971:

"The answer is and must be: economic power—El Paso's economic power—unchallenged, unchecked, unrelenting, highly disciplined, mobilized and advancing upon the members of the U.S. Congress."

The committee held a special hearing Nov. 23, 1971, into the only specific charge Moore made when pressed by committee members: that a bank official told him that an El Paso representative had indicated the company would deposit $100,000 interest free in his bank "if that official would come out in favor of this bill."

Scott Cuming, vice president and general counsel of El Paso, immediately testified that the charge was "an absolute, unmitigated lie." The accusation led the committee to delay action on S 2404. The special inquiry produced apparently contradictory testimony under oath, which a committee spokesman said was to be turned over to the Justice Department. There has been no subsequent action, and the committee did not publish the November hearing proceedings.

John H. Klas, Utah state Democratic chairman and vice president in charge of obtaining new accounts for the Continental Bank and Trust Company of Salt Lake City, testified that Daniel Berman, a Salt Lake City attorney who had represented El Paso, made over morning coffee what Klas considered "a serious offer" to be helpful in getting a $100,000 interest free deposit in Klas' bank. Klas, opposed to the merger bill, said there was no comment concerning any change of his position but that he assumed "there would be some sort of a quid pro quo expected." Another bank officer supported Klas' testimony.

Berman testified he had done little work for El Paso and that it was "an absolute lie" to say he ever offered Klas or anyone else anything in connection with his position on the legislation. He noted there were other influential Democratic figures opposed to the bill, including the state's national Democratic committeeman, the former national committeeman and James P. Cowley, former law partner of Sen. Frank E. Moss (D Utah) and Moss' campaign manager in 1958, 1964 and 1970.

El Paso Chairman Boyd testified "El Paso has not promised or suggested any financial inducement to anyone in exchange for support for this legislation." He said such an action would be "repugnant to our sense of decency and integrity and I categorically disavow the use of any such tactics for the furtherance of this legislation or any other matter...."

Supreme Court Decision

A final decision in the 16-year-old antitrust battle came March 5 when the Supreme Court refused to consider El Paso's appeal to allow a lower court to recommend an alternative solution—other than divestiture—in the case. Although El Paso may ask the court to rehear the case, such petitions are rarely granted.

The court unanimously affirmed without opinion a federal district court plan under which El Paso was required to sell Pacific Northwest's gas reserves, pipeline facilities and other property to the Apco Group. Justices William J. Brennan Jr., Byron R. White and Thurgood Marshall did not participate in the decision.

John C. McMillian, president of the Apco Group, March 5 said the decision "makes possible the establishment of an independent...company to serve the gas supply needs of the west...(and) preserves the integrity of the nation's antitrust laws."

Howard Boyd, chairman of the board of El Paso, the same day stressed that the court's ruling would not change the company's plans to continue its search for new sources of energy.

The court's decision appeared to rule out further congressional efforts to legalize the merger. Neither Sen. Magnuson nor Rep. Brock Adams (D Wash.)—the two chief proponents of legislation to preserve the merger—had reintroduced their bills as of March 6, and spokesmen for both members indicated that such a move was unlikely. "The bill is a little deader than it was before," an aide to Adams told Congressional Quarterly.

Congress in September 1972 had completed hearings on measures—strongly opposed by the Justice Department—to legalize the El Paso acquisition, but no bill was reported by the committees involved. Hearings held that month before the House Interstate and Foreign Commerce Subcommittee on Communications and Power dealt with El Paso's expenditures in 1971 of $893,862 on efforts to promote the legislation.

ENERGY, ENVIRONMENT GROUPS CLASH ON STRIP MINING

Strip mining—ripping off the earth's surface to extract coal or other minerals—is at the heart of one of America's most nagging and difficult domestic dilemmas. The problem is how to balance energy needs with environmental protection. Stripping, as the controversial mining method is often called, has inflicted severe damage upon the environments of Appalachia and the Midwest, and now is moving relentlessly into the Far West. But the nation is increasingly hungry for power and electricity, and coal—our most abundant natural energy resource—can be supplied most easily and cheaply by strip mining. As America moves closer to a long-predicted energy crisis, "King Coal" is being called upon to save the country from the power shortages which seem imminent. Many people, however, are beginning to ask if it will be necessary to destroy the land in order to save it.

Environmentalists contend that the ecological trauma visited upon many areas of the countryside by strip mining is widespread and undeniable. The very nature of the process makes some adverse effects inevitable: trees, brush and topsoil (called the "overburden") are torn away by bulldozers or giant earth-moving machines so that explosive charges, huge power shovels or mammoth auger drills can blast, claw and bore out the minerals, leaving great gashes on mountainsides ("highwalls") and piles of discarded earth ("spoil banks") which cause landslides, erosion, water pollution and esthetic blight. Environmentally, stripping is anathema to plant life, wildlife, fish and—ultimately—humans. Nothing and no one can live long in stripped areas where the vegetation has been denuded, the water poisoned by mine acid or thickened by silt and the soil itself rendered unstable, unproductive and ugly. West Virginia Democrat Ken Hechler, who has fought strip mining interests in his state and in Congress, in a November 1971 House speech called it "a cancer of the earth...a menacing disease—a pathology deriving from our lust for energy at the cheapest monetary cost regardless of the social cost."

But strip mining proponents contend the land can be reclaimed, and thus stripping should be allowed to continue. Indeed, the other horn of the dilemma is America's seemingly insatiable demand for power—electricity to light, heat or cool homes and offices and drive a vast array of modern appliances, natural gas for cooking and heating systems and petroleum products for automobiles and machinery. Coal, which less than a decade ago largely had been written off in favor of cheaper natural gas and oil and promising nuclear power, has suddenly become the *prima donna* of the American energy industry. The main reason is that there's so much of it—more than 3 trillion tons, according to U.S. Geological Survey estimates of current domestic reserves, or 88 percent of total U.S. energy resources, according to the National Coal Association. The other reason is a sharp rise in coal demand—by electric utilities which burn it in power plants, by industries such as steel mills which need coking coal, and recently by new facilities which convert coal to gas or liquid as substitutes for natural gas and oil products.

But electricity has been and will continue to be the pampered first child of the current coal boom. More than half of the total electric output of the nation comes from coal, and nearly 60 per cent of that coal comes from strip mines. In 1971, for the first time in history, strip mining together with auger mining surpassed underground mining as the nation's leading method of coal production. [1] *(Footnote sources p. 37)*

Ironically, one reason for the increase was that tightened air pollution standards increased the demand of large urban utilities in the East for the low-sulfur (and

One Man's View

"So far as I know, there are only two philosophies of land use. One holds that the earth is the Lord's or it holds that the earth belongs to those yet to be born as well as to those now living. The present owners, according to this view, only have the land in trust, both for all the living who are dependent on it now, and for the unborn who will be dependent on it in time to come.

"The model of this sort of use is a good farm—a farm that, by the return of wastes and by other safeguards, preserves the land in production without diminishing its ability to produce. The standard of this sort of land use is fertility, which preserves the interest of the future.

"The other philosophy is that of exploitation, which holds that the interest of the present owner is the only interest to be considered. The standard, according to this view, is profit, and it is assumed that whatever is profitable is good. The most fanatical believers in the rule of profit are the strip miners. The earth, those people would have us believe, is not the Lord's, nor do the unborn have any share in it. It belongs, instead, to rich organizations with names like Peabody, Kentucky River Coal, Elkhorn Coal, National Steel, Bethlehem Steel, Occidental Petroleum, The Berwin Corporation, Tennessee Valley Authority, Chesapeake & Ohio, Ford Motor Company, and many others.

"And the earth, they would say, is theirs not just for a time, but forever, and in proof of their claim they do not hesitate to destroy it forever—that is, if it is profitable to do so, and earth destruction has so far been exceedingly profitable to those organizations."

—Wendell Berry, poet and novelist

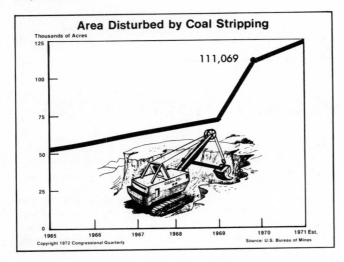

Area Disturbed by Coal Stripping

Thousands of Acres

111,069

125
100
75
50
25
0

1965 1966 1967 1968 1969 1970 1971 Est.

Copyright 1972 Congressional Quarterly   Source: U.S. Bureau of Mines

thus low-polluting) coal and lignite of the West. More than 77 percent of the country's 45 billion tons of "economically strippable" coal reserves is in 13 states west of the Mississippi, according to the Bureau of Mines. But the U.S. Geological Survey estimates that strippable reserves total 128 billion tons—or some 25 times the total amount of coal which has been stripped so far in the nation. No one knows how much coal ultimately will be strip mined, but with the nation's energy consumption increasing by about 7 percent annually, demand for coal is expected to at least double by 1985 and increase as much as eight-fold by the year 2000, according to some projections. Edwin R. Phelps, president of Peabody Coal Company, the nation's largest coal producer, told a House Interior subcommittee in November 1971: "The United States not only must continue to have coal, in increasing amounts, but a major portion of that coal must come from surface mines. Surface-mined coal is a public benefit. The needs of our society demand it."

Projections, of course, can be wrong, as those who continually have had to lower U.S. population trends can testify, and many environmentalists maintain that projected energy "demands" are merely self-fulfilling prophecies of energy industry public relations men. Instead, they call for stepped-up research on new sources of energy, such as solar, wind, geothermal power, hydrogen fuel and nuclear fusion. In the meantime, they contend that the nation's coal needs can be met by increased deep mining and that Americans could decrease their energy consumption by curtailing use of luxury appliances, improving the efficiency of building insulation, changing price rates to reward small consumers of electricity and simply turning out more lights more often. In September 1971, Hechler asked the House: "Are we prisoners of an onrushing technology which demands that we must devastate our planet in order to feed the 'energy crisis'; or do we have the will to control our future destiny and put a stop to further rape of the land?"

Many of the environmental effects of strip mining have been documented; others are merely ominous predictions. Obtaining reliable figures is sometimes difficult, but however viewed, the statistics of surface mining are truly staggering. The Geological Survey reported in 1971 that an area of land the size of Delaware and Rhode Island combined, about 3,200 square miles, had been dis-

turbed by stripping. The Soil Conservation Service in 1972 estimated that the area affected had reached 7,820 square miles, more nearly the size of New Jersey. If stretched out across the country, that would constitute a barren swath more than two miles wide from New York to San Francisco. Moreover, if all the remaining recoverable reserves were mined, stripped land would total 71,000 square miles—an area larger than the state of Missouri. That would increase the hypothetical cross-country "stripway" to a width of more than 20 miles. The Interior Department estimates that surface mining destroys outdoor recreation resources valued at $35-million annually, including $22.5-million worth of fish and wildlife benefits. According to Hechler, stripping has damaged at least 145,000 acres of lakes and ponds with silt and acid runoff and has polluted more than 13,000 miles of streams, with some 1,500 tons of mineral acid produced every day.

Social and Economic Legacies. But beyond the environmental issues, strip mining has generated fierce and continuing controversy over broader ramifications which affect society as a whole. Strip miners say the process is more efficient, less costly and much safer than underground mining, and that it provides badly-needed jobs. There is little question of stripping's cost-efficiency. In 1970, surface mined coal made up 44 percent of the year's production, but there were only 32,332 surface miners compared to 107,808 underground miners. Production per man per day was about 35 tons by surface miners compared to less than 14 tons by deep miners.[2] Yet the selling price of stripped coal was $4.69 a ton compared to $7.40 a ton for deep-mined coal.

As for safety, strip mining advocates argue that the practice is much safer than underground mining and reduces the high fatality rate from fires and cave-ins which long has plagued the mining industry, and the statistics bear them out. In an eight-month period in 1972, there were only 15 fatalities in surface mining operations compared to 87 underground fatalities—the fatality rate was thus .37 per million man hours for stripping compared with .65 for underground. Stripping opponents counter that strict enforcement of the Coal Mine Health and Safety Act of 1969 (PL 91-173) and use of safer machinery would eliminate this problem. But the coal companies claim that meeting the law's requirements has cost them more than $1-billion already and is drastically cutting productivity. Some industry leaders fault the law itself. "Unfortunately, many things in the 1969 law sound good on paper, but aren't really having any significant improvement in safety," says John Corcoran, president of Consolidation Coal Company, a subsidiary of Continental Oil. "We've had to change our whole method of mining, but the safety record is no better."[3] *(Footnotes p. 37)*

To some extent, the law may have set in motion a vicious circle—stripping increased as the costs and problems of deep mining multiplied, but then underground mine operators cut corners in an effort to remain competitive and safety conditions deteriorated. Other evidence suggests that lack of enforcement of the law by the Bureau of Mines may be the real problem. A General Accounting Office study found that out of $12.5-million in fines charged the coal industry since 1969, the Bureau of Mines canceled $2.7-million and collected only $1.4-million.

Strip mining's effect on jobs is another hotly-debated topic. The industry generally maintains that mining creates new jobs and boosts local economies. But critics counter that strip mining jobs are only temporary. "Strip mining is like taking seven or eight stiff drinks," Hechler says. "You are riding high as long as the coal lasts, but the hangover comes when the coal is gone, the land is gone and the jobs are gone and the bitter truth of the morning after leaves a barren landscape and a mouth full of ashes." In heavily strip mined areas, population figures indicate that the rates of outmigration are higher than normal. Nine out of West Virginia's ten highest strip coal producing areas had population losses between 6.2 and 29 percent from 1960 to 1970—with an average loss of 17.6 percent, or three times the statewide average. But in other areas where stripping is relatively recent, such as in the West and Southwest, it has created many new jobs and boosted the local economies, at least temporarily.

The other social problems caused by strip mining are often ignored or unknown. The Conservation Foundation's Malcom Baldwin believes that many social effects of strip mining are impossible to calculate. Among these additional costs are such things as the loss of other new industry, decrease in recreation and tourism, discouragement of investment, destruction of land for agriculture or development, and reduction of the tax base through lower assessments and outmigration.

Western Coal Fields

Publicity about strip mining has centered in Appalachia, but the newest and greatest battleground for stripping is the Northern Great Plains of the Far West— primarily the huge low-sulfur coal fields of Montana, Wyoming, North Dakota and South Dakota. Under the vast grasslands and high plateaus of the plains lie more than one trillion tons of coal—40 percent of the nation's supply. According to the Bureau of Mines, the area contains 77 percent of the country's "economically strippable" reserves—about 35 billion tons—and most of it is in thick (50-200 foot) seams just below the surface. Ownership of land and mineral rights in the area is extremely complex, with federal and state governments, Indians, railroad companies, ranchers and other private individuals holding surface and mining rights in at least 20 different combinations. The federal government owns about 30 percent of the lands, administered chiefly by the Bureau of Land Management and Bureau of Indian Affairs, and at least 50 percent of the mineral rights.

In the mid-1960s, major oil, coal and utility companies quietly began buying up leases on the coal rights of much Northern Great Plains land. Competitive bids quickly jumped from a few dollars an acre to more than $500 in cost and from about 100 acres to more than 5,000 acres in size. Federal coal leasing and prospecting permit actions now total more than 285. Total annual mineral production from Montana and Wyoming alone exceeded $200-million in 1969 and was projected to top $600-million in 1972, according to the Interior Department. In 1970, the department's Bureau of Reclamation began the North Central Power Study, aimed at assessing the region's electricity needs and potential output. Among the 35 participants in the study were private, public, regional and municipal utilities from as far away as Wisconsin,

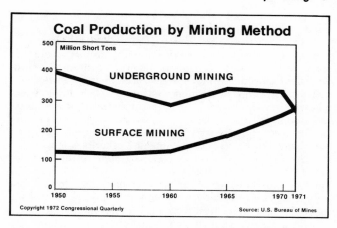

Coal Production by Mining Method

Copyright 1972 Congressional Quarterly   Source: U.S. Bureau of Mines

Illinois, Missouri, Utah and Oregon. The first phase of the study, completed in the fall of 1971, found no major obstacles to the development of a 53,000-megawatt power generating complex and a wide transmission grid system, estimating the total electric generating capacity by the year 2000 to be more than 180 million kilowatts, more than is now produced in either Japan, Germany or Great Britain.[4] The report projected extensive stripping of coal and construction of huge "minemouth" powerplants, aqueducts, reservoirs, power lines and new communities.

The only problem with the North Central Power Study, which the Interior Department de-emphasized, was that it virtually ignored environmental, social, economic and political impacts of the proposed complex. Much of the area consists of delicate ecosystems which could be permanently damaged by strip mining. It is one of the few regions left in the country where air pollution is still low, but the clear skies could be clouded by coal-burning plants whose smoke stacks emit fly ash, sulfur dioxide and nitrogen oxides. Water resources in the area are as yet unpolluted or undiverted, and it contains a diverse fish and wildlife population. But finally, potential development of the region promises an enormous impact on the people, with the population of about 130,000 at least doubling, according to some projections. This would require new residential, commercial and community facilities, schools, water and sanitation systems and raise other land use problems.

Many ranchers in the area had begun to complain, as big mining companies which had obtained mineral rights came to claim surface rights as well, which they legally could do under the laws of most states. Homesteaders who settled on the land in the 19th century knew they didn't own mineral rights, but that was before strip mining was widely practiced and most felt any mining would be underground. Merle Cox, a Sarpy Creek, Mont., rancher, sold his land to Westmoreland Resources, a conglomerate of eastern coal, oil and construction companies. "They said if I didn't sell they'd condemn it and take it, so I went and saw a lawyer. He said they could do it. It looked like selling was the only thing I could do," Cox said in an interview published in September 1972 by the *Los Angeles Times*. Another rancher, John R. Redding, refused to sell out. He told *Newsweek* in October 1972: "They want my coal real bad. We got a 60-foot seam. It looks like a boom coming? To me it looks more like a disaster. It will be a boom for a few companies but not for us. Goddammit, they have no legal right to condemn our land."

In addition, the North Central study raised a storm of protests from environmental groups, state and local officials and even some federal agencies. A study by the Environmental Defense Fund found "serious potential for large scale degradation of both human and natural environments" and recommended coordinated development planning for the entire area and detailed studies of actual strip mining reclamation, regional weather factors, river ecosystems and other problems.

As a result, the Interior Department retrenched and on Oct. 3, 1972, Secretary Rogers C.B. Morton announced the creation of an "inter-agency task force to assess the potential social, economic and environmental impacts" which might result from future development.

The study, termed the Northern Great Plains Resource Program, was to be conducted by Interior, the Environmental Protection Agency, the Old West Regional Commission, with other federal agencies to be called in as needed with ample provision for public involvement. Morton said the study was expected to take about three years, with preliminary results to be incorporated into

regional planning after the first year. Others estimated that the project could take up to five years, however, while stripping and leasing activity continued.

Four Corners: Power-Hungry Future? One area where large scale strip mining already is underway is the Four Corners region of the Southwest, where the borders of Arizona, New Mexico, Colorado and Utah meet in a cross. Six huge coal-burning electric powerplants are planned for the area, with two—the Four Corners and Mojave plants—already operating and the others scheduled for completion between 1974 and 1980. Nearly half of the power generated will serve southern California. The Four Corners project was begun by a consortium of 23 power companies called WEST, for Western Energy Supply and Transmission Association. The generating capacity of the six major plants will be about 14,000 megawatts, but by 1985 WEST plans to add enough smaller plants to bring the load up to 40,000 megawatts. Like the Northern Great Plains, the Southwest power project has aroused fierce controversy. One of the biggest objections is air pollution. Smoke from the plants has been recognized as far away as Albuquerque, 150 miles south, and Bryce Canyon, 215 miles west. The Four Corners plant probably is the worst single source of air pollution in the world, and if all six plants were operating at full capacity, their total daily emissions of fly ash (240 tons), sulfur dioxide (2,166 tons) and nitrogen oxides (1,000 tons) would be greater than those of New York and Los Angeles combined. In addition to loss of visibility, such pollution can be a health hazard. The Southwest Energy Committee in Flagstaff, Ariz., found evidence that tiny particulates in combination with sulfur dioxide were directly responsible for respiratory disease. At one hospital, the admission rate for acute and chronic respiratory illness in children doubled between 1965 and 1970; the first power plant began operation in 1963.[5] The plants have begun to install scrubbers and other pollution control equipment that will remove most of the pollutants, but small sub-micron sized particles can still escape. Another pollution problem is water, a scarce and valuable resource in the area. The powerplants need large quantities from the Colorado River and its tributaries for cooling purposes. The largest plant, Kaiparowitz, will consume 102,000 acre-feet annually, enough to serve the needs of San Francisco for a year. Withdrawal of such enormous quantities could sharply reduce the water table of the region, lessen amounts available to present users and increase the already-high salinity of the Colorado River.

But by far the most controversial issue in the region is strip mining. The two existing plants and at least two of the future plants will use strip-mined coal. Peabody Coal Company holds a lease on nearly 25,000 acres of joint Navajo-Hopi Indian lands and another 40,000 acres of Navajo land, all on top of historic Black Mesa, which now is the nation's largest strip mine. The mesa contains 337 million tons of bituminous coal in about 100 square miles. Peabody leased the land under an agreement with the tribal councils, but many Indians say the councils are controlled by white men and do not represent majority views. Peabody is paying one of the highest royalties ever paid on Indian lands—25 cents a ton, but the tribes will receive only about $73-million during the 35-year lease while Peabody will get $750-million. The company guarantees to hire 75 percent Indians for the 400 available

Coal Production by State

Production of bituminous coal and lignite
in the United States, 1971

(Thousand short tons)

State	Underground	Strip	Auger	Total
Ala.	6,751	11,121	73	17,945
Alaska	———	698	———	698
Ariz.	———	1,146	———	1,146
Ark.	41	236	———	276
Colo.	3,329	2,008	———	5,337
Ill.	29,446	28,956	———	58,402
Ind.	1,765	19,631	———	21,396
Iowa	418	571	———	989
Kans.	———	1,151	———	1,151
Ky.	53,216	56,766	9,406	119,389
Md.	176	1,365	102	1,644
Mo.	———	4,036	———	4,036
Mont.	20	7,044	———	7,064
N.M.	977	7,198	———	8,175
N. Dak. (lignite)	———	6,075	———	6,075
Ohio	12,862	37,595	973	51,431
Okla.	193	2,039	2	2,234
Pa.	44,289	28,002	544	72,835
Tenn.	3,543	5,412	316	9,271
Utah	4,620	6	———	4,626
Va.	21,631	7,168	1,829	30,628
Wash.	32	1,102	———	1,134
W. Va.	92,437	21,747	4,074	118,258
Wyo.	141	7,899	12	8,052
Total [1]	**275,888**	**258,972**	**17,332**	**552,192**

1 Data may not add to totals shown because of independent rounding.

SOURCE: "Coal-Bituminous and Lignite in 1971," Mineral Industry Surveys, Bureau of Mines, U.S. Department of Interior, Sept. 27, 1972, p. 11.

jobs, but so far only about 100 have been hired out of 130,000 Navajos and 5,000 Hopis. Indian attitudes are mixed. Chester Interpreter, a welder, told the *Wall Street Journal* in April 1971: "If it didn't come from here it'd just come from some place on white man's land. Why shouldn't we get the money and the jobs?" But Robert Salabye, a Navajo, said: "We have overcome hardships, yet none of the hardships previously encountered has ripped into the insides of our religion and way of life like the power shovels and deep wells. None have destroyed the source of life like the power plants and strip mining."[6] To many Indians, Black Mesa is a religious and spiritual shrine, literally the center of the universe. The Navajo believe that the mesa is the body of the Earth Mother; Hopi consider themselves stewards of the land and consider mining a desecration. The Indian poet Smoholla wrote:

You ask me to plow the ground.
Shall I take a knife and tear my Mother's breast?
Then when I die she will not take me to her bosom to rest.
You ask me to dig for stones?
Shall I dig under her skin for bones?
Then when I die, I cannot enter her body to be born again.

A study of the Southwest region by the Senate Interior and Insular Affairs Committee which was released in August 1972 (S Rept 92-1015) found that the environmental damage to the area was severe but said there was no other source for the needed power. It was too late now, the report said, but had there been better planning, different decisions probably would have been made. It recommended a thorough study of the long range economic and environmental impact of the energy complex, but said what was really needed were new federal laws on land use, power plant siting, strip mining control and public land management. Another recent report was that of the Interior Department's Southwest Energy Study Task Force, released in December 1972. It found that energy consumption in the area would increase from about 28,000 megawatts today to about 59,000 by 1980 and 110,000 by 1990, with southern California consuming about 60 per cent of the totals. "Relatively little effort has been made to reduce consumer demands and unless a major change in the use trend is achieved during the next decade, the 1980 estimated requirement for generation appears realistic," the report said. The report also said that regrading of stripped areas was "proceeding satisfactorily," but "no significant progress" had been made in revegetating the arid land. Peabody's employment program "would reduce by only a small percentage the large resident Indian unemployment problem," the report stated. While "no evidence was obtained that areas or sites of religious or sacred significance would be seriously altered by power development activities, the report admitted that "there appears to be no consensus in the Indian community concerning benefit and loss to Indian culture from Southwest electric energy generation."

Strip Mining History

In the Appalachian Mountains, rich natural resources and stark human poverty are juxtaposed. Under part of the mountain range, from western Pennsylvania through eastern Ohio, Maryland, West Virginia, Virginia, Kentucky, Tennessee and into Alabama lies nearly 40

Corporate Reserves and Production
(parent companies in parenthesis)

Company	Estimated Reserves (billion tons)	Percent Low-Sulphur	Coal Production in 1971 (million tons)	Coal Sales in 1971 (millions)
Burlington Northern	11.0	100%	none	none
Union Pacific	10.0	50	none	none
Peabody Coal (Kennecott Copper)	8.7	27	54.8	$268.8
Consolidation Coal (Continental Oil)	8.1	35	54.8	360.3
Monterey Coal (Exxon)	7.0	na	1.2	na[1]
Amax Coal (American Metal Climax)	4.0	50	12.5	na
Island Creek Coal (Occidental Petroleum)	3.3	28	22.8	247.2
United States Steel	3.0	na	16.6	na
Pittsburg & Midway Coal (Gulf Oil)	2.6	8	7.0	33.5
North American Coal	2.5	80	8.8	63.6
Reynolds Metals	2.1	95	none	none
Bethlehem Steel	1.8	na	12.0	none
Pacific Power & Light	1.6	100	1.7	none

1 Not applicable.

SOURCE: *Forbes* magazine, Nov. 15, 1972, p. 41.

percent of the nation's coal reserves. But the area long has been one of the nation's poorest. The residents of Appalachia traditionally have provided cheap labor for out-of-state entrepreneurs, who, according to some estimates, have extracted $500-billion worth or ores, fuels and timber from its hills over the past 130 years while paying nearly nothing in return. Coal mining in Appalachia traditionally has meant underground mining, but stripping in the area actually began in the early 19th century. Strip mining in Kentucky began as early as 1800, according to Harry M. Caudill, the Whitesburg, Ky., lawyer and author whose classic book *Night Comes to the Cumberlands* (1963) first brought national attention to strip mining and whose more recent *My Land Is Dying* (1971) calls for abolition of stripping in Appalachia. Coal was dug from shallow beds on hillsides and along streams, then shipped downriver on rafts to the growing cities where it was sold by the bushel for stoves and furnaces. Picks and shovels were the first tools of the strip miners, but around 1825 a mule-drawn scraper was devised which in conjunction with drills and black powder made stripping more efficient. But because of the continued inability to move large quanitites of soil to expose coal seams, stripping on a large scale still was not feasible, and the industrial boom which followed the Civil War was fueled chiefly by deep-mined coal. Hundreds of new deep mines opened in those years, reaching their highest output during the two world wars. But stripping did not wholly disappear. In 1877, an Otis steam shovel was peeling away prairie soil from a coal bed at Pittsburg, Kans., and by 1905, an entirely

(Continued on p. 33)

Coal Fields of the United States

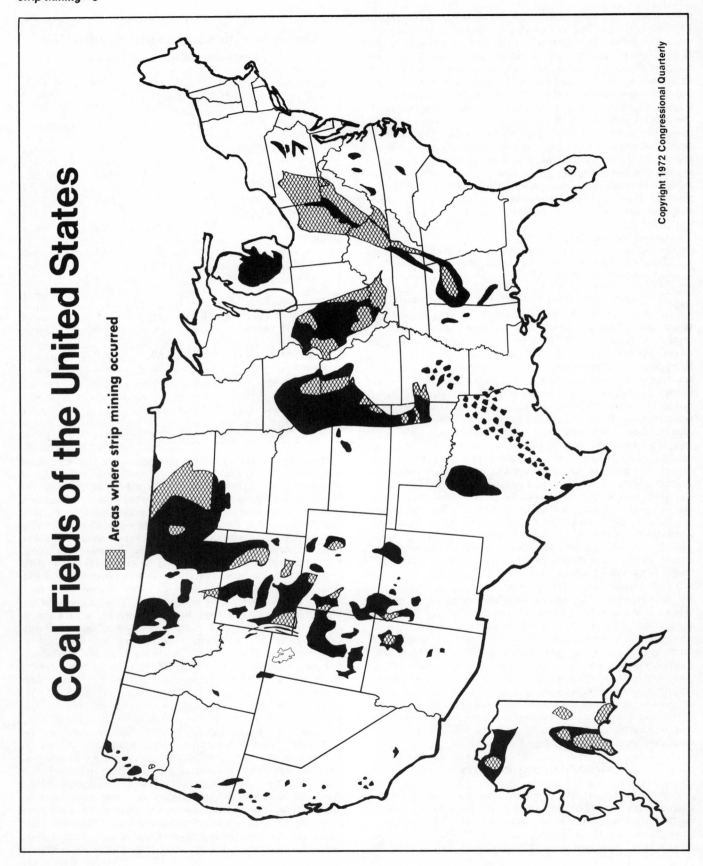

■ Areas where strip mining occurred

(Continued from p. 31)

mechanical strip mine was opened in Laurel County, Ky., with a steam drill and a Vulcan shovel mounted on a railroad spur. For the rest of this century, mining has become a race between the technologies of deep and surface mining, with the former winning out until about 1955, when stripping and augering began the precipitate increase which enabled them to surpass underground mining in 1971.

But as the technology of stripping progressed, the living standards of Appalachia's residents deteriorated. In intensive strip mining areas, economic alternatives are limited. Land values drop, new housing and industry are discouraged, water supplies are polluted and natural beauty is eroded. In West Virginia, recreation and tourism employ more than 19,000 people, while strip mining employs only about 4,000, but the incompatibility of the two industries is obvious. Few tourists would derive enjoyment from visiting scarred strip mined areas, although this possibility has been suggested by some mining industry executives. At the 1971 House hearings, Peabody's Coal's president Edwin R. Phelps said: "Beauty is indeed in the eye of the beholder and impossible to define. Nature created the Bad Lands of South Dakota and they were made a national monument, but if any surface miner duplicated them even on a small scale, it would be called a national disgrace. Requiring that lands be returned to productive use can be enforced; requiring that they be restored to a natural beauty makes enforcement a matter of taste."

In eastern Ohio, particularly extensive stripping has occurred, with little benefit to locals. A group of students from Case Western Reserve University in Cleveland found that in Belmont County, the value of coal has risen steadily but the average per capita and per family incomes remained below the average for all of Appalachia. They reported that coal companies made from 70 to 100 percent profit on their investment, grossing about $65,-000 per acre of coal. But the strippers paid only from $50 to $1,000 per acre, less than $17 per acre in taxes and were required to spend less than $300 per acre on reclamation. "In a sense," the report said, "the people are indirectly subsidizing the strippers for much of the damage they inflict. With land left useless, the population declining, the fluctuating tax base becoming ever more dependent on the coal industry, the economy of the strip mined area plummets, no one knowing when it will hit bottom."[7] Of the county's 341,000 acres, 200,000 have been leased or sold to strippers. A study by Prof. Samuel Brock, a West Virginia University economist, found that in one year two strip mine operators made net profits of more than 100 per cent. Stripping made millionaires out of 50 residents in Pikeville, Ky., (pop. 5,000) in a county where more than half are classified as poor under federal poverty program standards.

New Stripping and Old Laws. A primary reason for the surge of strip mining in the past decade has been the development of massive machinery which literally can peel off layers of earth up to 200 feet thick to get at beds of coal. In the early 1900s, steam shovels had a capacity of only a few cubic yards per "bite," but by 1957 the largest could lift 70 cubic yards in its bucket and in 1965 the size was increased to 180 cubic yards, which meant that 16,000 tons of overburden could be removed in an hour. The biggest machine operating today is the American Electric Power Company's "Big

Muskie," so called because it strips in Muskingum County, Ohio. It weighs 27 million pounds, stands 32 stories high, has a 310-foot boom, 170 electric motors and cost $25-million to build. Another famous stripping machine is the GEM of Egypt (for Giant Earth Mover, operating in Egypt Valley, Ohio), which weighs nearly 14 tons and has a body so big it contains a shower room for the crew. It has a 7,200-volt power plant and consumes more electricity per day than a town of nearly 5,000 residents. Some local residents have tried to fight the strippers, but the complexity of the laws and the power of the companies have been awesome opponents. "There just ain't nothin' we can do," one elderly Ohio citizen told *Newsweek* in June 1971: "They have the power and the money. We don't have nothin'."

An historical reason for the spread of stripping in Appalachia was the "broad form deed," under which mining agents years ago bought up the mineral rights to vast areas for as little as 10 to 50 cents an acre. The poor mountain people jumped at the chance to make what then seemed a large amount of money and still be able to live on their land. But many who signed the deeds were illiterate, and affixed their signature marks under fine print which gave away rights to do "any and all things necessary, or...deemed necessary or convenient in mining and removing the coal." The buyer had the same rights not just from the present owner, but from all "heirs, successors and assigns forever," and a further clause gave the buyer immunity from damage suits relating to mining operations. Under this or similar systems, most of the Appalachian coal regions were locked up by large eastern corporations long before modern stripping technology was conceived. Today, Kentucky is the only remaining coal state which still honors the broad form deed, although the power of mineral rights owners in the West to condemn surface lands is in effect the same basic principle.

The mining companies also took steps to ensure that they were supported by the state legislatures and courts. Harry M. Caudill describes in *My Land is Dying* how this process took place in eastern Kentucky, as the educated young left the region, leaving behind the old, disabled and helpless who were dependent on welfare or public works and thus became pawns of political machines:

> Independence counted for little at the polls among those who feared that a wrong vote might bring loss of subsistence—and the machines that delivered the vote were, not surprisingly, more finely attuned to the concerns of the mine operators and the land companies whose holdings they worked than to the needs of the voters whose lives they controlled. The men whom the machines sent to the state legislature were likewise attuned to the interests of the mining industry. They constructed a revenue system that had no scruples about ordinary citizens but that tenderly exempted the purchases of the coal companies. Thus, for example, a 5 per cent retail sales tax was passed that applied to a dental drill but not to a coal auger, to a miner's shovel but not to a 20-ton mechanical loader."

The courts were equally accomodating, especially in the post-war years when strip mining became such big business. The first "landmark" case was *Russell Fork Coal vs. Hawkins,* a decision handed down by the Kentucky Court of Appeals in 1949. The coal company had stripped 12 acres of steep land at the head of a narrow valley, and on the night of Aug. 2, 1945, a cloudburst brought on a flash flood which destroyed all the houses in the valley, although no lives were lost. Several damage suits by the victims were upheld in the lower courts and by a circuit jury, but when the company went to the appellate court the verdict was reversed. Caudill wrote: "The decision of the state judges in effect delcared that the masses of soil, the uprooted trees, and the slabs of rock and slate had been harmless until set in motion by the force of water. It was nature that had unleashed the water; thus the damage to the plaintiffs was solemnly declared to be an act of God—for which no coal operator...could be held responsible. The ruling absolved the stripper of all damages and sent his hapless victims onto the welfare rolls." Another important ruling came in 1953 in the case of *Buchanan vs. Watson,* in which the court dealt squarely for the first time with the problem of mineral rights versus surface rights. A small farmer had been virtually ruined by the company that stripped the coal from his land, and he sued for full damage payments. The trial judge ruled in his favor and so did the appellate court at first. But the company petitioned for a rehearing and lobbied intensively around the state capital. As a result, the original opinion was withdrawn and the new ruling absolved the company of any responsibility. The judgment said first that the land was of relatively low value and second that a decision against the company "would create great confusion and much hardship in a segment of the industry that can ill afford such a blow." Caudill wrote: "Thus the highest court in the state of Kentucky boldly and arrogantly based a landmark decision on considerations that were patently economic." But the implications of the decision for the coal industry and for Appalachia were profound. Stripping flourished as never before, cheap coal flooded the market and the price remained stable for more than a decade.

TVA and Appalachian Coal. Much of this inexpensive coal was destined for the Tennessee Valley Authority (TVA), today the nation's largest single consumer of coal and its largest producer of electric power. Founded in 1933 during the New Deal, TVA's original purpose was both political and social, aimed at bringing an entire area out of poverty with a series of hydroelectric dams and transmission lines, cheap fertilizer plants and programs to restore and conserve lands eroded by poor agriculture. But as the demand for electricity increased after World War II, TVA found water power insufficient and began building coal-fired generating plants. Of the 99-billion kilowatt hours now produced annually, more than 80 per cent are derived from coal and half of that comes from strip mines. In 1971 TVA bought 32.5 million tons of coal, or about 10 percent of the total burned by the entire electrical industry.

But TVA's insistence on cheap power led to criticism of the agency for promoting poor strip mining practices. TVA virtually controls the fate of Appalachian coal-bearing regions—setting market trends, changing prices, influencing technology development and effectively prescribing standards to which several industries must adhere. Wanting to obtain cheap coal in large quantities, TVA in the early 1950s began requesting industry bids on specified tonnages of coal to be delivered over several years. Mining companies submitted the lowest bids possible, but then the agency accepted bids only for part of the needed coal, made the price public and the competitive bid process started again. In this manner, the price of coal was depressed from about $4.80 to $2.50 a ton in less than a decade, while from 1951 to 1956 TVA increased its annual purchases from one million to 18 million tons. In the mountains, this trend virtually guaranteed that coal companies had to cut their overhead costs drastically, which usually meant stripping. "In eastern Kentucky," Caudill wrote, "as elsewhere in central Appalachia, its role has been nothing short of disastrous. The same cheap fuel that made possible an era of prosperity in the TVA region has wrecked the coalfields, impoverished entire communities and forced thousands of mountain people to desert the place of their birth." Even James Garvey, vice president of the National Coal Association, expressed doubts: "TVA has taken advantage of the willingness of non-career coal companies to 'cream the contours' (and) has lived off the very inexpensive coal which could be, and was, obtained from strip mining the contours of the hills." [8]

In the early 1960s, however, the agency began to realize the amount of damage its stripping contractors were causing. In a 1963 "Appraisal of Coal Strip Mining," the agency conceded that stream pollution, soil erosion, lowered land values and esthetic damage did result, but said the land was of little value anyway, selling for only a few dollars an acre but containing coal valued at up to $9,000 an acre. But criticism continued and in 1965, TVA chairman of the board Aubrey J. Wagner declared it the agency's position that "all strip mined lands must be restored" but left responsibility up to the states or Congress. But three years later, TVA's reclamation director, James Curry, told a reporter for *The Nation:* "Strip mining is part of the American way—an integral aspect of the American economy." In 1968 the agency issued a set of contract reclamation requirements and in 1970 announced that it was revising and toughening its provisions, but the regulations still contained many loopholes and were difficult to enforce. A resident of Tennessee's strip mining region told the *Nashville Tennessean* in September 1971: "This is what TVA is doing to us. They tell us they are making the strip miners grow it back. They can never make that mountain green again. And they can never take that slop out of our river again." TVA board member Frank Smith said in 1971 that the six years during which reclamation had been required by TVA contracts was not enough time to tell whether it would or wouldn't work.

Reclamation And Control

Reclamation is the key word in the lexicon of strip mining today. But the word means different things to different people, for there are as many degrees of reclamation as there are types of land. In flat or rolling regions which are "area mined," some reclamation efforts have been quite successful. But in mountainous terrain with steep slopes which are "contour mined," reclamation is difficult if not impossible. The mining industry generally talks in terms of reconditioning the land by repairing major damage, grading the surface and replanting some vegetation. But many environmentalists want total restoration of the land to its original or a better condition, a goal which in some places may be mutually exclusive with stripping. Hechler told the *Washington Post* in March 1972 that reclamation "is like putting lipstick on a corpse." Caudill compares the process to restoring a virgin to her original condition after she has been raped. But coal company executives contend that stripping and reclamation now go hand in hand. "It's hard to defend what happened in the past," concedes Carl E. Bagge, president of the National Coal Association, "but the future will be different." Edwin R. Phelps of Peabody Coal told the House Interior Committee in 1971: "To my mind, good reclamation is an integral part of the mining process." But Ralph Hatch, president of Hanna Coal Company, admitted: "Theoretically, reclamation of area mined land should be a simple process. The land is graded to a usable land form, the soil is planted and then nature takes its course. In reality the job is seldom that easy."

The process of good reclamation, both sides generally agree, should start long before any mining begins. The soil, climate, vegetation and other elements of the ecosystem should be analyzed and reclamation goals set. "Preplanning is the first step in reclamation," says Dr. Ronald D. Hill of the Environmental Protection Agency. In most cases, fertile topsoil should be set aside and saved separately from the rest of the overburden, which may contain toxic or acid-producing minerals. Actual reclamation should begin as soon as possible after mining because fresh earth is easier to handle and otherwise erosion may begin. The land should be graded to its original contour, topsoil replaced and then fertilized and seeded with appropriate grass, legumes or trees. But reclamation is a tricky business, and many projects which tried to follow this general procedure failed, as grading packed the surface too tightly for seeds to take root, or the fertilizer ran off after rains and the vegetation died. A study in Belmont County, Ohio, compared two watersheds, one natural and one reclaimed, over a five-year period. The "reclaimed" area's streams were highly acidic and the soil contained toxic elements which killed tomato plants and increased eutrophication of a nearby lake. In Montana's great plains, the Knife River Coal Company planted trees and legumes, "often with total failure but occasionally with surprising success," according to company reclamation officer Thomas A. Gwynn.[9] But a local rancher, Wallace McRae, countered: "Strip mining as practiced in the past has completely destroyed the productivity of the land for agricultural crop and livestock purposes." In the arid Four Corners region, where ecosystems are even more delicate and rainfall more scarce, the problems are intensified. Elwood A. Seaman, chief ecologist for the Bureau of Reclamation, has expressed doubt that any native plants could be reestablished in Black Mesa's stripped lands.

On the other hand, some reclamation programs undeniably have been successful. Pacific Power & Light Company, a major Northwest utility, since 1965 has been reclaiming stripped lands in Wyoming, where it has extensive low-sulfur coal holdings. Topsoil is replaced and then mulched with straw which is disced into the ground to help reduce wind erosion and protect the wheatgrass seedlings. The company spends as much as $700 per acre, and has established a cooperative research program with the University of Wyoming to study reclamation problems on other lands to be stripped where conditions differ. The company has been praised by local environmentalists and government officials alike for its

efforts. "We're part of the community," the company's Bob Peterson told Editorial Research Reports. "It's only the decent thing to do to put the land back the way it was." Agronomist Lee Hansen said: "We want to know it's done right and will stay that way."[10] Other companies also have had some success with reclamation. Since 1943 the Central Ohio Coal Company has planted 32 million tree seedlings in reclaiming 18,000 of 22,000 stripped acres with survival rates ranging from 50 percent among oaks to 95 percent for locusts, which it now plans to harvest as a timber crop. In West Virginia, the "head of the hollow" method of stripping entire mountain tops and filling up the surrounding valleys with the overburden, thus creating flat areas upon which it envisions industrial or housing developments or entire new towns. "It's worked so well that some of our neighbors have asked if we won't strip mine their land, too, and fix it up this way afterward," company president Paul Morton told *U.S. News & World Report* in September 1972. Other projects have included filling stripped areas with solid wastes as land fill or fertilizing them with sewage sludge to increase agricultural growth.

Despite these accomplishments in reclamation, some critics complain of an industry smokescreen. "Much progress has been made in reclaiming strip mined lands, there is no questioning this fact," admits Hechler. "There is also a vast and rising amount of money going into the first two letters of the word 'progress.' If all the money being spent by strip mine companies on color photos, brochures, helicopter trips for legislators, bus trips for schoolchildren and service clubs, radio, television, newspaper ads, and public relations representatives were being spent on reclamation itself, perhaps there would be even more genuine progress instead of just 'PR'."

The experiences of England and West Germany, where strip mining has been carried on for many years under strict reclamation controls, prove that it can be done. But the European attitude toward use of limited land resources is fundamentally different from our own. The Sierra Club's Peter Borelli points out: "The key to the West German and British experience in land restoration lies in meticulously detailed planning...there is no American control comparable to the European systems." Borelli told Editorial Research Reports that land use planning was an integral part of strip mining control: "Strip mining is a land use that severely reduces your future options. You can't talk about reclamation until you talk about where you mine, how you mine and under what conditions you mine. The technology has to be improved, we have to plug in land use planning, and we have to get a financial and spiritual commitment on the part of the industry."

State Attempts to Control. Most of the nation's coal-producing states have tried to pass laws to control strip mining to some degree, but of 28 states with existing statutes, few are considered adequately restrictive by environmentalists or particularly burdensome by the mining industry. Several state legislatures will consider strip mining bills during 1973 sessions. Although abolition bills have been introduced in many states, none has gone as far as banning strip mining, although West Virginia in 1971 did forbid stripping in 22 low coal-bearing counties not yet disturbed. State laws generally emphasize reclamation, but most are hampered by weak backup regulations and poor enforcement. Even in states where laws are considered strong, such as Pennsylvania, Kentucky, Virginia, West Virginia, Ohio and Tennessee, strict enforcement is often lacking. Hechler has said: "It is extremely difficult for state legislators, and those who administer the law, to withstand the kind of heavy pressure (from the mining industry) which is immediate, insistent, belligerent, unbending, emotional, determined and coupled with political threats which are also linked with hints of heavy campaign contributions to political opponents. The state and its elected public officials almost always seem to bend under this type of pressure, frequently expressing the fear that the strip mining industry will simply move on with its jobs to some other state."

Pennsylvania—the state with the most deep and strip mined lands—is generally thought to have the most stringent law, requiring strip mine operators to submit detailed reclamation plans before any work begins, including a statement of the "highest and best" use of the land prior to mining, the intended use after stripping and reclamation, the manner of conserving and compacting soil, a complete revegetation program, plans to prevent erosion and siltation and a detailed timetable. The law flatly prohibits water pollution, sets a reclamation bond fee and provides fines and prison terms for violations. It allows other uses of the land after reclamation, such as commercial or recreational development, but gives local governments power to zone out stripping if they desire. One engineering firm estimated that to meet the state's requirements, an operator must spend as much as $5,000 an acre. The law has been on the books in some form since 1963, and enforcement is considered among the best in the nation.

Ohio in April 1972 passed a new strip mining law at least as tough as Pennsylvania's, although some environmentalists took a wait-and-see attitude on enforcement. Democratic Gov. John J. Gilligan called it "a model for other states" and said it "will put an end to destruction of vast areas of our state by careless strip mining practices." The bill gives new authority to the Department of Natural Resources to reject mining permits where environmental damage cannot be prevented, increases penalties and bonds required for reclamation. Kentucky's legislature, on the other hand, in 1972 failed to pass any of the numerous bills introduced to toughen its model 1966 law, although the state in 1971 took over the national lead in coal production, with stripping ahead of underground for the first time ever. The legislature does not meet again until 1974. Defeat of the bills came after an intensive lobbying campaign by the Kentucky Coal Association and the apparent cooperation of Democratic Gov. Wendell Ford. The *Louisville Courier-Journal* editorialized on March 20, 1972: "One promise he (Ford) did not keep was that he would move aggressively in the area of strip mining. The single most reprehensible performance in this session was that of the House Agriculture and Natural Resources Committee, which squeezed the life out of all significant strip mine bills by sitting on them. This could not have been done without the Governor's approval." A study by the newspaper in May 1972 found that the laws of Tennessee, Virginia, West Virginia and Ohio all were stronger than Kentucky's. All five state laws provide that reclamation should be done without cost to taxpayers

and require cash or surety bonds. The study concluded that each law, if properly enforced, should be adequate, but found that widespread erosion and flooding still occurred. "Administrators agree in general that the legislators who made the laws failed to provide enough money for enforcement," it said.

A recent study done for West Virginia's Division of Reclamation found that the state was not getting satisfactory results from its law, especially in attempting to restore high walls. "When it comes to restraining strip mine operators," Caudill has said, "the Division of Reclamation is as worthless as a cupful of cold spit." And Norman Williams, a former Natural Resources Department official who now is director of the Mid-Appalachian Environmental Service in Charleston, said: "The blame is on the entire state apparatus. The governor and the legislature are ultimately responsible. Until a governor is able to stand up to the enormous pressures— and the pressures are mounting every day—there won't be a change. There is an industry coalition which has an enormous amount of leverage."[11]

Congress and Strip Mining

These and similar problems have led many people to believe that federal strip mining control legislation is the only answer to the problem nationwide, and it appears virtually certain that the 93rd Congress will pass a bill in some form. Senate Democratic Majority Leader Mike Mansfield of Montana has called the issue a "must" for 1973 and said it would be "one of the first orders of business." Lobbyists for environmental groups and the mining industry also are gearing up for major campaigns to influence the legislation. "We'll be making an enormous effort here on strip mining," Brent Blackwelder of the Environmental Policy Center told Congressional Quarterly. The Sierra Club's Borelli told Editorial Research Reports that his organization was working with others in the Coalition Against Strip Mining to write a bill of their own and have it introduced, but first wanted to see how key congressional committee assignments shaped up and what action the Nixon administration would take. "We're not rushing it," he said. "What we're trying to do is cull the best of all the available sources. It's all beginning to jell."

The foundation for federal legislation was laid in the 92nd Congress when the House on Oct. 11, 1972 passed a relatively tough control bill (HR 6482) by a 265-75 roll-call vote, despite strong opposition from the mining industry. But the Senate took no action on HR 6482 or its own bill (S 630) and the measure died when Congress adjourned. The House-passed bill gave the secretary of interior power to administer a federal regulatory and permit program, but allowed states to run their own programs if they met federal standards. For the first time, mine operators would have been required to obtain permits and to submit reclamation plans and purchase bonds. No strip mining would have been permitted on slopes greater than 20 degrees unless the mine operator could prove that environmental damage would be prevented and the land reclaimed. The National Coal Association (NCA) and the American Mining Congress (AMC) which had claimed all along that they endorsed passage of the legislation, changed their position a week before the vote and actively opposed the bill.

In an Oct. 6 letter to members of Congress, AMC president J. Allen Overton Jr. wrote: "There is grave danger that...the national economy and national security may be jeopardized through adoption of legislation which contains serious and unnecessary threats to the ability of the mining industry to furnish the increasing amounts of energy and minerals our nation so sorely needs." In a round of telegrams the same day, Overton and NCA president Carl E. Bagge called the bill "punitive" and "unrealistic" and said it would "summarily halt much of vital U.S. coal production." But the Environmental Policy Center and the Coalition Against Strip Mining, in an Oct. 11 letter to members of the House, said: "The mining industry's sudden opposition...represents a surprising admission by the surface coal mine operators that: 1) they have not been reclaiming their lands... 2) they do not intend to reclaim...and 3) they are currently surface mining coal in areas that they find impossible to reclaim."

Several new strip mining control bills were introduced in the first few weeks of the 93rd Congress. Hechler, with 25 co-sponsors, introduced a slightly weaker version of his abolition bill, which would ban mountain stripping within six months but would allow 18 months for phasing out area mining in flatter terrain. Ohio Democrat Wayne Hays, original sponsor of HR 6482, reintroduced the bill, but said in January 1973 it might be amended: "I think the Committee on Interior will get this out promptly. No legislation is perfect. I have no desire to stop it (strip mining) because I realize the need for coal." On the Senate side, Interior Committee chairman Henry M. Jackson, a Washington Democrat, asked the President's Council on Environmental Quality to study the impact of blanket prohibitions and slope limitations. He said that HR 6482 "was adopted without a full and realistic appreciation of all its consequences and the serious policy questions it poses." If Congress does enact a law it will be the first federal regulation of strip mining in history, although control bills were introduced as early as 1940 and bills have been introduced in every Congress since the 86th.

Coordinated National Energy Policy

Whatever action is taken to control strip mining, most observers believe that no ultimate solution can be achieved until the nation develops a long-range and comprehensive energy policy which carefully considers coal and other fuels in the future of America's energy supply needs. Some forecasts say that U.S. oil and natural gas reserves will last only for another two or three decades at present consumption rates and barring new discoveries, but coal has a "lifetime" of some 3700 years. Thus it is evident that coal will play a major role in energy use for some time to come, but how this coal is mined and how it is used still are debatable issues. Many people believe that a conversion from strip mining back to more deep mining is a possible path to follow. A May 1972 study by the Environmental Policy Center calculated that deep-mined coal was "the only realistic substitute" "for surface-mined coal." The report said that an examination of low-sulfur deep-mine coal found "more than ample" reserves to take the place of "all surface-mined

coal used to produce electricity for hundreds of years, assuming present economic and technological conditions, and assuming that national energy demand levels continue to grow." The report said there were about 30.8 billion tons of low sulfur coal and lignite which could be stripped and about 221.5 billion tons which must be deep mined. The average cost of deep mined electric utility coal was about 20 to 30 per cent higher than stripped coal, the study said, so if strip mining was banned the cost of power to consumers would increase by about $200-million, or less than $1 per individual per year, or $100-million if only mountain stripping were banned.

But a study by the National Coal Association countered that it was not realistic to replace strip mining with underground mining because "264 deep mines of one million tons capacity each would be required," with capitalization costs of between $3.2- and $3.7-billion ($12 to $14 per ton of annual capacity). The process would take three to five years before full production could be reached and more than 78,000 trained miners would be needed, the NCA report said, costing an additional $497-million in wages and salaries. But the Environmental Policy Center study said the NCA estimates were too high because they were based on opening up all *new* underground mines and brining them to *full* production. "Many old and inactive mines can be reopened and expanded so that the burden of substitution does not fall entirely on new mines. Furthermore, limited production from deep mines can be achieved within months; immediate full production is not essential."

Interior Secretary Morton seemed to support the environmentalists' conclusions when he told *Newsweek* in October 1972: "We must develop a new mining ethic in this country.... It is the greatest challenge the Interior Department has ever faced. By demanding reclamation, we can easily get the technology to reclaim the land.... If we can get a grip on public lands, with new authority Congress hasn't granted yet, I think we can set the standard for a new mining ethic so that the deep seams can be mined and closely followed by an environmental program that is compatible esthetically and with proper land use. The land will have a second purpose. It must. That is all there is to it." But beyond the problems of coal and strip mining, it seems clear that the nation must begin to limit and stabilize its total energy consumption and develop new, safe and clean sources of power. When that is done, the dilemma of strip mining will solve itself.

---

[1] With 276.3 million short tons compared with 275.9 from underground mines. For this and other statistics, see "Coal-Bituminous and Lignite in 1971," *Mineral Industry Surveys*, Bureau of Mines, U.S. Department of the Interior, Sept. 27, 1972, and Bureau of Mines *Minerals Yearbook*.

[2] "Coal—Bituminous and Lignite in 1971," *op. cit.*, p. 7, 61.

[3] Quoted in *Business Week*, "The Coal Industry Makes a Dramatic Comeback," Nov. 4, 1972, p. 55.

[4] A watt is the rate of work represented by a current of one ampere under a pressure of one volt. A kilowatt is 1,000 watts and a megawatt is 1,000,000 watts. The total electric capacity of the United States today is about 340,000 megawatts.

[5] "What Is the Future of the Southwest?" Southwest Energy Committee (1972), p. 2.

[6] Quoted by Melissa Savage, "Black Mesa Mainline: Tracks on the Earth, *Clear Creek*, No. 13, p. 14.

[7] Timothy A. Albright, "The Hidden Costs of Strip Mining: A Socio-Economic Study of Belmont County, Ohio," January 1971.

[8] Quoted by Osborn Segerberg Jr., "Power Corrupts," *Esquire*, March 1972, p. 138.

[9] "Proceedings of the Montana Coal Symposium," Billings, Mont., November 1969, p. 101, 108.

[10] Pacific Power & Light *Bulletin*, November 1972, p. 6.

[11] Quoted in *Conservation Foundation Letter*, January 1972, p. 5.

COMMON OWNERSHIP OF FUEL SOURCES A GROWING TREND

Various investigators see a trend toward common ownership and control of competing fuel sources at a time when many speak of an energy crisis.

For example, a subcommittee on special small business problems of the House Select Committee on Small Business in a report Dec. 8, 1971, listed the following coal property acquisitions by oil companies and conglomerates. The report said that on the basis of the list the subcommittee "finds that a trend toward concentration in the coal industry is readily apparent."

Acquiring firm	Acquired firm	Acquired firm percent of market[1]	Date of acquisition
Gulf Oil Co.	Pittsburg & Midway Coal Co.	1.7	1963
Continental Oil Co.	Consolidation Coal Co.	11.0	1966
Kennecott Copper Co.	Peabody Coal Co.	11.0	1968
Occidental Petroleum Co.	Island Creek Coal Co.	5.0	1968
Standard Oil Co. (Ohio)	Old Ben Coal Co.	2.0	1968
American Metal Climax	Ayrshire Collieries	1.9	1968
Ashland Oil & Refining Co.	Archer Mineral	1.0	1968
Occidental Petroleum Co.	Maust Coal & Coke Corp.	1.3	1969

1 Based on 1968 total national coal tonnage.
SOURCE: Moody's Industrial Manuals; and Beck and Rawlings.

The subcommittee, headed by Rep. Neal Smith (D Iowa), also noted oil company acquisitions of uranium and natural gas holdings. It said in its report that the growing fuel market concentration "may result in the dwindling of available fuel supplies, the maintenance of artificially high price levels and the eventual reduction in the number of competitors through merger, acquisition or bankruptcy." The committee found that major oil companies account for:

• Approximately 84 percent of U.S. refining capacity.
• About 72 percent of natural gas production and ownership of reserves.
• Thirty percent of domestic coal reserves.
• More than 20 percent of domestic coal production capacity.
• More than 50 percent of uranium reserves.
• Twenty-five percent of uranium milling capacity.

An early acquisition of a coal company by an oil company, as shown by the subcommittee's table, was Gulf Oil Corporation's purchase of the Pittsburg & Midway Coal Company in 1963. This was followed by others, including the Continental Oil Company's acquisition in 1966 of the big Consolidation Coal Company, one of the largest coal producers in the United States.

The Justice Department's antitrust division had concluded in 1966 that no antitrust action was warranted in the Continental-Consolidation Coal transaction. It found that companies were not in significant competition.

Among those which challenged that position was a House Select Small Business subcommittee. In a report, it said it believed the "failure of the Justice Department

Energy Debate Interests

The interests that stand to be affected by the current debate over a National Energy Policy are uncountable, ranging from the farmer who needs fuel for his tractor to the city apartment dweller who relies on electricity to go to work or avoid a 20-story climb to his home. Many of these consumers lack organized voices on the subject.

Organized interests with stakes in the outcome are also numerous. They include energy companies, including those dealing in oil, natural gas, coal and other minerals; private and public electric power companies; environmental groups and other citizens' action groups; foundations; industries, including the automotive industry; trade associations, and oil nations in the Middle East, among others.

A sampling of organized interests involved is shown (below) by some of those represented at April 1972 energy hearings of one of several congressional committees concerned—the House Interior and Insular Affairs Committee:

• American Petroleum Institute
• National Coal Association
• American Public Power Association
• Edison Electric Institute
• American Gas Association
• National Wildlife Federation
• AFL-CIO
• Friends of the Earth
• Atomic Industrial Forum
• National League of Cities and U.S. Conference of Mayors
• Independent Natural Gas Association
• Consumer Federation of America
• Independent Petroleum Association of America

to recognize the anti-competitive effects of such an oil/coal merger may have encouraged other oil companies to acquire coal reserves and production capacity...."

By arrangement with the Justice Department, the Federal Trade Commission in 1971 assumed responsibility for re-evaluating the main acquisitions by major oil companies of competing fuel resources. Alan S. Ward, director of the FTC's bureau of competition, said in March 1972 the FTC was investigating the effects of the Continental-Consolidation Coal transaction and expected to finish its study shortly.

The FTC in May 1971 ruled that Kennecott's acquisition—for more than $600-million—of the Peabody Coal Company was an antitrust violation in that it removed the coal company as a potential competitor in the energy field. The FTC said the action violated Section 7 of the

What Directors Do

State laws commonly provide that the business of corporations "shall be managed" by a board of directors. Prof. Myles L. Mace of the Harvard Business School says neither the laws nor 150 years of legal history show "precisely what directors do or do not do when they 'manage.'"

Mace wrote in *Harvard Business Review* (March-April 1972) he found "a considerable gap" between myth and reality on directors' functioning.

"In most companies, boards of directors serve as a source of advice and counsel, offer some sort of discipline value, and act in crisis situations...," Mace said. "I found that most presidents and outside board members agree that the role of directors is largely advisory and not of a decision-making nature." Exceptions are directors with large stock holdings.

Clayton Act and "substantially lessened competition in the U.S. coal industry." Kennecott appealed the FTC ruling requiring Kennecott to divest itself of Peabody to the federal courts. A similar suit by the Justice Department against General Dynamics' acquisition of the United Electric and Freeman Coal groups awaited U.S. district court decision.

Walker B. Comegys, acting assistant attorney general in charge of the antitrust division, said March 1 that future conglomerate mergers in the fuel and energy field will be evaluated on the basis of "whether such mergers eliminate potential competition, entrench leading firms, enhance reciprocity power and tend to encourage even further large mergers."

Interlocking Directorates. The following list indicates the range of interests and positions of officers or directors of six of the larger seven parent companies included in the Smith subcommittee report *(p. 38)*. The two other companies listed—Consolidated Edison Company of New York, Inc. and Commonwealth Edison Company of Chicago—are two of the largest U.S. power companies.

• **Gulf Oil Corporation,** Pittsburgh, 235,000-plus stockholders, 61,000-plus employees. It is both an operating and a holding company with interests in oil, natural gas production and processing, refineries, pipelines, tankers, chemicals, coal, electric power plants and other areas.

It controlled, generally through 100-percent ownership, about 175 subsidiaries in many countries at the beginning of 1971 and had sizable investments in other companies. A financing arrangement with Holiday Inns of America Inc. included provisions for locating Gulf service stations adjacent to hundreds of the motor hotels.

In 1967 Gulf acquired General Dynamics Corporation's General Atomic division at San Diego, Calif., which is engaged in nuclear research, development of nuclear fuel and building of nuclear steam systems for electric generating plants.

President and chief executive officer: Bob Rawls Dorsey; president since 1966; president of Gulf Exploration Company, engaged in oil exploration; president of Gulf Italia Company, fuel and petroleum; director, Allegheny Ludlum Industries; director, Corpus Christi Bank & Trust Company; director, Tex-Ex Corporation; director, General Foods Corporation; trustee, Southwest Research Institute, San Antonio, Texas; director, Mellon National Bank & Trust Company; director, Aluminum Company of America.

Other directors include:

Charles M. Beeghly; president, 1960-63, chairman of board and chief executive officer, 1963-69, chairman of executive committee and director after that, Jones & Laughlin Steel Corporation; vice president and governor, T. Mellon & Sons; former director, Mellon National Bank & Trust Company; director, PPG Industries Inc.; director, Cleveland Cliffs Iron Company.

James H. Higgins; president and director, Mellon National Bank & Trust Company; president and director, Mellon Bank International; director, Joy Manufacturing Company; director, White Consolidated Industries Inc.

Beverley Matthews, senior partner, McCarthy & McCarthy, Toronto, Canada; director, Gulf Oil Canada Ltd.; vice president and director, Toronto-Dominion Bank; director, Trans-Canada Pipe Lines Ltd.; director, Canadian Gypsum Company Ltd.; chairman, Canadian Niagara Power Company Ltd.; director, Westinghouse Canada Ltd.; director, Minnesota Mining & Manufacturing of Canada Ltd.

Nathan W. Pearson; director, Aluminum Company of America; director, Mellon National Bank & Trust Company; with T. Mellon & Sons, 1948—.

Ernest C. Brockett, former chairman and chief executive officer of Gulf Oil Corporation, was president and director of Mellon National Bank & Trust Company and a director of Aluminum Company of America.

Other former Gulf directors in addition to Brockett since 1970 included:

Frank R. Denton, chairman emeritus, Mellon National Bank & Trust Company; director, Pullman Inc.; director, Westinghouse Electric Corporation; former director, Jones & Laughlin Steel Corporation.

Richard K. Mellon; a governor of T. Mellon & Sons; president, Mellon National Bank, 1934-46; chairman of board, Mellon National Bank & Trust Company, 1946-66.

• **Continental Oil Company,** 85,000-plus common stockholders, 38,000-plus employees. An operating and holding company with operations in about 40 countries, with interests in these fields: chemicals, oil, gas, liquefied petroleum gas, plastics, gasoline, pipelines, rubber products, plant foods, pesticides and uranium exploration.

In 1971 the company negotiated a proposed merger with Burmah Oil Company Ltd. of Scotland, owner of 23 percent equity in the British Petroleum Company Ltd. Burmah also negotiated on a possible merger with British Petroleum Company Ltd., in which the British government is the major stockholder with about 49 percent ownership. Continental announced in 1972 that the merger talks with Burmah were dropped after failure to come to terms.

Chairman: Leonard F. McCollum; director, Morgan Guaranty Trust Company; director, J. P. Morgan & Company Inc.; chairman, Capital National Bank; director, Lincoln Consolidated Inc.

President and chief executive officer: John G. McLean; director, Boston Company Inc.; director, General Reinsurance Corporation; director, Bank of America (New York); director, Owens-Corning Fiberglas Corporation.

President of Conoco Chemical Division: Howard W. Blauvelt; director, Hudson's Bay Oil & Gas Company Ltd., a subsidiary.

President of Consolidation Coal, a subsidiary: John Corcoran; director, Mellon National Bank & Trust Company; director, St. Joseph Minerals Corporation.

Other directors include:

Charles A. Anderson; president and director, Stanford Research Institute; director, Continental Capital Corporation; director, Cutler-Hammer Inc.; director, National Cash Register Company.

J. Paul Austin, chairman and chief executive officer, Coca-Cola Company, Atlanta, Ga.; director, Coca-Cola Export Corporation; director, Morgan Guaranty Trust Company of New York; director, General Electric Company; director, J. P. Morgan & Company Inc.; director, Trust Company of Georgia.

William A. Hewitt, chairman and chief executive officer, Deere & Company, Moline, Ill.; director, Continental Illinois

National Bank & Trust Company; director, American Telephone & Telegraph Company; member of international advisory commission, Chase Manhattan Bank; director, Conill Corporation.

Gilbert E. Jones, president and director, IBM World Trade Corporation, 1963—; senior vice president, IBM Corporation, 1967—.

Plato Malozenmoff, member of executive committee; born in Russia, 1909, chairman and president, Newmont Mining Corporation, New York City; president and director, Resurrection Mining Company; chairman, Idarado Mining Company; president and director, Carlin Gold Mining Company; chairman, Granduc Operating Company; president and director, Newmont South Africa Ltd.; president and director, Similkameen Mining Company Ltd.; director, Southern Peru Copper Corporation; director, Canadian Export Gas & Oil Ltd.; director, Cassian Asbestos Corporation; vice president and director, Magma Copper Company; director, Atlantic Cement Company; director, Bankers Trust Company; director, Foote Mineral Company; director, Bankers Trust New York Corporation.

Neil J. McKinnon, chairman, Canadian Imperial Bank of Commerce, Toronto, Canada; director, Brascan Ltd. (generates and distributes electric light and power, Ontario, Canada); director, Canada Life Assurance Company; director, Allied Chemical Canada Ltd.; director, TransCanada PipeLines Ltd.; director, Campbell Soup Company; director, Ford Motor Company of Canada Ltd.; director, Honeywell Inc.; director, Falconbridge Nickel Mines Ltd.

Lauris Norstad, chairman, Owens-Corning Fiberglas Corporation, Toledo, Ohio; director, United Air Lines Inc.; trustee, Rand Corporation; director, Abitibi Paper Company Ltd. A retired general, he was supreme allied commander, Europe, SHAPE, 1956-63; president, Owens-Corning Fiberglas Corporation, 1964-67, chairman, 1967—.

Frank Pace Jr.; director, Colgate-Palmolive Company; chairman, Corporation for Public Broadcasting; director, Time Inc.; director, Bullock Fund Ltd.; director, Nation-Wide Securities Company. A past chairman and chief executive officer of General Dynamics Corporation, Pace was assistant director, 1948-49, and director, 1949-50, of U.S. Bureau of Budget; secretary of the army, 1950-53.

Andrew W. Tarkington, vice chairman of board; chairman, Hudson's Bay Oil & Gas Company Ltd.; director, Bankers Trust Company; director, Bankers Trust New York Corporation; director, Tri-Continental Corporation.

● **Kennecott Copper Corporation,** about 85,000 stockholders, 30,000-plus employees. An operating and holding company, with holdings which include 41 coal mining operations.

President: Frank R. Milliken; director, Peabody Coal Company, a subsidiary; director, Chase Brass & Copper Company, a subsidiary; chairman, Braden Copper Company, a subsidiary; director, Procter & Gamble Company.

President, Metal Mining Division: Charles D. Michaelson; president, Braden Copper Company; president, British Columbia Molybdenum Company; president, Ozark Lead Company.

Other directors include:

Russell DeYoung, chairman and chief executive officer, Goodyear Tire & Rubber Company, Akron, Ohio; director, Lykes-Youngstown Corporation; director, Aluminum Company of America.

J. Peter Grace, chairman and chief executive officer, W. R. Grace & Company, New York City; director, First National City Bank of New York; director, Deering Milliken Inc.; director, Magnavox Company; director, First National City Corporation; director, Brascan Ltd.; director, Chemed Corporation; director, Ingersoll-Rand Company.

Ellison L. Hazard; director, Continental Can Company Inc., formerly its board chairman and president; director, Goodyear Tire & Rubber Company; director, Irving Trust Company; director, Charter New York Corporation.

Arthur F. Mayne, president, A. F. Mayne & Associates Ltd., Montreal, Canada; director, Phillips Petroleum Company, many others.

Clifton W. Phalen; director, Chubb Corporation; director, Eastern Air Lines Inc.; director, Marine Midland Grace Trust Company.

John M. Schiff, partner, Kuhn, Loeb & Company, New York City; director, Westinghouse Electric Corporation; director, C.I.T. Financial Corporation; director, Uniroyal Inc.; director, Great Atlantic & Pacific Tea Company; director, Getty Oil Company.

Roy W. Simmons, president, Zions First National Bank, Salt Lake City; president, Zions Utah Bancorporation; director, Denver & Rio Grande Railroad.

Glenn P. Bakken, president, Chase Brass & Copper Company, Cleveland.

John Jeppson II, chairman, Norton Company, Worcester, Mass.; chairman, Guaranty Bank & Trust Company.

Walter H. Page, president, Morgan Guaranty Trust Company, New York City; director, Braden Copper Company; director, Merck & Company; president, J. P. Morgan & Company Inc.

Gavin K. MacBain, chairman and chief executive officer, Bristol-Myers Company, New York City.

● **Occidental Petroleum Corporation,** Los Angeles, 300,000-plus common stockholders, 33,000 employees. An operating and holding company with interests in, among other things, oil, natural gas, coal, refining, chemicals, plastics, fertilizers, real estate investment and development, and hotels in Switzerland. It has operating arrangements with Holiday Inns in Europe, Africa and the Middle East.

Chairman of board and chief executive officer: Armand Hammer; chairman of board and president, Mutual Broadcasting System, 1957-58; director, City National Bank, Beverly Hills, Calif.

President and chief operating officer: William Bellano; president, Gulf Sulphur Coal Company, 1958-60; president, Glen Alden Coal Company, 1961-64; various posts, 1965-68, culminating in presidency of Island Creek Coal Company, acquired by Occidental in 1968.

Other directors include James L. Hamilton, retired chairman and chief executive officer of Island Creek Coal Company.

● **Standard Oil Company of Ohio (Sohio),** about 43,000 common stockholders, 20,000-plus employees. An operating and holding company with interests that include oil, uranium, coal, chemicals, plastics, pipelines, gasoline, Hospitality Motor Inns Inc. and Dutch Pantry restaurants. The company is controlled by British Petroleum Corporation, and merger of Sohio with British Petroleum's main subsidiaries in the United States was completed Jan. 1, 1970.

British Petroleum Company Ltd., headquartered in London, has about 102,000 ordinary stockholders and about 160,000 employees outside the United States. Its global interests include oil, gas, chemicals, plastics, pipelines, tankers, tanker insurance, refineries, properties and finance. Sir Eric Drake is its chairman.

Chairman and chief executive officer of Standard Oil of Ohio: Charles E. Spahr; director, National City Bank of Cleveland; director, White Motor Corporation; director, Ohio Bell Telephone Company; director, Cleveland Electric Illuminating Company; director, Republic Steel Corporation.

Other Sohio directors include:

Lawrence A. Appley, chairman of the board, American Management Association.

DeWitt W. Buchanan Jr., president of Old Ben Coal Corporation, a subsidiary.

W. Fraser, a managing director of British Petroleum Company Ltd.

T. Keith Glennan, chairman of board, Aerospace Corporation; director, American Export Isbrandtsen Inc.; director, Republic Steel Corporation; trustee, Rand Corporation; assistant to chairman of Urban Coalition. He was president of Case Institute of Technology, Cleveland, 1947-66, with absences including service on the Atomic Energy Commission, 1950-52, and administrator, National Aeronautics and Space Administration, 1958-61.

M. M. Pennell, a managing director, BP Exploration Company.

Horace A. Shepard, chairman of board and chief executive officer, TRW Inc.

Hobart Taylor Jr., partner in Dawson, Quinn, Riddell, Taylor & Davis; director, Aetna Fund Inc.; director, Westinghouse Electric Corporation.

Lord Strathalmond, a managing director, British Petroleum Company Ltd.

• **American Metal Climax Inc.,** with interests in various metals and minerals including aluminum, bauxite, copper, lead, nickel, zinc, coal, molybdenum, potash and in fuels, chemicals, real estate and shipping. It sold most of its oil and gas holdings in the United States and Canada in the 1960s.

Chairman and chief executive officer: Ian MacGregor, head of various subsidiaries; director, American Broadcasting Company; director, American Cyanamid Company.

Other directors include:

John Black Aird, Toronto, Canada.

Alfred C. Beatty of London, chairman of Selection Trust Ltd. and of many holdings.

T. H. Bradford of London.

William A. M. Burden, director, Lockheed Aircraft Corporation; director, Columbia Broadcasting System Inc.

J. P. DuCane of London.

Gabriel Hauge, president, Manufacturers Hanover Trust Company; director, Manufacturers Hanover International Finance Corporation; director, Manufacturers Hanover International Banking Corporation; director, New York Life Insurance Company; director, American Home Products Corporation; director, New York Telephone Company.

E. C. Wharton of London.

Arthur H. Dean, partner, Sullivan & Cromwell; director, Bank of New York; director, Bank of New York International Corporation; director, Crown Zellerbach Corporation; director, El Paso Natural Gas Company; director, Campbell Soup Company; director, National Union Electric Corporation; director, Fund for Peaceful Atomic Development Inc.; director, Council of Foreign Relations. Dean represented the United States at various disarmament talks.

Harold J. Szold, partner, Lehman Brothers; director, General Cigar Company.

• **Consolidated Edison Company of New York Inc.,** electricity, gas and steam.

Chairman and chief executive officer: Charles F. Luce; administrator, Bonneville Power Administration, Interior Department, 1961-66; under secretary of interior, 1966-67; present position, 1967—; director, Metropolitan Life Insurance Company; director, United Air Lines.

President: Louis H. Roddis Jr. A retired navy engineer, he helped design the nuclear reactor for the U.S.S. Nautilus. He was deputy director of the division for reactor development, Atomic Energy Commission, 1955-58, later president, then chairman, of Pennsylvania Electric Company and director of nuclear power activities for General Public Utilities Corporation, New York City. President of Atomic Industrial Forum, 1962-64.

Other trustees include:

E. Virgil Conway, chairman and president, Seamen's Bank for Savings.

Hobart D. Lewis, editor-in-chief and president, Reader's Digest.

John M. Doar, president of Bedford-Stuyvesant Development and Services Corporation, Brooklyn, N.Y.; assistant U.S. attorney general (civil rights), 1965-67, first assistant to assistant attorney general before that; trustee, Robert F. Kennedy Memorial Foundation.

Frederick M. Eaton, partner, Shearman & Sterling; director, First National City Bank; director, Monsanto Company; director, New York Life Insurance Company; trustee, Carnegie Corporation of New York.

Marian Sulzberger Heiskell, director and director of special activities, *New York Times* Company, 1963—; wife of Andrew Heiskell, chairman and chief executive officer of Time Inc.

Grayson L. Kirk, president emeritus, Columbia University;

director, International Business Machines Corporation; director, Mobil Oil Corporation.

Milton C. Mumford, chairman, Lever Brothers Company, a subsidiary of UniLever N.V.; director, Crown Zellerbach Corporation; director, Equitable Life Assurance Society of U.S.; director, Federal Reserve Bank of New York.

J. Wilson Newman, chairman of finance committee and director, Dun & Bradstreet Inc.; director, General Foods Corporation; director, Chemical New York Corporation; director, Chemical Bank; director, Fidelity Union Bancorporation; director, Fidelity Union Trust Company; trustee, Mutual Life Insurance Company of New York.

Richard K. Paynter Jr., director, New York Life Insurance Company.

Richard S. Perkins, director, New York Life Insurance Company; director, International Telephone & Telegraph Corporation; director, Southern Pacific Company; director, Allied Chemical Corporation; trustee, Carnegie Institution of Washington; trustee, Vincent Astor Foundation.

William S. Renchard, chairman, Chemical Bank; director, Borden Inc.; director, Armstrong Rubber Company; director, New York Life Insurance Company; director, Foote Mineral Company; director, Federal Reserve Bank of New York; director, Cleveland-Cliffs Iron Company.

Ralph A. Weller, president, Otis Elevator Company; trustee, Penn Mutual Life Insurance Company; member, Rockefeller Center Advisory Board, Chemical Bank.

Lawrence A. Wien, lawyer; director, Borden Company.

• **Commonwealth Edison Company (Chicago)**

Chairman: J. Harris Ward, director, International Harvester Company; director, New York Life Insurance Company; director, Northern Trust Company; director, Union Carbide Corporation.

Chairman, finance committee: Gordon R. Corey, director, Conill Corporation; director, Continental Illinois National Bank & Trust Company, a subsidiary of Conill; director, Inland Steel Company; director, Universal Oil Products.

President: Thomas G. Ayers; director, First National Bank, Chicago; director, Zenith Radio Corporation; director, G. D. Searle & Company; president, Leadership Council for Metropolitan Open Communities.

Other directors include:

John A. Barr, dean of Northwestern University's Graduate School of Management; director, Northern Trust Company; director, Swift and Company; director, Stewart-Warner Corporation. Was president, 1955-61, and chairman of board, 1961-65, Montgomery Ward & Company.

Joseph L. Block, director, Inland Steel Company; director, First National Bank, Chicago. Was president, 1953-59, and chairman and chief executive officer, 1959-67, Inland Steel Company, then chairman of executive committee.

Lowell T. Coggeshall, director, Abbott Laboratories; director, Field Foundation of Illinois Inc.

Albert B. Dick III, chairman, A. B. Dick Company; director, Northern Trust Company; director, Marshall Field & Company.

Brooks McCormick, president and chief executive officer, International Harvester Company; director, Swift and Company; director, First National Bank, Chicago. Was chairman of National Safety Council, 1964-67.

Edward Byron Smith, chairman, Northern Trust Company; director, Illinois Tool Works; director, Federal Reserve Bank, Chicago.

Norris A. Aldeen, president, Amerock Corporation.

Joseph S. Wright, chairman and chief executive officer, Zenith Radio Corporation; director, Continental Illinois National Bank & Trust Company; director, Standard Oil Company (Indiana). Was secretary to Sen. Burton K. Wheeler (D Mont. 1923-47), 1933-36; attorney, 1936-42, and assistant general counsel and chief of compliance division, Federal Trade Commission, 1947-52; assistant general counsel, 1952-53; general counsel and director, 1953-58, president, 1959-68, chairman 1968—, Zenith Radio Corporation.

CRITICS QUESTION PROCEDURES, CONFLICTING ROLES

The Atomic Energy Commission (AEC) has long been familiar with problems posed by nuclear fallout. It is now learning that it must cope with political and legal fallout from environmentalists, politicians and even some AEC scientists who disagree with the commission on scientific matters.

Environmentalists are asking about the effects of thermal pollution from nuclear power plants on rivers, lakes and bays. Several Representatives have introduced legislation which would permit states to set their own limits for radiation hazards within their states even though these limits may be stricter than AEC standards.

The Issues

Three major issues have emerged from the struggle between the AEC and its critics.

● Critics have said that the AEC's dual authority regarding the promotion and development of nuclear power along with the regulation of nuclear power plants represents a conflict of roles.

● Many environmentalists have charged that nuclear power plants are being constructed and operated in a manner which might result in the destruction of the environment and the health and safety of the American people.

● Critics have contended that the AEC's radioactive waste disposal practices are inadequate and will result in contamination of underground water supplies.

Conflicting Roles. Critics of the AEC have suggested that its role in the promotional development of nuclear power should be separated from its authority to regulate nuclear power plants. Dr. Ralph E. Lapp, a nuclear physicist, suggested in the Jan. 23 issue of *The New Republic* that the AEC's regulatory power be transferred to the new Environmental Protection Agency (EPA).

The EPA was given the authority to set radiation protection standards when it was formed. At that time, the authority was transferred to it from the AEC and the now defunct Federal Radiation Council.

Nuclear Plant Safety. Nuclear power plants are designed with checks and doublechecks to guard against the accidental release of radioactivity. However, nuclear power plants routinely release radioactive effluents into the air and water under controlled circumstances.

Disagreement exists among scientists as to the long-range effects that the routine release of radioactive effluents into the air will have on the health of Americans. The environmental problems involving nuclear power plants center upon fears that thermal pollution will destroy marine life and rivers, lakes and bays.

Radioactive Waste Disposal. Within the past 18 months or so, debate over radioactive waste disposal

Fission versus Fusion

A battle for research funds to develop reactors has been going on between advocates of nuclear fission and nuclear fusion. Research in the area of fission is more advanced.

Fission involves splitting the nucleus of an atom into nuclei of lighter atoms. Nuclear fusion is a reaction in which the nuclei of light atoms join to form nuclei of heavier atoms.

The Administration has decided to provide strong financial support for the development of fast breeder reactors, a sophisticated version of present nuclear reactors, which provide energy from fission. This decision was made because, despite some disadvantages, research on these reactors was much further along than on fusion reactors.

The disadvantages of fission reactors involve hazards to those who mine fuels such as uranium, problems with the disposal of radioactive waste and the chance of nuclear accidents.

The AEC has stated that the fast breeder reactors can be made safe and that safe programs of radioactive waste disposal can be developed for them.

Fusion reactions have several advantages. No radioactive wastes are produced as a result of the fuel cycles, and they are safe with respect to nuclear accidents from runaway reactions. Fusion reactors appeal to environmentalists because they would produce less thermal pollution than fission reactors.

Disadvantages of fusion reactors include the difficulty in producing controlled fusion reactions and the length of research time necessary before fusion reactors could produce the amount of additional power needed.

The AEC, the nuclear industry and the electric utilities have said that a safe fast breeder reactor can be generating electric power on a commercial scale by 1984.

Advocates of the fusion reactor have said that "depending upon the level of effort...the time it would take to produce a reactor could range from as much as 50 years to as little as 10 years." Given the Administration's decision to emphasize fast breeder fission reactors, it may be closer to 50.

methods has involved the AEC, the congressional Joint Committee on Atomic Energy and Senators and Representatives who are not committee members.

Critics of the AEC's radioactive waste disposal practices cite the possibility of radioactive contamination of underground water sources and deplore the AEC's failure to establish long-range plans to combat this problem.

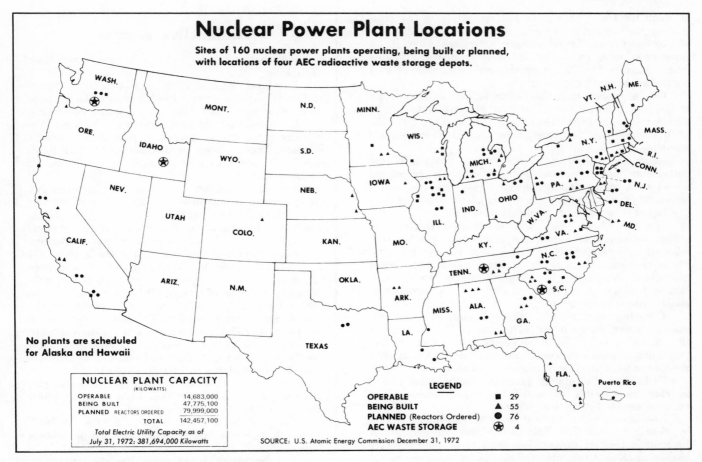

Nuclear Power Plant Locations

Sites of 160 nuclear power plants operating, being built or planned, with locations of four AEC radioactive waste storage depots.

No plants are scheduled for Alaska and Hawaii

NUCLEAR PLANT CAPACITY (KILOWATTS)	
OPERABLE	14,683,000
BEING BUILT	47,775,100
PLANNED REACTORS ORDERED	79,999,000
TOTAL	142,457,100

Total Electric Utility Capacity as of July 31, 1972: 381,694,000 Kilowatts

LEGEND

OPERABLE	■	29
BEING BUILT	▲	55
PLANNED (Reactors Ordered)	●	76
AEC WASTE STORAGE	✪	4

SOURCE: U.S. Atomic Energy Commission December 31, 1972

Nuclear Safety Problems

Americans are using more electricity than ever. But they are worried about what nuclear power plants will do to their health and their environment. They want more electricity, but they are worried about more than the money they may have to pay for it.

Questions regarding the safety and environmental aspects of nuclear power plants are sophisticated technologically, and it is difficult for a layman to confront an expert representing the AEC or a utility at a public hearing.

Before construction is permitted by the AEC, the utility is required to file a Preliminary Safety Analysis Report which is checked by the AEC. This step often takes a year or more and involves many conferences between the AEC regulatory staff and the utility. The Preliminary Safety Analysis Report and the AEC regulatory staff study then are subjected to review by an independent Committee on Reactor Safeguards.

Public hearings follow before a three-man panel selected from members of the AEC's Atomic Safety and Licensing Board. Citizens and associations are permitted to testify at the hearings. The final step involves a public hearing before an operating license is awarded to a utility for a nuclear power plant.

Despite these AEC procedures for checking the safety of plant designs and the provisions for public hearings, the public has very little information about nuclear safety.

In the Feb. 7 issue of *The New York Times Magazine,* Dr. Lapp suggested that the Environmental Protection Agency undertake a major review of reactor safety. "Although much progress has been made in accident-proofing reactors, the public remains poorly informed on the issue of the accidental release of radioactivity. Furthermore, it has little confidence in the spokesmen for either the utilities or the AEC," he wrote.

Radiation Standards Debate. A vigorous national debate is stirring over the issue of how much radiation a person can safely tolerate in his lifetime.

Everyone receives natural background radiation from the sun and from radioactive elements in the earth. Many receive extra man-made radiation from sources such as medical X-rays. The routine discharge of radioactive effluents from nuclear power plants will undoubtedly add more man-made radiation to the environment.

Proponents of nuclear power plants contend that the radiation risks from nuclear power plant discharges are slight compared to the benefits derived from expanded networks of electrical power.

One of the units that scientists use to measure radiation received by people is the rad. A rad is a specific unit of measurable radiation. For the general population, the AEC considers 0.17 rads a safe, permissible level.

Two scientists, Dr. John W. Gofman and Dr. Arthur R. Tamplin of the AEC's Lawrence Radiation Laboratory in California, have charged that the 0.17 rads guideline is much too high. They have become active in the anti-nuclear power plant movement.

Gofman and Tamplin have estimated that if all Americans were irradiated by nuclear power effluents from 16,000 to 32,000 additional radiation-related deaths would result each year.

Others replied that the Gofman-Tamplin figures are misleading because not all of the population would be within the range of reactor effluents, even when the bulk of the electricity in America is generated by nuclear plants.

Lapp has stated, "I have made an analysis of the community dose from nuclear power effluents, projecting ahead to a major deployment of power reactors, and I arrive at a maximum national mortality rate of five deaths per year and more likely less than one."

However, Lapp still believes that further efforts should be taken to reduce the small level of radiation released to communities located near nuclear reactors. "It is probably not feasible to make a powerful reactor absolutely 'clean'—i.e., involving no release of effluent—but technology is certainly available to achieve near-zero release of radiopollutants."

Locating the Plants. Finding suitable sites for nuclear power plants might turn into a difficult proposition. Lapp stated, "So far as safety is concerned, I feel that nuclear plants do constitute a hazard and that they should not be sited close in to metropolitan areas."

Utilities would ideally prefer to locate their plants as close as possible to heavily populated areas where the peak demand for power occurs.

The San Onofre nuclear generating station owned by Southern California Edison and San Diego Gas and Electric is located three miles from the western White House at San Clemente. Advocates of nuclear power plants have pointed to this proximity to show how safe nuclear plants are.

Challenges from States. The AEC has been challenged by state governments which would like authority to set their own radiation standards, which may be stricter than radiopollutant levels that the AEC permits for nuclear power plants.

One case being watched with interest involves the state of Minnesota and the Northern States Power Company. Minnesota attempted to limit the Northern States Power Company nuclear plant at Monticello, Minn., to a radioactive emissions level of 2 percent of the volume permitted under AEC standards. The company sued the state.

A federal district court ruled in favor of the company because it was complying with the AEC's operational standards. The case is under appeal to the Eighth U.S. Circuit Court of Appeals.

Environmental Aspects. Environmentalists think that nuclear power plants will overheat and possibly destroy aquatic environments because water that has been heated in the plant's steam condenser is released directly into adjoining bodies of water.

When the water temperature is raised, the supply of oxygen in the water is reduced. Sometimes, chemicals are added to the water in the reactor to control growth formations on the pipe surfaces. It is not known exactly what effect these have on marine life.

Environmentalists have two new laws on their side. The National Environmental Policy Act of 1969 (PL 91-

Radioactive Wastes

Radioactive wastes may be divided into three categories:
• Low-level wastes have a radioactive content sufficiently low to permit discharge into the environment after reasonable dilution or simple processing.
• Intermediate-level wastes have too high a radioactivity concentration to permit release after simple dilution. These wastes are disposed of through treatment such as filtration or ion exchange, or are buried in the ground.
• High-level liquid wastes cannot be released into the environment because of their high radioactivity concentration. The AEC stores high-level liquid wastes underground in large steel-lined, concrete tanks, but this is considered only an interim solution.

Radioisotopes in nuclear waste that are of the greatest concern for public health and safety reasons are those which are highly toxic or have a long half-life. The half-life of a radioactive substance is the period required for the disintegration of half of the atoms. Strontium-90, cesium-137 and plutonium-239 are common radioactive wastes which pose problems for nuclear scientists. Strontium-90 and cesium-137 are hazardous for 600 years and plutonium-239 takes 500,000 years to decay to a harmless level.

The storage methods for radioactive waste now utilized by the AEC are still in a research phase and they differ at various plant sites:
• The Hanford nuclear plant converts its high-level liquid wastes to a solid form within storage tanks.
• The Savannah River plant has its radioactive waste stored in underground tanks while it explores the feasibility of storing radioactive waste in bedrock caverns below the Tuscaloosa Aquifer.
• The Idaho facility converts its liquid wastes into a solid form and stores them in underground concrete vaults.
• The Oak Ridge National Laboratory used hydraulic fracturing to dispose of radioactive wastes until recently. The wastes were mixed with cement and other additives and then pumped down a well into the ground and out into subterranean rock formations.

190) requires federal agencies to prepare environmental impact statements for projects in their areas of responsibility. The Water Quality Improvement Act of 1970 (PL 91-224), forces the AEC to revise its procedures for approving utility applications for power reactor construction permits and operation licenses.

Radioactive Waste Problems

Sen. Frank Church (D Idaho) in a Senate speech March 6, 1970, questioned the AEC's radioactive waste disposal practices at the National Reactor Testing Station west of Idaho Falls, Idaho.

Church said newspaper articles had revealed the possibility of radioactive contamination of the Snake

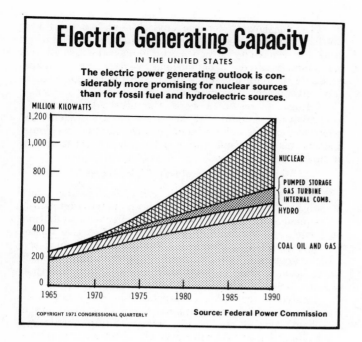

Electric Generating Capacity
IN THE UNITED STATES

The electric power generating outlook is considerably more promising for nuclear sources than for fossil fuel and hydroelectric sources.

MILLION KILOWATTS

NUCLEAR

PUMPED STORAGE
GAS TURBINE
INTERNAL COMB.

HYDRO

COAL OIL AND GAS

1965   1970   1975   1980   1985   1990

COPYRIGHT 1971 CONGRESSIONAL QUARTERLY   **Source: Federal Power Commission**

Plain Aquifer, a subterranean geologic formation which serves as a water source.

In addition to the Idaho site, radioactive wastes are stored by the AEC at the Hanford nuclear plant near Richland, Wash., the Savannah River nuclear plant near Aiken, S.C., and the Oak Ridge National Laboratory in Tennessee.

Criticizing the AEC. In his Senate speech, Church said that the AEC had not made public for three years a 1966 report from the National Academy of Science's Committee on Geologic Aspects of Radioactive Waste Disposal which was critical of AEC waste disposal practices.

Chairman Glenn T. Seaborg of the AEC replied that the commission had not suppressed the report. Seaborg said many reports from advisory committees are not published in cases where the AEC is seeking advice pertaining to its own programs. He also said that the study group had exceeded its authority.

The report made several basic criticisms of the AEC's waste disposal program. The committee said:

• "None of the (four) major sites at which radioactive wastes are being stored or disposed of is geologically suited for safe disposal of any manner of radioactive wastes other than very dilute, very low-level liquids....

• "The current practices of disposing of intermediate and low-level liquid wastes and all manner of solid wastes directly into the ground above or in the fresh-water zones, although momentarily safe, will lead in the long run to a serious fouling of man's environment.

• "At all sites where continuous disposal of low-level wastes or frequent unscheduled releases to the earth materials underlying the site occur, there is always the danger of a build-up of concentrations in the soil and underlying rocks.

• "When safety is involved, cost is secondary....Waste disposal costs are now a small part of the over-all expense budget of the nuclear industries, and any compromise with safety for the sake of economy could lead,

in the long run, to a mushrooming of waste disposal into the most costly item in the use of nuclear power."

AEC Reply. The AEC replied, "To comply with the committee's recommendations, AEC would have had to abandon fuel reprocessing and radioactive waste management facilities and activities at each (of four) sites. It would have had to acquire an extensive new site or sites, presumably located over either salt beds or deep underground basins, since such locations appeared more attractive to the committee for disposal.

"It would have had to construct new processing and waste management facilities at the new site and move existing radioactive wastes from current sites to the new site for disposal. Such an undertaking would have involved the expenditure of billions of dollars."

The National Academy of Science committee that issued the report critical of the AEC was replaced in 1968 by another committee from the academy called the Committee on Radioactive Waste Management. The purpose of the new committee is to "advise the AEC concerning long-range waste management plans and programs for an expanding nuclear energy industry."

GAO Report. In October of 1969, the congressional Joint Committee on Atomic Energy asked the General Accounting Office to review the AEC's radioactive waste management activities.

The GAO report was released in January 1971. It said, "Although AEC has assigned a high priority to radioactive-waste management, the level of effort given to the program should be increased in view of its extraordinarily complex characteristics.

"The problems and delays being experienced in the implementation of AEC's policies for the management of radioactive wastes are primarily attributable to a need for more definitive technology on such matters...."

The AEC's Division of Waste and Scrap Management, which was established in May 1970, has over-all responsibility for overseeing waste management, burial and storage programs.

The AEC has concluded that liquid storage of radioactive wastes in underground tanks is acceptable only as an interim measure. From the standpoint of safety, AEC has decided that solidification of high-level radioactive liquid wastes followed by its storage in salt formations is the best way to isolate the waste.

In June 1970, the AEC announced the tentative selection of a site near Lyons, Kan., for an initial salt mine repository demonstration project. This facility would accomodate both solidified high-level liquid wastes and plutonium-contaminated solid wastes.

Although the Lyons site was abandoned because of a water threat to the salt beds, the fiscal 1972 budget provided $3.5-million for the initiation, design and land acquisition of the repository. AEC estimates that preparation of a salt mine requires four years, at a cost of $25-million. The AEC is looking at sites in southeastern New Mexico.

While the salt mine radioactive waste disposal project is getting under way, the AEC continues to use interim storage methods at its other four sites. The GAO report said, "It does not appear that the AEC headquarters reviews of these (radioactive waste disposal) plans were made in sufficient depth to fully evaluate the plans and differences among the operational sites....

"Because of the technical factors involved, we are not in a position to comment on the adequacy of the interim storage practices at AEC installations. However, as the tanks and engineered systems increase in age and are utilized more because of the accumulation of new wastes and movement of wastes between tanks, there is an increased possibility of tank incidents occurring until all liquid wastes are removed from these old tanks."

Congressional Proposals

Representatives Jonathan B. Bingham (D N.Y.), Joseph E. Karth (D Minn.) and Bertram L. Podell (D N.Y.) have introduced bills which would amend the Atomic Energy Act of 1954 to permit a state, under agreement with the Atomic Energy Commission, to control radiation hazards. The bill would permit states to impose standards for regulating the discharge of radioactive waste from nuclear facilities which are more restrictive than the corresponding standards imposed by the AEC.

These bills strike at the heart of the court case between the state of Minnesota and the Northern States Power Company.

Representatives Bingham and Lester L. Wolff (D N.Y.) have introduced bills to transfer regulation of nuclear power, except those which relate to source material, from the AEC to the Department of Health, Education and Welfare to be administered through the Public Health Service subject to disapproval in certain cases by the Federal Power Commission or the Secretary of the Interior.

Rep. John P. Saylor (R Pa.) has introduced a resolution to "create a Federal Committee on Nuclear Development to review and re-evaluate the existing civilian nuclear program of the United States."

All of this proposed legislation has been referred to the congressional Joint Committee on Atomic Energy. No hearings had been scheduled on the legislation by mid-March.

A spokesman for the joint committee said that "surely there will be some discussion of these matters during the authorization hearings on the budget." However, neither the joint committee nor the AEC have been very receptive to suggested changes involving their authority.

Sen. Mike Gravel (D Alaska) announced that he would sponsor a bill to impose a moratorium on the construction of nuclear power plants and to make utilities financially responsible for nuclear accidents.

AEC Reaction

The AEC is moving forward steadily but a bit more cautiously despite challenges from environmental and congressional critics. The AEC seems to realize that its authority may be the subject of future disputes, but it apparently is not yet ready to make too many policy changes regarding radioactive waste disposal and its nuclear power plant development program.

AEC Commissioner James T. Ramey told a California Environmental Quality Council meeting that "the continuing availability of abundant and low-cost electrical energy is critical to the well-being and growth of our society.

"In our concern for the environment, we must not overlook another crisis—that of meeting the accelerating need for electricity which accompanies the growth of our industrialized, technological society and makes available to more and more of our people the necessities and conveniences of modern life."

Ramey expressed a hope that the AEC and environmentalists could "strike a balance between the need to explore site-related environmental problems and the need to avoid undue delays in the construction of nuclear power plants."

Steps to Combat Criticism

In order to combat public criticism, the AEC has emphasized its program of research on the environmental consequences of nuclear power, the effects of radiation on health and methods of disposal for radioactive waste.

Environmental Research. Nuclear plants, which are now in operation, require about 50 percent more cooling water because their thermal efficiency is lower than that of fossil-fueled plants.

Heated water which is returned to nearby bodies of water from nuclear power plants cannot retain as much dissolved oxygen as cooler water. Environmentalists have charged that this will adversely affect aquatic plants and animals.

The AEC has set up a new research facility at its Savannah River plant to study the effects of thermal pollution. The AEC also is encouraging the use of cooling towers and spray ponds to provide additional cooling for water heated in nuclear plants already in operation.

Reactors being designed for use in the future will utilize water more efficiently. Therefore, less water will be required to operate nuclear power plants.

Radiation Research. In its annual report to Congress, submitted in January 1971, the AEC reported: "During 1970, the AEC was sponsoring more than 1,070 individual research studies directly or indirectly concerning the environmental aspects of radiation...."

The AEC is cooperating in a study of the adequacy of radiation standards which is being conducted by the National Academy of Sciences. Preliminary work on the study started in 1970 and the review is expected to require two years for completion.

The relationship between radiation from nuclear power plants and public health is a most sensitive subject with the AEC. The AEC stated in its report to Congress that "the word 'radiation' continued, through erroneous assumptions and misrepresentations of facts, to conjure a feeling that nuclear power, if allowed to continue its growth, would unduly endanger the health and welfare of the nation's population.

"Many of the questions raised overlooked the fact that the risks associated with radiation—not only with regard to nuclear power plants but also in connection with all types of atomic activities—have probably been more thoroughly studied and are better understood than any other potential industrial environmental factor."

Waste Disposal. In 1970, the AEC announced that "research has proven the feasibility of converting liquid radioactive wastes into solid form."

The AEC has been conducting research on the storage of solid radioactive waste in salt formations as preparation for its salt mine repository demonstration project at Lyons, Kan.

ATOMIC ENERGY OFFERS HOPE OF UNLIMITED FUEL SUPPLIES

Nuclear energy currently provides only a fraction of the electrical energy consumed in the United States—about three-tenths of one percent. But it is expected to produce 20 percent of the nation's electricity in 1980 and perhaps 50 percent by the year 2000. America is greeting this age of nuclear energy with a curious mixture of resignation, fear and hope. The atom promises to deliver us from the "energy crisis" that has resulted in summer "brownouts" and cascading power failures. But every nuclear plant has what physicist Ralph E. Lapp calls a "Hiroshima halo" around it. For atomic power is still associated with the awesome explosion that ended World War II and launched the world into the nuclear era.

"Nuclear power came just in time," according to Glenn T. Seaborg, the outgoing chairman of the Atomic Energy Commission. "Civilization as we know it will grind to a halt unless we can develop nuclear power." The thrust of his argument is that the nation's supply of fossil fuels—petroleum and coal, the traditional sources of energy—is finite and nonrenewable. Estimates vary and are highly controversial. Commission officials frequently say that reserves of oil and gas will run out in 30 years and coal in 80 years. At the other extreme, a study commissioned by President Kennedy reported in 1966 that fuel reserves were sufficient to last for some seven thousand years. [1]

The energy crisis involves many factors but is not yet the result of an over-all insufficiency of fossil fuel. In some cases it is the result of a maldistribution of power. In other cases it stems from an inadequate fuel-supply system. In still others, it is the result of an insufficient generating capacity. At least in part, shortfalls in the supply of electricity result from the successful efforts of environmentalists to block the construction of pollution-causing generating facilities. Here again, nuclear power is cast in the role of a rescuer because it is widely admitted that the atom is the cleanest source of power available—at least in the sense that a nuclear plant does not belch sulfur dioxides and other pollutants into the air as many fossil-fuel plants do.

A high-power nuclear reactor, however, burns as much nuclear fuel in a year as is consumed in the detonation of more than 1,000 Nagasaki-type A-bombs. AEC officials dislike that analogy because, they contend, atomic explosions are impossible in the 22 nuclear plants now generating electricity in the United States. Nevertheless, men like Lapp worry about the possibility of freak accidents that could release large amounts of lethal radiation. Lapp considers the accumulation of immense amounts of radioactivity in the reactor core "a potential threat without precedent in urban life." [2]

Moreover, nuclear power plants produce more waste heat than fossil-fuel plants and this is a form of pollution. Reactors also constantly "leak" tiny amounts of radiation. While this leakage constitutes only a small fraction of the "background" radiation received from the environment, there is a bitter scientific controversy about how dangerous these small doses are. There is a growing debate about how much protection should be built into nuclear reactors and about who should decide that question. Some critics complain that the AEC's function as the promoter of nuclear energy conflicts with its role as the watchdog over nuclear safety. There are questions about safeguards in the mining, manufacture, transportation, use and disposal of atomic fuels. All of these questions are posed within the context of a larger argument about whether America should—or even can—cut down on its consumption of energy, now doubling about every decade.

Federal Efforts to Develop Breeder Reactors. In a message delivered to Congress on June 4, 1971, President Nixon committed the United States to a further development of nuclear power over the next 10 years. Among his proposals "to ensure an adequate supply of clean energy," he requested supplemental appropriations of almost $100-million in fiscal 1972—more than $75-million of it for various aspects of nuclear power. Over the coming decade, he envisioned an investment of $3-billion in federal funds to develop "clean energy" from all sources. Two billion dollars of that would be the federal contribution to the construction of a commercial "fast breeder" nuclear reactor by 1980. Nixon described the advanced reactor as "our best hope for meeting the nation's growing demand for economical clean energy."

Without the breeder reactor, nuclear fuels would not significantly enlarge the nation's fuel supply. AEC officials estimate the rare form of uranium consumed in present-day nuclear power plants will run out in about 40 years. The breeder, however, creates more fuel than it consumes. [3] Estimates vary but breeders are expected to extend the supply of nuclear fuel from decades to centuries.

The Atomic Energy Commission has placed a high priority on the breeder reactor for years. Since 1949, the federal government has spent some $600-million on the development of a liquid-metal fast breeder. [4] The only operating commercial power plant using a breeder reactor

---

1 *Energy R & D and National Progress: Findings and Conclusions,* September 1966, p. 8. The report's estimate of fuel reserves included those that are prohibitively expensive to recover with present technology —such as low-grade oil shale at depths of 20,000 feet.

2 Ralph E. Lapp, "How Safe Are Nuclear Power Plants?" *The New Republic,* Jan. 23, 1971, p. 19.

3 "Breeding" is accomplished by the careful selection and placement of fissionable and "fertile" elements into the reactor core. Neutrons not necessary to keep the nuclear reaction going are absorbed by fertile material to produce more fissionable material. Thus, when the isotope of uranium (U-238), a fertile material, absorbs neutrons, it is converted into fissionable plutonium.

4 "Liquid metal" refers to the primary coolant used to transfer heat from the reactor core—in this case, liquid sodium.

is the Enrico Fermi plant on Lake Erie, about 35 miles southwest of Detroit. It is owned jointly by the Detroit Edison and the Power Reactor Development companies. The Fermi plant is capable of generating nearly 61,000 kilowatts of electricity while at the same time converting "fertile" material into nuclear fuel.

Yet the plant has been a disappointment, Seth Lipsky wrote in *The Wall Street Journal*, July 27, 1971. "The Fermi plant's unhappy history is one of foulups, miscalculations and accidents. It was supposed to cost some $50-million. Close to $130-million actually has been spent. When it was first switched on eight years ago, it was supposed to have grossed, by 1970, $48.6-million from the sale of steam to Detroit Edison and $43.5-million from the sale of plutonium to the government. But during that eight years the plant has operated at full power for the equivalent of only 21 days. It has taken in a paltry $65,000 from the sale of heat, and it has sold not a dime's worth of plutonium."

Instead of leading the world in breeder reactors (Lipsky continued), the U.S. now is racing to catch up with England, France and Russia where bigger breeders are being built partly because the prototype Fermi plant has failed. Indeed, government-supported efforts are now under way to get a brand-new demonstration breeder that really works....

Types of Nuclear Plants

Boiling Water: Water is heated as it passes up through the reactor. Steam is drawn off the top of the reactor vessel and forced into a turbine. The least expensive to build but the plant must be relatively large.

Pressurized Water. Water passing through the reactor is kept under pressure which allows it to be heated without boiling. This highly pressurized water is forced through a coil or tubes in a steam generator which converts water to steam.

Gas-Cooled: Instead of water, a gas like helium or carbon dioxide is circulated by blowers through the reactor. The gas is superheated and produces steam as hot as 1,000 degress Fahrenheit in a steam generator.

Heavy Water: Deuterium, an isotope of hydrogen, is commonly called heavy water. It is a very efficient moderator for slowing down neutrons so they can split U-235 atoms. Usually, the fuel elements are placed in tubes running through a tank of heavy water. The coolant—either gas, water or heavy water—passes up the tubes past the fuel and into a steam generator.

Liquid Metal Fast Breeder: The coolant in this case is a metal, usually sodium. It is heated to about 1,000 degrees Fahrenheit and is forced through a "heat exchanger" where it transfers its heat to another "loop" or closed-system of liquid metal. The intermediate loop transfers heat to a steam generator. Liquid metal efficiently removes heat from the reactor but it has a violent reaction on contact with air or water. Thus an intermediate loop is necessary to protect the reactor from any explosion caused by an accidental leakage of sodium into the steam generator.

President Nixon, in his request for supplemental appropriations, specified that $27-million would be spent "so that the necessary engineering groundwork for demonstration plants can soon be laid." AEC officials have talked in terms of a plant capable of producing 300 to 500 megawatts of electrical power—five to eight times more than the Fermi plant. (A kilowatt is a unit of power equal to one thousand watts. A megawatt is one million watts.)

Seaborg told a news conference on the day the President's message went to Congress that a plant of that size would cost $400-million to $500-million—of which about half would be supplied by utility and reactor manufacturers. General Electric, Westinghouse, and North American Rockwell are the three major candidates vying to build the demonstration breeder.

Some scientists consider the breeder to be a temporary facility to provide energy only until they can develop thermonuclear fusion—an experimental but potentially much more powerful source of energy. At present, atoms are split to produce heat in a nuclear plant. In a fusion reactor, atoms would be welded together to achieve the same result. Since fusion power would use hydrogen atoms easily extracted from the sea, it promises to supply abundant, cheap electricity for millions of years. A number of fusion-minded scientists have urged an "Apollo-type" commitment to develop fusion power quickly. Its low priority has been called a "disgrace" by some, who predict that the Soviet Union may be the first to perfect the fusion technology. High-energy physicists predict that fusion power will be available in the 1980s, even though it has never been achieved experimentally. Most scientists, however, doubt that fusion will be practical until after the turn of the century and some question whether it will ever produce electricity.

Current State of Nuclear Energy. Since the first full-scale commercial nuclear power plant went into operation in 1957,[5] 21 others of various types have started functioning. As of mid-1971, 55 additional plants were under construction and 44 more were being designed. The generating capacity of existing, rising and planned facilities totals nearly 100 million kilowatts. Contracts were signed in the first six months of 1971 for 13 new atomic reactors, compared with 14 during the entire previous year.

This growth has taken place despite opposition from some environmentalists and despite rising costs of nuclear-plant construction. Capital costs of a large nuclear plant have risen in the last three years from about $120 per kilowatt of capacity to more than $200—in some cases to more than $300. Construction costs for fossil fuel plants are usually much less. Operating costs are also usually less for fossil fuel plants. The compensating factor is that the cost of nuclear fuel typically is less. The enrichment and fabrication of fuel are currently the largest factors in the cost of atomic fuel. Uranium concentrate is worth about $9 a pound. The enrichment process increases the value to about $115 per pound. And the fabrication process increases the cost to $165 a pound.

Costs have been a major drawback to private investment. Jeremy Main described in the November 1969 issue of *Fortune* a "premature rush" that had been under

---

5 At Shippingport, Pa. The 90,000 kilowatt facility is jointly owned by the Duquesne Light Company and the AEC.

way on the part of many major utilities to build nuclear plants ahead of their rivals. "The stampede set off after Jersey Central Power & Light Co....accepted in 1963 a $60-million...offer by General Electric to build a 640-megawatt plant at Oyster Creek (N.J.)," he wrote.

"According to an analysis published soon after the contract was signed, Oyster Creek would produce electricity by mid-1967, at a cost of four mills per kilowatt-hour, which was cheaper than the cost of a comparable coal-burning plant and half the average current cost. The estimate aroused such enthusiasm for nuclear power that almost half the total generating capacity ordered by private utilities in 1967 and 1968 was nuclear."

"But Oyster Creek did not work out," Main continued. It first produced power in the autumn of 1969, more than two years behind schedule. He said the experience at Oyster Creek might be an extreme example of the utilities' problems with nuclear plants. But he added that of the 47 nuclear plants then under construction, most of them expected to start producing electricity from six months to two years late.

Writing in the same issue of the magazine, Harold B. Meyers said: "The long-awaited transition of the U.S. electric-power industry into the nuclear age has been slowed by a number of factors, including technological difficulties and public resistance. But a special and unexpected cause for delay has been one company's crucial failure to deliver a single vital component of nuclear plants." He identified the company as Babcock & Wilson, a maker of steam-generating boilers for conventional power plants. It received contracts to make nuclear pressure vessels: huge steel pots—some are more than 70 feet long and weigh more than 700 tons—to contain atomic reactions.

B & W built a plant at Mount Vernon, Ind. to make them "but nothing seemed to go right," Meyers recounted. "Plagued by labor shortages and malfunctioning machines, the plant produced just three pressure vessels in its first three years of operation.... Last May (1969), B & W was forced to make a humiliating disclosure. Every one of the 28 nuclear pressure vessels then in the Mount Vernon works was behind schedule, as much as 17 months. For the utility industry, the news from B & W meant intolerable delays in bringing 28 badly needed nuclear plants into service."

Nuclear Energy Policy

The Atomic Energy Act of 1946 gave the government monopoly control over nuclear materials, making it impossible for a private company to build and operate a nuclear power plant. This condition presented no problem at first because nuclear production of electricity on a large-scale basis was not then a reality.[6] By 1953, however, the possibility of future production was in sight and arrangements had to be made for future methods of production and sale. The following year Congress changed the law after lengthy hearings. The issue was the future structure and development of the nation's civilian atomic energy program and, in particular, whether private firms should be permitted to market commercial nuclear power when it finally became available.

Advocates of public power, such as the American Public Power Association and the National Rural Electric Cooperative Association, saw the atom as a way to bring

---

AEC Licensing Procedure

1. Utility files a detailed Preliminary Safety Analysis Report which undergoes intensive study by the AEC's regulatory staff. This review takes up to a full year and involves conferences between the AEC and the utility and the construction company.

2. The utility's report, plus the AEC regulatory report on the project, undergoes examination by the Advisory Committee on Reactor Safeguards, a group of 14 nuclear experts. The Advisory Committee has the power to force changes in the reactor design and to deny a construction permit.

3. Public hearings are held prior to the issuance of a construction permit. These are held before a three-man board selected from a 23-man Atomic Safety and Licensing Board panel. Intervenors can argue against the issuance of a permit.

4. After the reactor has been constructed, it is monitored by AEC officials to ensure that it has been built to specification. Another public hearing is held before the awarding of an operations license. Several reactors have been held back from operating because of interventions at this stage.

---

really low-cost power to consumers. With this in mind, they favored a government development program to solve technical problems and put nuclear energy on the market quickly. They contended that since the secrets of the atom had been revealed at great expense to the government in World War II, the whole nation should enjoy any financial benefits to arise from atomic power. They argued that if sales were left to private companies, power prices would be higher and private industry would reap the benefits.

Public vs. Private Development of Atomic Power. The private electric industry, through the Edison Electric Institute and the National Association of Electric Companies, pressed for an amendment to the 1946 act authorizing private industry to build and operate commercial nuclear plants. The industry opposed government construction and operation of nuclear electric plants on a commercial basis. President Eisenhower took a position similar to that held by the private power industry.

As finally enacted, the Atomic Energy Act of 1954 let private industry enter the nuclear power business. However, private companies would be subject to AEC regulations, and the ownership of special nuclear materials would be retained by the government. The public power forces also won a number of important victories on patent rights, regulation of nuclear power rates by the Federal Power Commission, and public power preferences in the granting of licenses to non-federal applicants desiring to build nuclear plants.

But on the question of government-owned plants, the public power advocates lost. The final bill contained a provision forbidding the AEC to engage in commercial production; it could only build and operate experimental

---

6 The first electric power in the world generated from nuclear power was accomplished on Dec. 20, 1951, with an experimental reactor at the National Reactor Testing Station in Idaho.

plants. Starting in 1955, private companies were invited to build, own, and operate atomic reactors. The AEC stood ready to assist by waiving use charges for special nuclear materials, performing research and development work at no charge, and contracting for additional research and development.

The Eisenhower administration and particularly AEC Chairman Lewis L. Strauss believed that private industry would do the job. But industry was slow to respond because of high costs, and Democrats in Congress began complaining that the nation's nuclear program was lagging. By late 1957, the AEC indicated that the government itself was prepared to undertake the building of certain reactors if proposals from private industry were not submitted or could not be negotiated.

Under the cooperative program as it developed, the AEC provided virtually every conceivable type of assistance except actual construction of private reactors. A commission suggestion that it provide construction funds for investor-owned power reactors was turned down by Congress in 1959. But in 1962 the commission was authorized to provide funds for engineering design of private demonstration reactors.

Safety and Pollution

With their potential, however remote, for inflicting death and destruction, nuclear power plants are subject to especially searching criticism. The hazards associated with nuclear power plants usually fall into three categories: 1) low levels of radiation leaked from the plant; 2) the dangers involved in transporting nuclear fuel and radioactive wastes to and from nuclear plants; and 3) the possibility of an accident—a non-nuclear explosion or a melting of the reactor core—which could release large amounts of radiation.

The AEC can point out that in 14 years of operating experience, there is no record of anyone having been injured by radiation from any commercial reactor. And since World War II, there has been no recorded major transportation accident in which people have been injured as a result of the radioactive contents of a shipment. However, critics draw little comfort from these statistics. While commercial reactors have taken no lives, there have been seven deaths connected with the operation of experimental reactors in the United States. And the transportation of all hazardous substances—not just nuclear cargo—is a matter of rising concern. Several train derailments in recent years have involved poisonous chemicals and explosives.

Expressing a prevalent AEC viewpoint, Seaborg has spoken of "excessive fear" by the public. He is convinced that nuclear reactors are safe but acknowledges that an accident could release radioactivity. He explains that this is why nuclear plants are constructed and designed with back-up safety systems to prevent or minimize the possibility of an accident. But other prestigious scientists have voiced concern about the risks involved. Dr. Edward Teller, a former director of the Livermore laboratory, notes that an economical breeder "needs quite a bit more than one ton of plutonium...I do not like the hazard involved."[7] And Walter Jordan, assistant director of the Oak Ridge National Laboratory, wrote recently that "the $64-million question still remains, and this is whether we have succeeded in reducing the risk to a

tolerable level—i.e., something less than one chance in 10,000 that a reactor will have a serious accident in any year." One chance in 10,000 would mean that if there were 100 nuclear reactors operating in the United States, an accident could be expected every 100 years.

Critics contend that if risks must be accepted in nuclear plants, they must be balanced against the benefits. Furthermore, the risks must be outlined and the public must be polled in some way as to whether it is willing to take them. The benefit-risk argument leads to a number of additional questions: Who takes the risks and who gets the benefits? Since some risk can be eliminated by additional but expensive safety systems, who will pay for the added measure of safety?

The fears of some critics would be eased if the regulatory role of the AEC were split off from its function of encouraging and promoting nuclear power. For them, this dual role represents conflict of interest which could lead to tragedy. Ralph E. Lapp made several suggestions for a more widely based safety review system for nuclear reactors in a series of articles published early in 1971 in *The New Republic*. He urged that a high-level review of reactor safety be made "by some independent group such as the National Academy of Engineering, funded by the Environmental Protection Agency."

Lapp also suggested that a permanent Nuclear Power Safety Board be established, that reactor size be limited to reduce the consequences of an accident, that no nuclear plants be placed near metropolitan areas, and that research into reactor safety be intensified. Robert Gillette of *Science* magazine wrote recently that while AEC officials continually assure the public that nuclear reactors are safe, "a number have been discreetly appealing for more money—preferably much more money—to support research on the safety of conventional, water-cooled nuclear reactors." AEC expenditures for safety research reached a peak of $37-million in fiscal 1970 and dropped to $36-million in 1971.

Safeguards Against Mishaps. One of the worst accidents that could occur in the light-water plants operating in the United States today is a "blowdown"—a sudden loss of coolant which would allow the reactor to overheat. If a reactor core heated to the melting point a number of things could happen. Within a minute, the core would begin to collapse to the bottom of the containment vessel. The molten radioactive material would eventually burn its way through the vessel and then through the slab of concrete under it. The ball of atomic fire would burn itself into the earth in what is known, perhaps tongue-in-cheek, as the "Chinese syndrome"—meaning it may continue to sink into the earth in the direction of Asia. One guess is that the molten material would sink to the water table where it would cause the venting of highly radioactive steam. Another possibility is that the material would congeal into a fiery glob that would burn for a decade or more.

Under normal conditions, reactor-maintenance experts could take action before the core melted. Control rods—as many as 90 of them—can be inserted into the core to soak up neutrons and thus shut down the nuclear reaction. Some experts say there still might be enough

---

7 Quoted by Gene Schrader, "Atomic Doubletalk," *The Center Magazine*, January/February 1971, p. 48.

residual heat in the core, along with heat released by decaying fission products and by chemical reaction between metal and remaining water, to melt it. Thus one of the key safety features of most reactors is a "backup coolant system" which is designed to flood the reactor vessel if the primary bath of coolant is lost.

This system became a controversial matter in 1971 when the congressional Joint Committee on Atomic Energy released a letter that Seaborg had written to Sen. John O. Pastore (D R.I.), the committee chairman. Seaborg said new techniques for calculating the temperature of cladding (tubes) in the reactor indicated that "the predicted margins of emergency core cooling systems performance may not be as large as those predicted previously." His letter stemmed from a series of small-scale experiments which the AEC conducted at its National Reactor Testing Station near Arco, Idaho.

Those experiments indicated, but did not prove, that high steam pressures inside the reactor vessel might delay the entry of the backup coolant. On the basis of an "interim policy statement" issued by the AEC June 19, 1971, five reactors were ordered to modernize their backup systems by July 1, 1974, and in the meantime to triple their inspections of pipes, pumps and valves. Four new power plants were ordered to hold their peak operating temperatures below normal.

Concern over nuclear reactor safety arose in the late 1950s. In response to a request by the Joint Committee, the AEC commissioned its Brookhaven National Laboratory on Long Island, N.Y., to study nuclear safety. The laboratory report, *Theoretical Possibilities and Consequences of Major Accidents in Large Nuclear Power Plants*, presented to the committee in March 1957, said an accident might cause no casualties or that conceivably it might leave as many as 3,400 persons dead and 43,000 injured. Property damages might range from $500,000 to $7-billion. A revision of this study was undertaken in 1965 but the results were never made public. In a letter dated June 18, 1965, Seaborg told Rep. Chet Holifield (D Calif.), who was then the committee chairman, that the larger reactors being planned at that time would produce greater damage in the event of an accident but that the likelihood of an accident was "still more remote" than before.

Sheldon Novick, in his book *The Careless Atom*, described the situation in 1957 this way: "The Joint Committee had reached an impasse; in order to have private industry participate in the reactor program, utilities would have to own and operate their own reactors. This they declined to do unless adequate insurance was available. But insurance companies refused to assume the risk." The result was the Price-Anderson Act, which Congress passed that year, stating that the aggregate liability for a single nuclear accident "shall not exceed the sum of $500-million." The act requires the operator of a reactor to obtain as much private insurance as possible. The Atomic Energy Commission then provides the remaining insurance up to a total of $500-million protection. As the matter worked out, private insurance now provides some $82-million in coverage for each nuclear reactor and the government provides $418-million.

Controversy Regarding Radioactive Discharges. Dr. Ernest J. Sternglass, a professor of radiation physics at the University of Pittsburgh, asserted in 1969 that 400,000 infant deaths and more than two million fetal

Radiation: Causes and Effects

Radiation is a wave of sub-atomic particles—photons, electrons, protons or neutrons—which penetrates matter, including living tissue, at nearly the speed of light. Radiation causes damage because the particles can either physically tear away molecules within a cell or ionize (split into charged fragments) tissue atoms. In either case, radiation injures, sometimes permanently, the body's atomic chemistry.

The most widely used unit of radiation measurement is the *rad*, an acronym for radiation absorbed dose. It is defined as that quantity of radiation which delivers 100 ergs of energy to one gram of substance. The *rem*, acronym for Roentgen equivalent man, is a measure that includes an estimate of the biological impact of different types of radiation. It is usually roughly equivalent to a rad. A *millirem* is one-thousandth of a rem.

Science has not yet been able to determine a "threshold" below which radiation is always harmless. The lowest absorbed dosage at which medically significant damage to humans has been observed lies somewhere between 50 and 100 rad, according to some experts. A whole-body single dose of 100 rad induces vomiting in about 10 percent of people so exposed. A whole-body single dose of 450 rad causes death to half those so exposed.

deaths had occurred in the United States as the result of strontium-90 fallout from nuclear weapons tests. Two AEC scientists, Dr. John W. Gofman and Dr. Arthur R. Tamplin, challenged his findings. But, in the process of digging into the statistics, they became convinced that radioactive emissions from nuclear power plants are potentially dangerous. Their findings, in turn, have been challenged. Robert W. Holcomb reported in *Science* magazine: "An analysis of their work reveals that most of the assumptions they use in making predictions can be neither proved nor disproved, but the consensus of their peers is that at least some of the assumptions are wrong." Gofman had asserted that if all Americans were irradiated to the AEC maximum, 32,000 extra cancer deaths would result yearly.

Radiation is a normal hazard of all earth dwellers. The "background" radiation—from cosmic rays, the earth and food—ranges from 90 to 200 millirems per year. Until recently, the Atomic Energy Commission standards for nuclear plants set maximum individual exposure at 500 millirems per year.[8] These were the upper limits when the commission, on Dec. 3, 1970, published design and operating requirements for nuclear power reactors to keep levels of radioactivity emissions "as low as practicable."

New operating criteria for nuclear reactors, issued by the AEC on June 9, 1971, would limit the exposure to people living nearby to no more than 5 percent of the

---

8 These exposure guides are established by the Federal Radiation Council, formed in 1959 to provide "guidance for all federal agencies in the formulation of radiation standards." The guidelines were originally formulated in the 1950s by the International Commission on Radiological Protection and the National Committee on Radiation Protection and Measurements.

amount of radiation that they normally receive from natural sources. Harold L. Price, AEC director of regulations, said all but two or three of the 22 power plants now in operation emit less than one percent of the radioactive wastes that they are allowed to release under the new guidelines. Price added that the companies would be allowed three years to make the necessary improvements to cut down on the emission of radioactivity.

The commission was quick to point out—and its critics to note—that the new regulations applied only to those nuclear plants cooled by ordinary water. Thus breeder reactors, isotope processing plants and waste disposal sites were not affected. The disposal of wastes has created a furor. These wastes are now kept in liquid form in large underground steel tanks near Richland, Wash., Idaho Falls, Idaho, and Aiken, S.C. Exactly how much radioactive waste is under storage is classified information. The AEC told Editorial Research Reports the amount was "in excess of 80 million gallons." Some experts suggest it is in excess of 200 million gallons.

Waste Disposal, Environmental Criticism. In budget hearings before the Joint Committee in March 1971, the AEC requested funds to buy a salt mine near Lyons, Kan., to dump radioactive wastes on a trial basis. Commission officials explained that studies indicated salt beds were the safest dumping grounds—better than placing waste-filled metal containers in the earth or burying them in the deep sea. They said salt seemed to be the ideal receptacle because it withstands high temperatures, becomes plastic and flows to heal fractures and to fill holes. It has compressive strength and radiation shielding properties comparable to concrete.

Many Kansans, including some state officials and congressmen, remained unconvinced that the wastes could be safely sealed away for all time. They questioned whether seepage might not occur and enter underground streams. Richard S. Lewis, writing in the *Bulletin of the Atomic Scientists*, noted that one question "unasked and unanswered during the budget hearing, but implicit in the debate was: Who would be responsible if 50, 500, 5,000 or 50,000 years from now, deformation from heat, an earthquake or a new ice age ruptured the rock seal and allowed the radioactivity to percolate through the aquifers into the environment?"

While the AEC's request for these funds was being considered by Congress, the U.S. Court of Appeals in the District of Columbia told the commission that it had failed in its duty to guard against environmental damage at the Calvert Cliffs plant being constructed on the Chesapeake Bay by the Baltimore Gas & Electric Company. The commission's interpretation of the National Environmental Policy Act of 1969 "makes a mockery of the act," the court said in a decision in the Calvert Cliffs case on July 26, 1971. "The very purpose of the...act was to tell federal agencies that environmental protection is as much a part of their responsibility as is protection and promotion of the industries they regulate," the court said. It ordered the AEC to revise its procedures for environmental protection.

Critics of the commission long have accused its members of insensitivity to environmental issues. President Nixon's new appointments to the commission were being viewed in Washington as a reflection of his awareness of this criticism. On announcing Seaborg's resignation, July 21, 1971, Nixon named as his successor—

pending Senate confirmation—James R. Schlesinger, an assistant director of the White House Office of Management and Budget. In that role, Schlesinger was credited with persuading the administration to reverse itself and return federal land to the Taos (N.M.) Indians—a cause that conservationists endorsed. Nixon also named William O. Doub, a Baltimore lawyer who has served on the presidential Air Quality Advisory Board, to replace commission member Theos J. Thompson, who was killed in a plane crash.

Promise of Fusion Power

The breeder reactor promises to provide energy for hundreds of years. But another source of energy—fusion —holds the promise of providing electricity for millions, perhaps billions, of years. According to physicists, fusion power will be inherently safe, cheap and abundant. Nuclear fission releases energy by the splitting apart of U-235 atoms. Fusion releases energy by fusing hydrogen

---

Principles of Nuclear Reaction

As physicists now know, not all atoms of an element are similar. The nucleus of one atom may have more or fewer *neutrons*—uncharged particles —packed into it than another does. Such different physical forms of the same chemical are called *isotopes*. Uranium atoms usually have 238 *protons*— positively charged particles—plus neutrons in their nucleus. But a few uranium atoms, about seven-tenths of one per cent of naturally occurring uranium, have three fewer neutrons. This is the isotope U-235 and it is the basic fuel for all atomic power. U-235 is *fissionable*, or capable of being split apart when struck by a slow-moving neutron.

If a neutron is moving too quickly, it is absorbed by U-238 atoms—converting them to *plutonium* atoms. If it is moving slowly enough to split a U-235 nucleus, it produces an enormous multiplication of energy. In the act of splitting apart into flying fission fragments, the destroyed nucleus of a U-235 atom releases two or three new neutrons. The fragments, containing some 200 million electron volts of kinetic energy, produce heat when they collide with surrounding atoms. The new neutrons, meanwhile, if sufficiently slowed down by passage through a "moderator" like graphite, are capable of splitting other U-235 atoms. When this occurs and goes on occurring, the result is a *nuclear reaction*.

A nuclear power reactor concentrates U-235 into a precise geometrical configuration so that: 1) the released neutrons can be slowed down and have a better chance of striking new U-235 atoms; 2) so that the reaction can be controlled by the placement of rods which absorb neutrons and 3) so that a *coolant*— either water, gas, or liquid metal—can be passed by the reaction to transfer heat from it. This heat is eventually converted into steam which is used to drive the blades of a turbine. In light-water plants such as are used in the United States, the water circulated through the reactor also acts as a moderator, slowing down neutrons.

nuclei together. It is the source of the power in an H-bomb explosion and it is the energy source of the sun and the stars.

Research on fusion power began secretly about 20 years ago and almost simultaneously in the United States, the United Kingdom and the Soviet Union. Secrecy was ended by international agreement in 1958 and there has been a high degree of international cooperation since then. According to Richard F. Post of the Lawrence Radiation Laboratory, around $210-million is being spent annually on worldwide fusion research—"about 50 percent in the Soviet Union, 25 percent in the United States and the rest in the U.K., Western Europe and Japan." [9]

In some respects, starting up a self-sustaining fusion reaction is similar to building a wood fire. The flame from a match must be hot enough and be held long enough, and the fuel must be closely spaced to heat itself and keep the fire going. The fuel in a fusion reactor, however, is deuterium and tritium, two isotopes of hydrogen.[10] "The general idea," wrote Francis F. Chen in *Scientific American*, "is to heat a plasma, or ionized gas, of deuterium or tritium to more than 100 million degrees centigrade and hold the plasma together by means of a magnetic field long enough for some of the ions to fuse, releasing energy in the form of radiation."

A plasma is sometimes described as the "fourth state of matter." It is a hot gas—so hot that it "ionizes" or breaks up into a mixture of negatively charged electrons and positively charged nuclei. Physicists say that if a deuterium-tritium plasma can be made dense enough, contained long enough and heated high enough, the deuterium and tritium nuclei would be forced to collide with each other, even though they are usually held apart by their positive charges. The fusing would create the nucleus of helium-4 which would instantly release a highly energized neutron. The neutron—in one theoretical design—would produce heat when it penetrated a "lithium blanket" surrounding the reaction. The lithium, in turn, would siphon the heat off to a steam-generating plant.

Actually, only part of the energy would be transferred to the lithium. The rest would be used to keep the fusion process going by heating the incoming gas to fusion temperature. Fusion theorists calculate they need to confine a plasma to a density at least as high as one hundred trillion particles per cubic centimeter. Furthermore, this density must be held for a full second and the plasma must be heated at the same time to about 40 million degrees centigrade. If all three conditions are met, the result would be a self-sustaining fusion reaction that would continue as long as more deuterium was fed into the reaction.

One or two of the three parameters of fusion—density, time and heat—have been achieved in various experiments. But no experiment has yet achieved all of them at the same time. The closest experiment to achieving these requirements was the Tokomak-3, a Russian fusion experiment in Moscow. The Tokomak features a torodial (doughnut-shaped) containment vessel in which the plasma is confined by means of powerful magnetic fields. In the summer of 1969, Russian scientists announced that the Tokomak had held a plasma of 50,000 billion particles per cubic centimeter at a temperature of 10 million degrees for 0.05 seconds—that is, the tempera-

---

Uranium Into Fuel

Enrichment. Since the isotope of fissionable uranium is rare, an enrichment process is necessary before the element can be used in the light-water reactors employed in the United States. Uranium ore is milled to produce a crude concentrate known as *yellow cake* which contains 70 to 90 percent uranium oxide. Yellow cake is refined into pure uranium trioxide, a fine orange powder known as *orange oxide*. This is subsequently converted to uranium dioxide by hydrogenation and the dioxide is finally converted into uranium tetrafluoride, called *green salt*, by reaction with hydrogen fluoride gas.

Green salt is shipped to one of the three large uranium enrichment plants at Oak Ridge, Tenn., Paducah, Ky., and Portsmouth, Ohio. There it is reacted with fluorine gas to produce *uranium hexafluoride*, a volatile compound which changes into a gas at low temperatures. This gas is fed into a series of chambers, a "cascade," which concentrates the fissionable U-235 isotope. Once enriched, the hexafluoride is converted back, step by step, to uranium dioxide powder.

Fabrication. This powder is compacted into cylindrical pellets and loaded into long zirconium alloy tubes. The tubes, called *cladding*, protect the fuel material from corrosion and lock in the radioactive fission products. Some 200 tubes are arranged in a *fuel assembly* which may weigh 1,300 pounds. The assemblies, perhaps 200 of them, are loaded into chambers in the reactor equipped with fittings which permit the coolant to enter and leave the assembly. The "geometry" of the core must be precise because a certain spatial relationship is necessary for a controlled chain reaction to take place. Also, hundreds of thousands of gallons of coolant must flow through the reactor each minute.

---

ture and density were near what would be required for sustained fusion and the time was about a tenth of the minimum. The containment time, however, was 10 times as long as was previously attained.

Richard F. Post has suggested that fusion power could make it possible to convert heat directly into electricity without the intermediate step of producing steam. Dr. Bernard J. Eastlund and Dr. William C. Gough of the AEC have suggested a plan whereby the intense heat of a fusion "torch" could be used to reduce garbage and other wastes to chemical elements which could later be recovered and reprocessed. While far from fanciful, these advanced concepts must await proof that fusion power is possible.

(Continued on p. 92)

---

9 Address before the National Academy of Science's Symposium on Energy for the Future, Washington, April 26, 1971. Cooperation in fusion research may soon be matched in the field of U-235 enrichment, a closely held U.S. secret. Victor Cohn of *The Washington Post* reported July 30, 1971, that the AEC was ready to begin talks with 10 friendly nations about sharing the secrets of nuclear enrichment.

10 Deuterium, or "heavy water," is easily separated from ordinary sea water. Tritium, the radioactive form of hydrogen, is rare.

SCIENCE SEARCHES FOR CLEAN ENERGY SOURCES

As America awakens to the growing reality of the energy crisis, the now urgent need for development of new and clean energy sources becomes increasingly clear. That the nation will someday run out of its traditional fossil fuel sources is incontrovertible—only the timing of depletion can be argued. This is not an easy concept to grasp. More than 95 percent of the current U.S. energy supply comes from oil, coal and natural gas, and Americans have grown used to a plentiful supply of cheap energy in all forms—especially electricity, natural gas, heating oil and gasoline. But no more. As research geophysicist M. King Hubbert wrote in *Scientific American* in September 1971: "It is difficult for people living now, who have become accustomed to the steady exponential growth in the consumption of energy...to realize how transitory the fossil-fuel epoch will eventually prove to be when it is viewed over a longer span of human history."

The winter of 1973 may have helped many people face up to the gravity of the fossil fuel shortages. Supply problems which had been predicted for years, finally became cruelly tangible as schools, factories and homes all over the country were hit by shutdowns or rationing. And with the coming of spring, the chilling fact began to hit home that the energy crisis now came in all seasons, that winter freeze-ups might be followed by summer brown-outs. Although the immediate causes of the short-term energy crisis continued to be debated—many blamed failures in delivery systems, lagging domestic explorations, restrictive import quotas, inadequate refining capacity and counterproductive government controls—it seemed evident that the long-term crisis could not be solved by reliance on traditional fuels or policies.

What was needed for the longer run, many energy analysts, environmentalists, economists and engineers agreed, was a stepped-up program of research and development on new energy sources—solar and geothermal power, nuclear power options including fusion, hydrogen as a fuel, wind and tidal power and other possible sources. It was expected that all energy would be more expensive in the final decades of the 20th century, and higher costs probably would encourage efforts to utilize energy more efficiently and to conserve it whenever possible. As former Commerce Secretary Peter G. Peterson put it in a November 1972 speech to the American Petroleum Institute: "We are moving into an era in which every energy option will have a cost. It may be a balance of payments cost, an environmental cost, a competitiveness cost, a discomfort cost, or all of these costs. But the cost will always be there.... The era of low cost clean energy sources is almost dead."

To a great extent, belief in the development of new energy sources depended almost entirely on one's faith in technology. Despite promising breakthroughs in the feasibility of several new sources, formidable obstacles still remain. And the amount of progress made in the next 10 years, or next 20 years, will have a great impact on the vital matter of resolving energy needs with environmental protection. Continued reliance on fossil fuels and nuclear fission, in particular, could have serious adverse effects on the nation's environment through increased strip mining and offshore drilling, thermal pollution or radiation hazards, and deteriorating air quality. And if a final showdown between energy and environment became necessary, there was little doubt which would win—at least in the short run. As someone once said, "Everyone is an environmentalist until the lights go out." Physicist Dr. Ralph Lapp graphically illustrated the potential for such backlash: "A hard-hat worker, sweating it out during an electrical blackout, deprived of TV and nursing a can of lukewarm beer, will have his own perspective on environmental risks."[1] Indeed, many people already seemed resolved to making some concessions on environmental quality in order to allow energy business-as-usual through the next decade. But for every pessimist there was an optimist. Herman Kahn of Hudson Institute told the annual meeting of the American Association for the Advancement of Science: "We can support reasonable growth rates for the next 50, 100 or 200 years and solve all the problems that come up along the way with current technology." The key word was reasonable. At present growth rates, Americans will be using five times as much energy by the year 2000. And more than anything else, that is why much current writing on the energy crisis reads like an eschatology of doom. *(Footnotes sources p. 62)*

Solar and Geothermal Power

Solar Energy. By far the most abundant of the potential new energy sources is solar power—the thermal energy of the sun. The total energy radiated to the earth from the sun is nearly 180,000 trillion watts, which is some 30,000 times the world's present electric power capacity.[2] Although this enormous energy is dispersed over an immense area, its power is so great that the amount falling on less than one half of one per cent of the land area of the United States is more than enough to meet the nation's total energy needs to the year 2000.[3] The energy in the sunlight falling on the surface of Lake Erie alone in a single day is greater than present annual U.S. energy consumption. "A solar energy system with an operating efficiency of 20 percent operating in the American Southwest could provide the equivalent of the total U.S. electrical output using an area of less than 4,000 square miles," Dr. Jerome Weingart of California Institute of Technology's Environmental Quality Laboratory wrote in the December 1972 issue of *Environmental Quality*.

Harnessing this power on a large scale to generate electricity is an awesome task, however. Professor and Mrs. Aden Meinel of the University of Arizona, both leading proponents of solar power, have proposed a 1,000-megawatt generating system using special lenses to focus sunlight onto chemically-coated, nitrogen-filled pipes that would transfer the heat to a central storage unit using molten salts. The solar farm, as the Meinels call it, would be about five miles square with an initial cost of $1-billion. Larger systems would require collection areas as much as 75 miles on a side. But they argue that the nation already has an energy program—agriculture—that consumes 500,000 square miles of land and supplies only one percent of energy needs—food. "Our plea is that people now begin to look at solar energy as a harvest of at least equal importance with agriculture," they wrote. [4]

Another research team led by Ernst Eckert of the University of Minnesota and Roger Schmidt of Honeywell Inc., has proposed a parabolic reflector to concentrate sunlight into air-filled heat pipes, each attached to small water storage tanks, to produce steam without the need for a central storage tank and the associated pumping costs. They maintain their system would be easier to construct and that a pilot plant could be built before 1980 and commercial solar power would be available by 1990. [5]

Perhaps the most ambitious scheme for harnessing solar energy is that of Peter Glaser of Arthur D. Little Inc., an industrial consulting firm. Glaser suggests a huge satellite system orbiting 22,000 miles above the earth which would use giant mirror panels and silicon converters to change sunlight into microwave energy and beam it back to earth. The plan, which would require an operable space shuttle system to be built, would provide 10,000 megawatts of power at a total cost of about $20-billion. Although it staggers the imagination, the plan is technically feasible and is now being studied by a consortium including Grumman, Textron and Raytheon. Glaser believes the system could be operational before the year 2000 if a strong commitment were made to its development.

But although large-scale use of solar power appears to be some time off, small-scale application is a much closer prospect, and actually has a lengthy history. In 1772 a solar furnace was built in Europe to melt metals for chemical experiments. From 1870 to about 1910 solar energy provided fresh water to a remote mining area in Chile through a series of troughs which collected evaporating ocean water condensed on panes of glass. Solar water heaters, widely used in California and Florida in the early 1900s, are used in Australia, Japan and Israel today. Solar space heaters also are highly developed, with most systems using a black metal surface under glass on the roof to absorb sunlight and create a "greenhouse" effect to heat water or air which is circulated during the day and stored at night. These systems can heat all the water needed by most homes and buildings but are only a supplementary space heating system. Solar air conditioning devices also have been demonstrated using the absorption-refrigeration process. Some experts believe that solar heating and cooling systems could supply up to half of the total energy needs now used for residential and commercial heating and air conditioning, which is 20 percent of U.S.

consumption. Weingart claims that if two-thirds of U.S. residences were given solar equipment in the next 30 years, "more energy would be saved each year than is currently produced." The main roadblocks are not technical, but social, such as convincing construction firms.

The possible environmental drawbacks of solar power are land use questions, waste heat from turbines and possible alterations in local thermal balance and climate. But neither appears insoluble. Waste heat could be used in water desalinization plants or other industrial purposes, while reflecting materials between solar collectors could restore the thermal balance. As for land use, the Meinels argue: "We think that any rational person flying over the vast deserts of the Southwest cannot be unimpressed by the great areas of arid land lying unused. It would seem to be an acceptable price for the harvest of sunshine that some 5 to 10 percent of this desert be impressed into the service of mankind." The only other possible problem is that a major influx of people into a solar farm area could create enough smog to ruin the system. But the regions generally proposed are arid deserts 35 degrees from the equator such as the Sahara, the Arabian Peninsula, Chile's Atacama Desert and Central Australia. But despite the optimism of some researchers, other scientists are skeptical. Lawrence Rocks and Richard Runyon of Long Island University wrote: "Many people have begun to believe that harnessing the sun is just around the chronological corner. This is a misassessment (sic) that could be fatal if we let it lull us into a false sense of security.... America could collapse while dreaming about it in philosophical detachment from practical matters." [6]

Geothermal Power. Another major power option is geothermal energy—heat from the interior of the earth. The total energy potential of the earth's core is enormous but it is accessible only where it comes close enough to the surface to be tapped. With present drills capable of going only about seven miles deep, the unlimited heat of the earth's mantle (30 miles down) still is out of reach. But geothermal energy recently has been receiving much attention as new drilling sites are discovered. It has high potential for electric power production, residential space heating, desalinization, refrigeration and air conditioning.

Geothermal energy has been utilized for many years on a small scale. In the United States, some 200 homes in Boise, Idaho have been heated by underground steam since 1890. The most significant large-scale development is The Geysers, 90 miles north of San Francisco, where steam generates electricity in a power plant. In operation since 1960, the plant now produces about 300 megawatts and estimates of its ultimate capacity range from 1,000 to 4,000 megawatts. But the world's largest installation is in Larderello, Italy, which was completed in 1904. New Zealand, Japan, Mexico, Iceland and the U.S.S.R. also have active geothermal power plants and total world production is well over 1,000 megawatts. One leading geothermal proponent is Joseph Barnea, director of the United Nations resource and transport division, who has written: "At the present rate of development it is likely that by the end of this decade the production of electric power from steam fields will be quadrupled." [7]

Geothermal resources are of three basic types—steam, hot water and hot rocks. Dry steam is the most useful but least common; wet steam must be separated into steam and water components before being filtered and run through turbines. Hot water wells generally have high mineral or salt contents, but can be used to heat other fluids with lower boiling points, such as isobutane. Use of deeper hot rocks is more difficult, but the Atomic Energy Commission's Los Alamos laboratory has suggested using hydrofracturing techniques to create underground cracks in rock beds and then circulate pressurized water through them. If successful, this method would open up hot rock resources at least 10 times the steam and hot water potential. [8]

United Nations. At a U.N. seminar on geothermal energy in January 1973 many experts urged rapid development of the resource. Representatives of U.S. petroleum and utility firms were among the 250 participants—their interest has been aroused by the Interior Department's plans to lease 58 million acres of federal lands in 14 western states in the spring of 1973. This was authorized by the Geothermal Steam Act of 1970 (PL 91-581), and the companies will have the same depletion allowance as the oil industry. A 1972 report from the National Science Foundation's Research Applied to National Needs (RANN) program estimated that 132,000 megawatts of geothermal electricity could be generated in the United States by 1985 and 395,000 megawatts by the year 2000, more than present U.S. capacity. The report recommended a $685-million federal research and development program. One of the directors of the RANN study, former Interior Secretary Walter J. Hickel, told *The New York Times* in December 1972: "From our current perspective, geothermal energy promises to be perhaps the most acceptable of all new energy sources from an environmental standpoint." Other estimates of geothermal's potential are lower, ranging from 19,000 megawatts by 1985 from the National Petroleum Council to 60,000 megawatts per year from the U.S. Geological Survey. [9] But enthusiasts charge that industry and government are overly cautious about geothermal potential.

Problems. Geothermal power is not completely without problems. The steam often smells like rotten eggs, and makes a lot of noise at the well sites. It usually contains hydrogen sulfide which can be hazardous if oxidized into sulfuric acid and discharged into the air or water. Other trace elements include nitrogen, boron, flourides and arsenic. Withdrawal of steam or water can drop the local water table and release excess brine which must be reinjected to prevent earth subsidence. Also, most geothermal resources are far from population centers, which would necessitate large transmission line systems. After an extensive study, two researchers from Washington University concluded: "Some reports readily conclude that geothermal power is completely clean and safe. This is far from certain at our present state of knowledge. Thus, it is absolutely imperative that those who...exploit geothermal resources be required to submit an environmental impact statement for public review prior to extensive development." [10]

Winds, Tides and Oceans

Other potential new energy sources are wind and tidal power and the thermal gradients of the ocean's depths. The World Meteorological Organization in 1961 estimated wind power available at favorable sites around the world at some 20 million megawatts, but most scientists agree that only a small percentage can ever be harnessed. Nonetheless, several researchers have proposed using the wind to generate electricity. Windmills have been used as small-scale power sources for many years—more than 30,000 were operating in Europe in the 19th century. Some time before World War II, the German engineer Herman Honnef proposed building wind towers to generate electricity and research picked up in Europe and the United States. In 1941 the world's largest windmill—110 feet high with a 175-foot diameter blade—was built atop Grandpa's Knob near Rutland Vermont, and it produced 1.3 megawatts until it was shut down in 1945. But several wind power proposals have been resurrected in recent years. Some Oregon utility companies have given a grant to meteorologist E. Wendell Hewson of Oregon State University to study the economic feasibility of wind generators. In September 1971, Professor Claude M. Summers of RPI wrote in *Scientific American:* "A propeller-driven turbine could convert the wind's energy into electricity at an efficiency of somewhere between 60 and 80 per cent." One of the most enthusiastic proponents is Professor William E. Heronemus of the University of Massachusetts, who suggests building windmills on floating towers in the ocean or on platforms on the continental shelf to generate electricity which would be used to electrolyze distilled sea water into hydrogen and oxygen. The hydrogen would be collected and sent ashore through pipelines to be burned directly or used in fuel cells, or compressed and stored for use during peak demand periods. [11] There may be disadvantages to wind power, however. Some have warned that if windmills were used in large systems on the land, air current patterns might be affected which could change temperature and humidity. Rows of huge steel towers with enormous blades would create aesthetic blight worse than transmission lines. But most scientists believe there is a need for more research into wind power. Dr. H. Guyford Stever, director of the National Science Foundation, expressed cautious optimism when he told a subcommittee of the House Committee on Science and Astronautics in 1972: "There are areas of the United States in which this particular source of energy could become competitive.... Such systems may become a significant factor in our energy supply on a regional basis." The Great Plains, some Rocky Mountain states, parts of New England, Alaska and Hawaii are such areas.

Most scientists agree that ocean tides could have only a small impact on total world energy needs. Tides have been used as small-scale energy sources for several centuries, but harnessing them on a large scale presents great problems. The average tidal height of most beaches—about three feet—is insufficient to produce the amount of back-and-forth water power necessary for electricity generation. The only commercial tidal-electric installation now operating is on the estuary of the Rance River near Saint-Malo, France, where the tides average 27 feet. This station, completed in 1966, has 24 adjustable-blade turbine units in a barrier separating the inland tidal basin from the sea, and generates 340 megawatts which are integrated into a large power grid. In the United States, the Passamaquoddy project on the Bay of Fundy between Maine and Canada was first proposed in 1919 and actually begun in the 1930s but finally halted by a lack of congressional appropriations. The project proposed exploitation of the 18 foot (average range) tides in the bay to generate at least 300 megawatts and perhaps as much as 1,000 megawatts of power. The proposal has been periodically revised for study by the U.S. or Canadian governments during each of the last three decades, but has not yet been deemed economically practical. Other areas which have been suggested for tidal power development include the Cook Inlet in Alaska, the San Jose Gulf in Argentina, the Severn River in England, numerous other estuaries in France and several places in the U.S.S.R., where a small experimental station already is in operation on the Kislaya Inlet near Murmansk. The environmental advantages of tidal power are that it consumes no exhaustible resources and produces no pollutant wastes, although its effects on aesthetic and ecological factors are largely speculative. However, even if all the world's potential tidal power areas were developed, they would produce only a small percentage of total power needs.

The colder waters of the oceans have been called the largest natural resource on earth. Ocean thermal gradients —the temperature differences between deep and surface water—range from 25 to 45 degrees Fahrenheit. Heat engines have been built which can work across these gradients, although they are of relatively low thermal efficiency—about three percent. The process was first demonstrated by Georges Claude of France in 1929. Thermal gradients in the Gulf Stream off the eastern coast of the United States theoretically could generate all of the energy needed in this country by the year 2000, according to Dr. Stever, of the National Science Foundation. But the process probably would be limited to tropical waters with high surface temperatures. Environmentally, the system appears to have few adverse effects, and the constant turnover of hot and cold water might actually stimulate marine life development in some areas.

Nuclear Power and Hydrogen

Fission, Breeders and Fusion. Nuclear energy currently produces only a small fraction of the electricity consumed in the United States—less then four percent. But it is expected to produce at least 10 percent of the nation's electric power by 1980, as much as 30 percent by 1985 and perhaps 50 percent by the year 2000, according to AEC estimates. A total of 29 nuclear power plants were operating at the end of 1972, with 55 under construction and 76 more being planned. For much of the last decade, nuclear power has been hailed as the panacea for the world's future energy supply problems. But its problems and costs, both economic and environmental, have risen steadily and today there is a growing schism in the scientific community over the wisdom of continued large-scale development of all forms of nuclear power. "Nuclear power came just in time," former AEC chairman Glenn T. Seaborg said in 1971. "Civili-

zation as we know it will grind to a halt unless we can develop nuclear power." In contrast, consumer advocate Ralph Nader told *The New York Times* in January 1973: "This is the first time that this country has permitted development of an industry that can wipe this country out.... The danger of catastrophic nuclear power plant accidents is a public safety problem of the utmost urgency in the country today."

Although nuclear power plants produce no air pollution as do conventional coal or oil burning plants, they have serious potential environmental drawbacks. They produce large amounts of waste heat, (about 60 percent more than other power plants), usually in the form of hot water, which can present thermal pollution problems if it is not dissipated in cooling towers or in an adjacent body of water, which some believe can adversely affect the climate or marine life. Reactors also "leak" tiny amounts of radiation, which is far less than the natural "background" radiation in the environment, but there is bitter controversy about the possible dangers of these small doses. Others question the safety of mining, manufacturing, transporting and disposing of atomic fuels, particularly handling the radioactive wastes produced by the reactors which must be stored in protective containers for as long as several centuries. Conventional nuclear reactors use only uranium-235, which is only seven-tenths of one percent of available uranium, and may be exhausted in as little as 40 years, according to the AEC. Other energy analysts believe the AEC may be exaggerating this shortage.

But the AEC is placing its nuclear power hopes of the near future on the fast breeder reactor, which converts U-238, (which makes up the other 99.3 percent of all uranium) into fissionable plutonium. The breeder is a kind of perpetual motion machine that produces, or breeds, more fuel than it consumes. First demonstrated experimentally in the 1950s, the breeder has been developed in several countries including England, France, Japan and the U.S.S.R. as well as the United States. In his "clean energy" message of June 4, 1971, President Nixon called the breeder "our best hope today for meeting the nation's growing demand for economical clean energy" and pledged a major federal effort to develop a breeder prototype by 1980. The first breeder will be built near Oak Ridge, Tenn. Its construction costs are estimated at close to $1-billion but its operating costs are still the subject of speculation. "Estimating the cost of the project is a little like Adam turning to Eve and saying, 'What's it going to cost us to have this baby?'" TVA chairman Aubrey J. Wagner has said.[12] The reason for this uncertainty is largely based on unknown costs of the amount of environmental protection that will be required for the breeder by the end of the 1970s. For today a growing controversy based on environmental and safety factors is generating around the breeder and criticism of the AEC's safety testing program is increasing. One critic of the breeder, former atom bomb physicist George Weil, who now is a nuclear energy consultant, says: "It's conceivable it could produce a nuclear explosion. Not a big explosion but a hell of a big bang." Others are more concerned about the production of vast amounts of plutonium, an extremely lethal material which has a radioactive half-life of more than 24,000 years. That means the waste could still be dangerous to humans for more than 200,000 years—or 50 times all recorded history to date. "It would place an unendurable burden on the safety and health of future generations," physicist and Nobel laureate Hannes Alfven has said.[13] On the other hand, Alvin Weinberg, director of the AEC's Oak Ridge National Laboratory, believes that the need for the breeder to fill the interim before development of solar or fusion power is so great that the risks are worth taking. "The only surveillance that would be required would be the rather minimal guarding of a few burial grounds for radioactive wastes, I do not consider this...to be at all unreasonable."[14] Another potential danger might come in transport of waste materials to storage sites (which have not yet been agreed upon—a Kansas salt mine site was dropped in 1972; the latest ideas are building massive steel and concrete storage facilities or rocketing radioactive wastes to the sun). The number of shipped containers, about 30 per year in 1970, could rise to 500 per week by the year 2000, making the chances of truck or railroad accidents almost a certainty, based on Department of Transportation accident rates.[15] In addition, the chances of sabotage or diversion of plutonium for illegal purposes increase greatly, since the material is extremely valuable (about $10,000 per kilogram) and is the basic stuff of making atomic bombs. Even AEC officials foresee the development of a plutonium black market, and others imagine such frightening scenarios as extremist groups building bombs and demanding enormous sums in return for not blowing up major cities. "Despite a distinct resemblance to science fiction, these are not hypothetical problems," Allen L. Hammond wrote in *Harper's* in January 1973. The final aspect of the breeder which has been the subject of criticism is the possibility of a failure in the cooling system which would produce a "meltdown"—the reactor core would overheat and melt through the bottom of the plant into the earth, releasing large amounts of radioactivity, into the atmosphere or the water table. The AEC claims this is virtually impossible, but past failure of other nuclear power plants have led to some skepticism.

The final nuclear option is fusion, or thermonuclear power, the reaction that produces hydrogen bomb explosions and is the energy source of the sun and other stars. It has been described as the "No. 1 Holy Grail" and the "Lost Dutchman Mine" of atomic science. Most scientists agree that it will eventually provide an ultimate source of clean, cheap and inexhaustible energy, but estimates of the time needed for its development vary from 10 to 100 years. Its radiation hazards would be negligible, its only waste product is innocuous helium gas and it carries no danger of a runaway reaction. Potential reactor efficiencies still are largely conjectural, but some believe they might convert 40 to 60 percent of their heat into electricity, and might someday eliminate the thermal pollution problem.

Research on fusion power began secretly more than 20 years ago and almost simultaneously in the United States, the United Kingdom and the Soviet Union. An international agreement in 1958 ended the secrecy and set a policy of cooperation which has endured. The Russians currently spend the most money on fusion research but U.S. expenditures have steadily increased. Some researchers believe that lack of funds is the primary roadblock to fusion development, while others see the need for fundamental breakthroughs in physics or engineer-

ing. The amount of money spent on fusion research increased more than seven-fold in the 1950s but leveled off after about 1962 and has remained fairly constant for the past decade.[16] Edward C. Creutz, the National Science Foundation's assistant director for research, believes an accelerated effort could bring electric power from fusion by 1990. Several encouraging experiments of the past few years have led many scientists to believe that fusion may be demonstratated by 1980 with magnetic containment systems to control the reaction or even earlier with laser beams to heat the fuel to reaction temperature. But these are the most optimistic predictions and both would be followed by long periods of tests and models before commercial power production would be possible. [17]

Hydrogen: The Ultimate Clean Fuel?

Although not itself a *source* of energy, hydrogen has been proposed as the ideal *fuel* for the future because it burns cleanly and completely, emits virtually no combustion pollutants and is abundant in coal, oil, natural gas and, most importantly, in water, which is composed of two hydrogen and one oxygen atoms. Hydrogen is a highly efficient energy converter in liquid or gas form. Most proposals for a so-called "hydrogen economy" emphasize its superiority to electricity for many large-scale energy applications such as transportation, space heating and heavy industry.[18] Its most appealing feature is that when burned it produces only steam, which returns to the atmosphere and is recycled naturally with other water vapor. *(Footnote sources, p. 62)*

The only problem with hydrogen is that it will require large amounts of energy—probably electricity—to produce it in sufficient quantities for widespread use. Although several techniques for production of hydrogen from water have been proposed, the only process proved in practice is electrolysis—decomposing water into hydrogen and oxygen by passing a strong electric current through it. Thus proposals for a hydrogen economy assume an abundant supply of nuclear or solar energy. The other problem with widespread public acceptance of hydrogen is the fear many people have of its supposed dangers as a highly flammable fuel, commonly referred to as the "Hindenburg syndrome" because it seems to be primarily based on memories of the Hindenburg zeppelin disaster of 1937 when the hydrogen-filled airship ignited and burned in less than two minutes. But hydrogen technology and safety measures have in the last decade improved so greatly—largely because of the space program—that the fuel now is no more hazardous to use, transport or store than gasoline or natural gas.[19]

Hydrogen first was suggested as an alternative fuel in 1933 by Rudolph Erren, a German inventor working in England, who wanted to run internal combustion engines on hydrogen to eliminate exhaust pollutants and decrease the British need for oil imports—both problems which, ironically, confront the United States today. Also in the 1930s, the English inventor F. T. Bacon, proposed hydrogen use in fuel cells. In the 1960s the Atomic Energy Commission proposed production of hydrogen as part of the operation of "nuplexes"—large nuclear-agricultural-industrial complexes built around a central nuclear reactor. Recent studies of hydrogen utilization have sprung up at many universities and industrial research laboratories in the U.S. and abroad, with U.S. efforts being directed by the Institute of Gas Technology under sponsorship of the American Gas Association.

Pipeline Use. Interest of the natural gas industry in hydrogen is understandable since the fuel could easily be supplied through the existing network of natural gas pipelines that reach most U.S. industries and about 80 percent of homes. Based on current pipeline costs, these could carry hydrogen at about one-eighth the cost of sending an equal amount of electricity through high-voltage power lines above ground, eliminating much of the need for cables, tower and poles, switching stations and other unsightly equipment. Hydrogen can be burned as a gas in home heating, cooking and cooling appliances with minor burner modifications. In a liquid form, it can be substituted for gasoline in automobile engines, as first demonstrated in 1969 by Dr. Roger J. Schoeppel of Oklahoma State University, and again in 1972 at an intercollegiate Urban Vehicle Design contest when a converted Volkswagon designed by a group of Brigham Young University students was the only car to beat the 1975-76 federal emission standards and actually emitted an exhaust cleaner than most city air.[20] The major problems with using hydrogen for automobiles include the need for an enlarged fuel tank (as much as 50 gallons) in the vehicles and larger storage units at service stations, as well as higher costs. But the liquid hydrogen currently derived in gaseous form from oil or natural gas and then liquified by a cryogenic (freezing) process is only about 50 percent more costly than gasoline on an energy-per-unit-weight basis. Initially at least, hydrogen appears most practical for large-tanked vehicles such as buses, trucks and trains. It has also been proposed as an airplane fuel. The main problems with use of hydrogen for transportation are fuel logistics and storage, as it is bulky in gas form, dissipates rapidly through leaks and requires costly cryogenic tanks in liquid form. For industrial uses, hydrogen might someday replace coal and coke to reduce iron ore in steel plants—U.S. Steel and Armco already are operating such an experimental plant in Mexico. The utility industry is becoming increasingly interested in hydrogen for use in electric generating plants, which often operate at only 50 percent of capacity because of the problems of storing electricity. Using hydrogen, "the industry could operate near 100 percent of its capacity at all times and the stored hydrogen could be used to meet peak demands for power," one observer believes.[21] In addition, hydrogen might also someday be used in thermonuclear fusion power plants.

Immense amounts of hydrogen will be needed if its use is ever to become widespread. Current world consumption is about 6 trillion cubic feet, with the U.S. consumption more than a third of that. The Institute of Gas Technology has estimated that 60 trillion cubic feet of hydrogen would provide the energy equivalent of U.S. natural gas consumption in 1968, and electrolysis production of that amount at current efficiencies would require more than one million megawatts of electricity, or more than three times present U.S. capacity. Hydrogen replacement of fossil fuels for all uses except electricity generation would require 295 trillion cubic feet by the year 2000.[22]

Progress In Energy Utilization

Improvements in Use of Traditional Sources. While the search for new energy sources continues, other scientists are at work improving efficiencies in the way old energy sources are utilized. Many believe there is considerable room for improvement in this area of energy conversion and savings would result which could provide more time for development of new sources. Part of this effort involves new technology such as magnetoydrodynamics (MHD) and fuel cells, but other proposals include improving the capabilities of old systems or consolidating power plants and industries so that waste heat and other byproducts can be fully utilized. During the 20th century, the efficiency with which fuels were consumed in this country has increased by a factor of four. But a more revealing measure is to compare energy consumption with gross national product to determine actual cost-efficiency of energy use. Between 1890 and 1960 the GNP grew at an average annual rate of 3.25 percent while fuel consumption increased at an annual rate of only 2.7 percent. But this ratio no longer holds. "Since 1967 annual increases in fuel consumption have risen faster than the GNP indicating that gains in fuel economy are becoming hard to achieve and that new goods and services are requiring a larger energy input, dollar for dollar, than those of the past," Claude M. Summers wrote. Unless efficiencies of power plants and lines, transportation and other energy uses are improved, this trend will continue. As Russell E. Train, chairman of the President's Council on Environmental Quality, said in May 1972: "We must increasingly shift our efforts from simply finding more energy supplies to use, to concerning ourselves with how to use energy in the most efficient way. For the efficiency of energy use will have profound effects on the quality of life for all Americans."

The efficiency of energy conversion varies widely. When wood or coal is burned in an open fireplace, less than 20 percent of the energy is radiated into the room as heat while the rest goes up the chimney. A good home furnace can capture about 75 percent of its fuel energy, but most furnaces are operated at low capacity and poorly serviced so their actual efficiencies may run as low as 35 to 50 percent.[23] Conversion of fossil fuels to electricity, only five percent efficient in 1900, has become more than 30 percent efficient today, but the efficiencies of electricity use vary greatly. Electric space heating and air conditioning are only 30 percent efficient at most, and about 10 percent of electricity is lost in transmission. Standard electric light bulbs convert only about 5 percent of their input into light and the rest into heat; flourescent bulbs are much better, reaching up to 36 percent efficiency. But perhaps the least efficient major user of energy today is the automobile, which accounts for most of the 25 percent of the U.S. energy budget consumed by transportation. The thermal efficiency of the internal combustion engine has risen only from about 22 to about 25 percent since 1920, while miles per gallon averages have declined from nearly 14 to just over 12, about half that of most European cars. Two Berkeley researchers have calculated that reducing the average size of American cars to 2,000 pounds (from 3,000), boosting average miles per gallon to 25 and building them to last 10 years (instead of 5) could reduce their total energy consumption by nearly two-thirds.[24]

Another potential area for improvement is in the "total energy" concept, or consolidation of urban and industrial systems in a kind of "energy park" aimed at making optimum use of heat, electricity and transportation. Power would be generated in a central plant and waste heat could be used to run supplementary turbines for such needs as space heating, aquaculture agriculture or desalinization. The overall thermal efficiency of such systems might be as high as 75 or 80 percent. Many others have recommended more recycling as a means of improving energy utilization, as this requires much less energy than producing products from scratch. All told, the potential for reducing energy demand by improving the efficiency of energy utilization might be as much as 25 percent of what would otherwise be consumed.

Two devices that have received considerable attention as energy efficiency improvers are the MHD generator and the fuel cell. Fuel cells convert chemical energy directly into electricity. First discovered by Sir William Grove in 1839, they remained a scientific curiosity until the first practical cell was demonstrated at Cambridge University in 1959. Since then they have been used in the space program but their high costs have made them prohibitive for commercial use. But recently some have begun to believe that cost problems could be overcome and fuel cells could be an available power source within a decade. At present only one company, Pratt & Whitney, is pursuing development on a full-time basis, but other firms are expected to increase their investments during the next few years. MHD only a decade ago was hailed as the energy converter of the future, but it has yet to be demonstrated as a practical technology, partly because of continuing engineering problems but also because of lack of funds. These generators convert hot combustion gases from fossil fuels directly into electricity by injecting a small amount of "seed" material to make the gas electrically conducting and then passing it through a magnetic field at high speed, producing an electric current. MHD could increase the overall efficiency of conventional power plants to 50 or 60 percent, as well as having environmental advantages which include elimination of sulfur oxide emissions and reduction of nitrogen oxide emissions and thermal pollution.

Vast Coal and Oil Shale Deposits. Another possible means of reducing energy problems in the near future is more efficient use of the nation's huge deposits of coal and development of its oil shale resources. Both have environmental problems but recent trends appear to be promising. Much effort has been devoted to coal gasification and liquefaction—turning coal into pipeline quality synthetic natural gas or synthetic oil products. Gasification technology is more advanced and by some estimates could supply 5 to 10 trillion cubic feet of gas by the year 2000, although this might be only a small percentage of consumption by then, as domestic use was more than 22 trillion cubic feet in 1971 and was projected at 40 trillion cubic feet by 1985. [25]

Gasification technology is fairly simple—carbon from coal is combined with water at high temperature to form methane, the principal ingredient of natural gas. Five major methods have been developed but only one is in commercial use—the Lurgi process in Europe. The other four methods are being tested in the United States and a commercial plant may be in operation by 1981, according to the Office of Coal Research. [26] Coal liquefaction is more complex and expensive and less efficient, but 10 small plants may be built by 1985.

Oil shale has been recognized as a possible energy source for more than a century. Government geologists estimate that two trillion barrels of oil lie encased in shale rock beneath 11 million acres in Colorado, Utah and Wyoming—an amount six times greater than all proved reserves of crude petroleum on earth. But oil shale development has been delayed because of uncertainties in extraction technology, production costs and government policies. Plans to lease federal acreage to the oil industry have been proposed several times but never implemented, but the Interior Department is now awaiting final comments on its draft environmental impact statements for a proposed leasing program to begin soon.

Oil shale is sedimentary rock containing a waxy substance called kerogen, which when processed will yield a fluid hydrocarbon called shale oil. But for each barrel produced, 1½ tons of rock must be processed, creating serious potential environmental problems. In addition, large amounts of water are needed in the production process, which could severely tax Colorado River Basin resources and possibly increase already high salinity. Finally, production of one million barrels a day by 1985 would disturb up to 50,000 acres of land and require careful reclamation procedures. At present, the only production is on an experimental plant on private land in Colorado which produces 1,000 barrels a day. Hollis M. Dole, assistant secretary of the Interior Department, has said: "I am very bullish on oil shale. I feel that it is now economic to develop oil from oil shale providing the environmental safeguards are met." [27]

Solid and Organic Waste Material. Other recommendations have emphasized production of fuels from solid and organic wastes such as garbage, manure, logging and wood residues, agricultural wastes and sewage. Many have proposed making methane—a possible natural gas substitute—from agricultural wastes. When digested by microorganisms in oxygen-free containers, they can produce a gas which is up to 72 percent methane, and 10 cubic feet can be made from each pound of wastes. [28] But the major problem with such schemes is collecting the wastes and making conversion plants economically feasible. Others have suggested using municipal wastes as a supplementary fuel in power plants. One project by the Union Electric Company in St. Louis, reported in January 1973 in *Business Week*, found that shredded garbage with metal removed by magnets can be burned along with coal in utility boilers—it has about half the heating value but can product up to 15 percent of the daily energy load. The Environmental Protection Agency is providing about two-thirds of the project costs, and EPA estimates that at least 20 coal-burning plants around the nation can easily be converted to burn garbage. But some researchers believe the potential of waste conversion has been overestimated. According to a recent study by Larry L. Anderson of the University of Utah, although the United States generates more than 2 billion tons of organic wastes annually, more than half of their total weight is water and less than 20 percent are readily collectible. [29] Thomas H. Maugh II reported in *Science* magazine that many solid waste proposals "have been highly simplistic... and have ignored the difficulties of marketing low-value energy resources.... While conversion of organic wastes to fuels is an ideal way to dispose of the wastes, it is probably not a feasible method of averting an energy crisis." [30]

Prospects For New Energy Policy

For several years various energy experts have been calling for the adoption of a comprehensive national energy policy aimed at averting fuel shortages and developing new energy sources. Today those calls have reached a national crescendo, with a wide variety of proposals from different segments of society. But nearly all of the suggestions entail consolidation of federal authority—which now is spread out among some 64 departments and agencies in government.

The National Petroleum Council, an oil industry advisory group, has been conducting a three-year study of energy problems for the Interior Department, and in December 1972 submitted a final summary report, "U.S. Energy Outlook." In addition to centralization of federal authority, the report's principal recommendations were increased domestic production, continued oil import quotas, expanded refining capacity, deregulation of natural gas prices, "realistic" environmental standards and health and safety regulations, voluntary energy conservation, wider access to reserves on federal lands (including uranium, oil shale and geothermal resources), increased leasing of Outer Continental Shelf and seabed lands, expanded private research and development and more tax incentives for industry resource development.

Former AEC chairman Glenn T. Seaborg, among others, suggested in *Science* in June 1972 that the AEC be given a broader role than just atomic development and be placed in charge of all energy matters. "The commission has the scientific expertise, technical capability and organizational strength to develop the other energy sources as well. No other agency of the federal government is in a more favorable position to launch a unified program for meeting the energy needs of the American people." Concurring with this suggestion is S. David Freeman, former White House energy advisor who is now director of the Energy Policy Project, a 15-month, $3.5-million study of energy problems sponsored by the Ford Foundation. "I also think we need a single federal energy research and development agency. It should be given the mandate to come up with a program that includes all the options and should have industry and government as partners in funding it.... I think that you must take the nucleus of the laboratories of the AEC and make them energy laboratories, instead of just nuclear energy centers. The scattered inadequate programs of research in Interior and elsewhere should be consolidated with the research programs in AEC, into an agency with an overall energy research mission." [31] The Energy Policy Project is studying various aspects of U.S. energy supply problems and will publish a final report in the summer of 1973. Among other groups, the Sierra Club's board of directors issued a statement in October 1972 calling for nationwide energy and land use planning to "avert environmental disaster," and urging more energy conservation, land use constraints, fuel extraction regulations and power plant siting controls.

Congress and the President. "Energy is about to replace ecology as the pet of Washington politics," *Forbes* magazine wryly commented in its Oct. 1, 1972,

issue. Environmentalists hope the replacement will not be complete, but admit the time seems ripe for establishment of a new national energy policy either through passage of legislation, executive action or both. The 93rd Congress is gearing up for action on numerous energy policy bills. In the Senate, Washington Democrat Henry M. Jackson, chairman of the Interior Committee, has called energy policy development "the most critical problem—domestic or international—facing the nation today." On NBC-TV's "Meet the Press" Dec. 10, 1972, Jackson said: "I believe the No. 1 order of business is, first, to appoint an 'Energy Czar'...the second thing we need to do is recognize the need for a very large domestic program with heavy emphasis on research and development.... The third is nuclear power. We need an Admiral Rickover running our civilian nuclear power program." In the House, several energy policy bills are expected to be considered by the Interior Public Works and Interstate and Foreign Commerce Committees early in the session.

The Nixon administration also seemed to be setting the stage for wide-ranging actions on energy policy. The major effort was expected to come in February with a special energy message from President Nixon. President Nixon on Jan. 5, 1973, named Agriculture Secretary Earl L. Butz as presidential counselor for natural resources, including energy policy, in an apparent effort to bypass Congress in his desire to establish a Department of Natural Resources. *(Boxes p. 3, 91)*

Conservation of Energy. A growing body of opinion is suggesting that wiser use of available energy is a desirable goal along with development of new energy sources and more efficient energy utilization. The long history of inexpensive and unlimited energy in this country has led many Americans to use more and care less about energy supply. If this trend could be even partly reversed, many scientists, economists, engineers and environmentalists are now saying, the nation could save as much as 25 to 30 percent of its energy. Americans are extremely profligate energy users, consuming about four times more per capita than the Japanese and two and one half times more than West Germans.

An October 1972 report from the Office of Emergency Preparedness (to be abolished by President Nixon as part of his executive reform plan) called "The Potential for Energy Conservation" said the nation by 1980 could reduce its energy demand by as much as the equivalent of 7.3 million barrels of oil a day—saving $10.7-billion annually by an accompanying decrease in the need for oil imports. The report said that short-range conservation measures could save up to 16 percent of the 1980 energy demand while long-range steps could cut 1990 energy requirements by as much as 25 percent. The OEP study suggested that major areas for energy conservation were industry and transportation. Industry could easily cut its demand by 10 to 15 percent of projected levels or more if given adequate incentives through such devices as an energy use tax or a tax to encourage recycling. At present, many industries are given a favorable rate for higher energy consumption on an "interruptible" basis—this means that service can be cut off during peak demand periods. Transportation, which accounts for 25 percent of the total annual energy budget, also could accomplish major savings, the report said. A shift to bus and rail travel from private automobiles, more shipments of freight by rail rather than trucks and planes, less "short-haul" air travel and more urban mass transit were recommended. By the year 2000, this could save more than one trillion barrels of oil per year. But the report admitted that the tastes and habits of the public were difficult to change and major action was unlikely for some time.

Residential and commercial uses of energy account for 21 percent of U.S. energy consumption annually, the report said, with possible savings of 20 percent by 1980 and 30 percent by 1990. These could be accomplished by better insulation in all new and some old buildings, more centralized heating and cooling systems and fewer single-family homes. Turning down all home thermostats two degrees in winter and up two degrees in summer could save 600,000 barrels of oil daily by 1980. Other simple steps for home and office included: shutting off lights when leaving rooms, drawing blinds in empty rooms to stop heat transfer through windows, operating washing machines, dryers and dishwashers only when fully loaded, repairing leaky faucets promptly, having furnaces adjusted and clean regularly, keeping unused fireplaces closed, cleaning all condensing coils on appliances, installing good weather stripping, taking showers instead of baths and using flourescent bulbs instead of standard light bulbs. Also, electric ignitions should be installed on gas-burning stoves instead of pilot lights, which can use up to one third of the total fuel.

Others have suggested that office buildings could be designed for much higher energy savings by using less glass, light colors on roofs and walls and cutting down on interior lighting. Consulting engineer Fred S. Dubin has written that 50 to 60 percent of the electricity consumed in an office building is for lighting, but this could be cut at least in half. "Better quality of illumination rather than higher intensities should be the goal.... Many recent experiments confirm that lighting levels between 10 and 40 foot candles are sufficient for visual acuity and physiological needs, where levels of 60 to 150 foot candles are now being provided."[32] In Great Britain, the minimum recommended lighting is 10 foot candles; in the United States, it is 70 foot candles and average commercial intensity is 125 foot candles today.

Among other studies, a two-volume report from the Rand Corporation on energy problems in California made recommendations similar to the OEP report. Done for the state government and the National Science Foundation, the Rand study concluded that the need for power plant construction envisioned by the state utility industry could be cut by two-thirds in the next 30 years by policies such as using more natural gas and less electricity for home uses, solar energy for space heating and cooling, better building insulation, improved air conditioning efficiencies, reducing electric requirements of lights and erecting more "low-energy" buildings.[33]

The Energy Policy Project's Freeman has said: "Once we recognize that conservation, rather than promotion, is a national objective, we could be just as successful in fashioning a way of life that will make it happen.... I happen to believe that we are using energy extremely wastefully in this country and that there are great opportunities for having our cake and eating it too. This will mean some changes in life style that will improve the quality of life.... We need to buy time to perfect cleaner sources."[34]

Another means of buying time is the virtually enforced conservation of energy which would come about if fuel prices rise sharply, as they are almost certain to do in the next several years. But this could have the unequal and unfair effect of forcing the poor to use less energy while the rich, if they so chose, could continue profligate consumption. More equitable measures would be rate structures which favored small users of energy and incentives for efficient buildings and consumer products. If cooperative, regulatory and persuasive measures such as these do not work, more drastic means of curbing energy use may be unavoidable. The Environmental Protection Agency—in the interest of air quality standards—already has proposed gasoline rationing for the Los Angeles area. Sometime during the closing years of the 20th century, Americans may be subjected to the involuntary indignities of daily driving restrictions, nightly television hours or even "lights out" curfews while waiting for science to harness the warmth of the sun, the heat of the earth and the power of the atom.

***

[1] Ralph E. Lapp, "Brainpower-An Answer to Our Energy Problem," *Nation's Business,* August 1972, p. 47.

[2] Lawrence Rocks and Richard P. Runyon, *The Energy Crisis* (1972), p. 49.

[3] Allen L. Hammond, "Solar Energy: The Largest Resource," *Science,* Sept. 22, 1972, p. 1088.

[4] Aden B. and Marjorie P. Meinel, "Is It Time for a New Look at Solar Energy?" *Bulletin of the Atomic Scientists,* October 1971, p. 35.

[5] Edmund Faltermeyer, "The Energy 'Joyride' Is Over," *Fortune,* September 1972, p. 191.

[6] Rocks and Runyon, *op. cit.* p. 48.

[7] Joseph Barnea, "Geothermal Power," *Scientific American,* January 1972, p. 70.

[8] Allen L. Hammond, "Geothermal Energy: An Emerging Major Resource," *Science* Sept. 15, 1972, p. 979.

[9] M. King Hubbert, "Energy Resources of the Earth," *Scientific American,* September 1971, p. 67.

[10] David Fenner and Joseph Klarmann, "Power From The Earth," *Environment,* December 1971, p. 34.

[11] William E. Heronemus, "Alternatives to Nuclear Energy," *Catalyst.* Vol. II., No. 3, p. 25.

[12] Quoted by David Brand, "Power Play," *The Wall Street Journal,* Nov. 29, 1972.

[13] Hannes Alfven, *Bulletin of the Atomic Scientists,* July 1972, p. 5.

[14] Letter to the Editor, *Science,* Dec. 1, 1972, p. 933.

[15] Hoyt C. Hottel and Jack B. Howard, "An Agenda for Energy," *Technology Review,* January 1972, p. 46.

[16] See William C. Gough and Bernard J. Eastland, "The Prospects for Fusion Power," *Scientific American,* February 1971, p. 64.

[17] William D. Metz, "Magnetic Containment Fusion; What Are the Prospects?" *Science,* Oct. 20, 1972, p. 291.

[18] Derek P. Gregory, "The Hydrogen Economy," *Scientific American,* Jan. 1973, p. 13.

[19] Lawrence Lessing, "The Coming Hydrogen Economy," *Fortune,* November 1972, p. 140.

[20] Lessing, *op. cit.,* p. 144.

[21] Thomas H. Maugh II, "Hydrogen: Synthetic Fuel of the Future," *Science,* Nov. 24, 1972, p. 851.

[22] Gregory, *op. cit.,* p. 18.

[23] Allen L. Hammond, "Conservation of Energy: The Potential for More Efficient Use," *Science,* Dec. 8, 1972, p. 1080.

[24] A. B. Makhijani and A. J. Lichtenberg, "Energy and Well-Being," *Environment,* June 1972, p. 16.

[25] G. Alex Mills, "Gas From Coal—Fuel of the Future," *Environmental Science and Technology,* December 1971, p. 1179.

[26] Thomas H. Maugh II, "Gasification: A Rediscovered Source of Clean Fuel," *Science,* Oct. 6, 1972, pp. 44-45.

[27] Quoted by Helene C. Monberg, "Oil Shale," *Western Resources Wrap-Up,* Sept. 6, 1972.

[28] Hinrich L. Bohn, "A Clean New Gas," *Environment,* December 1971.

[29] L. L. Anderson, U.S. Bureau of Mines Circular 8549 (1972), p. 13.

[30] Thomas H. Maugh II, "Fuel from Wastes: A Minor Energy Source," *Science* Nov. 10, 1972, p. 599.

[31] Quoted by Jack Shepherd, "Energy 1," *Intellectual Digest,* December 1972, p. 33.

[32] Fred S. Dubin, "If You Want to Save Energy," *American Institute of Architects Journal,* December 1972, p. 19.

[33] "California's Electricity Quandry: Estimating Future Demand" (Vol. I) and "Slowing the Growth Rate" (Vol. II), Rand Corporation, 1972.

[34] Quoted by Jack Shepherd, *op. cit.,* pp. 31-33.

ENVIRONMENTAL PROBLEMS WORLDWIDE IN SCOPE

The world is awakening to a sense of crisis about the state of the environment. Dozens of countries, including the United States, have taken steps to control pollution. Scores of national and international meetings have examined in detail the deterioration of the environment. International agencies, ranging from the North Atlantic Treaty Organization to the United Nations Economic Commission for Asia and the Far East, from the Organization of American States to the World Bank, have instituted environmental programs. "The environment," remarks Barry Commoner, one of America's leading ecologists, "has just been rediscovered by the people who live in it." The rediscovery culminated in 1972 in the United Nations Conference on the Human Environment. *(Conference p. 68)*

The big question for the U.N. conference, and for all subsequent attempts to stop worldwide pollution, is whether the concern about the environment has come too late to do much good. Has man, in fact, gone too far to turn back? Can the nations make the hard political decisions that are necessary to establish worldwide cooperation in the face of the present crisis? Anything less than a full-scale international effort seems futile. The world's ecosystem is one; it is such that no nation alone can clean up its environment. The atmosphere carries industrial pollutants and pesticides all over the earth. Virtually every international waterway is polluted, and becoming worse year by year.

Pollution on All Continents

Lake Erie is "dead,"[1] and so is the Lake of Zurich. The Baltic and Mediterranean Seas are dying. Lake Baikal in Soviet Siberia, the world's largest fresh-water lake, is being poisoned by effluent from pulp mills and industries. In the heart of Africa, the Zambesi River is polluted by raw sewage as it flows over Victoria Falls. Coastal waters of the South Seas are fouled by human and chemical wastes, and coral reefs are dying as a result. The once-lovely Rhine River is Europe's drainpipe to the sea, carrying the filth of cities and factories in such quantity that Germans say it ought to be called the Rinne, their word for sewer. By the time Rhine waters reach Amsterdam, they are so polluted that a Dutch newspaper reports it is able to develop photographic film in them.

Nearly every big city has severe smog problems. London has made improvements since the "killer smog" of 1952 contributed to the death of 4,000 persons. But conditions have worsened in many other places. Some of the worst smog problems today are found in Mexico City, Tokyo and Santiago, Chile. In the United States, for the first time, the federal government on Nov. 18, 1971, ordered 23 industrial plants and steel mills shut down temporarily at Birmingham, Ala., to relieve a smog crisis in the eastern United States. But air pollution is not confined to individual metropolitan areas or nations. In Sweden, the nation's pine forests are withering under rainfall that bears sulphur compounds blown from Germany's Ruhr Valley. Pesticides from Africa have been found in the West Indies, 3,600 miles away.

The worldwide ecological movement is relatively new. The word ecology[2] entered the English language about a century ago. But the modern ecological movement is scarcely a decade old. In the United States, it is sometimes dated from 1962, the year Rachel Carson's book *Silent Spring* appeared, bringing the environmental crisis to public attention. Underlying the world environmental concern is the growing awareness that the capacity of the earth to support human life is finite. There are definite limits to the earth's resources, whether man abuses them or not. And there is suspicion that man may be approaching the limits of those resources in several areas, including food and water. Even those who have written glowingly of the so-called green revolution, which has doubled and tripled agricultural yields in certain regions, freely admit that improved agricultural technology may only have bought a few years of time for man to solve the problems of rapid population growth.

Depletion of Earth's Resources

Per capita consumption of the earth's resources is many times greater in the developed than in the developing countries. Efforts to close the economic gap between the world's rich and poor nations will inevitably increase the strain on resources. One scientist, Preston Cloud, has estimated that to bring the rest of the world up to the current U.S. level of consumption would require a yearly world output of 60 billion tons of iron, a billion tons of lead, 700 million tons of zinc and more than 50 million tons of tin—between 200 and 400 times the present world production levels. Dr. Philip Hauser, a sociologist, estimates that the world's resources could support a population of only half a billion people if they all consumed at the U.S. level. The present estimated world population is 3.7 billion. Loren Eiseley, the anthropologist, has called man a "flame" that will eventually consume the world.

Depletion of the earth's resources is one side of the ecological dilemma; pollution is the other. Man the consumer is also man the poisoner. Pollutants that enter the earth's ecosystem at any point may be expected to spread across the globe. Air pollution and water pollution are generally treated as distinct problems by environmental-

---

1 A condition caused by pollution-induced plant growth which shuts off sunlight and allows algae to decompose below the surface, exhausting the oxygen in the water. See "Coastal Conservation."

2 Derived from the Greek word *oikos*, for household, it is a branch of science concerned with the inter-relationship of organisms and their environment.

ists. However, French oceanographer Jacques Cousteau recently declared that "there is only one pollution because every single thing, every chemical whether in the air or on land will end up in the ocean."

Cousteau fears that the damage being done to the oceans and world's great rivers by industrial wastes, oil spills, pesticides and other chemicals may be irreversible. "Twenty-five percent of all the DDT compounds so far produced are already in the sea. They will all end up in the sea finally. But already 25 percent has reached the sea—cadmium, mercury, all these problems." Another great oceanographer and marine scientist, Dr. Jacques Piccard, warned just a few weeks earlier that at the current rate of pollution, there would be no life in the oceans in 25 years. He said that the shallow Baltic Sea would be the first to die, and that the Adriatic and the Mediterranean would be next.

International Nature of Pollution

A United Nations report on marine pollution explains how an ocean can be "killed": "The ecological balance of the oceans can be upset in many ways. Some pollutants simply poison the animals and plants with which they come into contact. Other pollutants make such a demand on the oxygen dissolved in sea water—oxygen which is essential to the life of marine animals—that the living competitors suffocate. Some pollutants accumulate in marine food chains and webs because they are not readily metabolized. Pollutants concentrated by food chains can reach levels which upset physiological functions."

The U.N. document emphasizes the hazards of oil pollution, from accidental spills from tankers and the rupture of offshore wells. "A recent estimate puts oil pollution from oil transport activities alone at one million metric tons per year and the total from all human activities at no less than 10 times this amount." Thor Heyerdahl, the Norweigian anthropologist-explorer, noted after his successful crossing of the Atlantic Ocean in the summer of 1970 that his papyrus raft, the Ra, encountered great blobs of tar-like material on the ocean surface on many of the 57 days it was at sea.

Experts are also concerned by the rising concentrations of the so-called "chlorinated hydrocarbons" in the sea. These consist mainly of the pesticides DDT, dieldrin and endrin. Another class of chemicals, the polychlorinated biphenyls, are also found in increasing amounts. Both classes of compounds are responsible for massive kills of marine life. "Levels of DDT contamination in marine fish may, in fact, be approaching levels associated with the collapse of fisheries for freshwater areas," the U.N. report states.

If possible, atmospheric pollution is even more ubiquitous than oceanic pollution. It comes from various sources—from industry, the heating of buildings, trash burning, jet airplanes. The principal culprit is the internal combustion engine. The U.S. Public Health Service has estimated that in the United States alone, the nation's motor vehicles spew into the atmosphere each year some 66 million tons of carbon monoxide, one million tons of sulphur oxides, six million tons of nitrogen oxides, 12 million tons of hydrocarbons, one million tons of particulate matter and assorted other dangerous substances, such as

tetraethyl lead. Under certain conditions of wind and temperature, the combination of these gases can produce "killer" smogs. One estimate is that the average resident of New York City, simply by breathing the air of his city, "smokes" the equivalent of 38 cigarettes a day.

The steadily rising combustion of fossil fuels—coal, gasoline, fuel oil—presents still another global problem, which is only dimly understood. The Air Conservation Committee of the American Academy for the Advancement of Science has found that the amount of carbon dioxide released into the air has tripled since the beginning of the century, industry and transport vehicles may be producing as much as 50 billion tons of carbon dioxide a year.

Technology Versus Ecology

The committee observed that combustion could raise the concentration of carbon dioxide in the atmosphere by as much as 17 times. No one is sure what the result of such high concentration would be. Some scientists believe it would act as a "heat trap," raising the temperature of the earth. One possible consequence could be the melting of the Greenland and Antarctic ice caps, raising the level of the oceans by as much as 250 feet and drowning every port city in the world.

Most pollution problems made their first appearance, or became very much worse, in the years following World War II. Especially in the developed nations of the world, the principal factor was the technological revolution that transformed the nature of agricultural and industrial production. As a result of the new technology, and of vastly altered consumption patterns, the output of certain items which contribute heavily to pollution problems zoomed upward. According to Barry Commoner, production of non-returnable soda bottles increased 53,000 percent in the quarter-century after the war; synthetic fiber output rose by 5,980 percent; mercury used in chlorine production, by 3,930 percent; and mercury used in mildew resistant paint by 3,120 percent. DDT, detergents and synthetic plastics made their appearance on the market. Authorities estimate that human beings are now exposed to over half a million chemical pollutants, and that the number is increasing by 400 to 500 a year.

The new technologies have transformed the face of agriculture, as well as industry, in the developed countries. The steadily rising use of pesticides and fertilizers is one part of the story. Another is the evolution of "agribusiness"—the assembly-line approach to the raising of crops and animals. Cattle, for example, are not turned out to graze but are kept in feed lots; with little exercise, they gain weight much faster. But the concentration of their wastes in one small area constitutes another strain on the environment. In the United States, the volume of animal waste that finds its way untreated into rivers and streams is estimated to be ten times as great as the volume of human wastes.

A special problem of the technological age is radiation pollution. One source of exposure to radiation is isotype therapy and X-ray diagnosis and therapy, which has increased significantly in recent years. Until the leading powers agreed in 1963 to discontinue above-ground testing, the radioactive fallout from atmospheric explosions of nuclear devices represented a growing threat to human health. Scientists found alarmingly high levels of cancer-causing strontium-90 in humans all over the earth. Atmospheric winds carried radioactive ash from Hiroshima around the world in barely two weeks.

The newest threat of radioactive contamination stems from the proliferation of nuclear power plants to generate electricity. As of November 1971, 23 commercial nuclear power plants were in operation in the United States, 54 were under construction and 48 were being designed. Reactors constantly "leak" tiny amounts of radiation. While this leakage constitutes only a small fraction of the "background" radiation received from the environment, there is a bitter scientific controversy about how dangerous these small doses are. A related argument concerns the disposal of radioactive byproducts of the power-generating process. The Atomic Energy Commission pins its hopes on storing the byproducts in underground salt mines. Given the long radioactive life of such substances, many scientists fear that such storage may merely postpone the day of reckoning.

Lord Ritchie-Calder, the British author-environmentalist, has pointed out that in some atomic wastes the radioactivity can persist for hundreds of thousands of years. "With the multiplication of power reactors, the wastes will increase," he wrote. "It is calculated that by the year 2000, the number of six-ton nuclear 'hearses' (trucks) in transit to 'burial grounds' at any given time on the highways of the United States will be well over 3,000 and the amount of radioactive products will be about a billion curies, which is a mighty lot of curies to be roaming around a populated country."

Still another pollutant of the modern age has only recently come to the attention of researchers: noise. In the crowded cities of the world, noise—from aircraft, construction, vehicles and amplified sound systems—is reaching levels beyond the capacity of humans to absorb without injury. Scientists have found that excessive noise can raise blood pressure, increase the cholesterol count, affect the heart and glands, harm unborn children and cause stress and irritability.

Problems of Poor Countries

A high rate of population increase puts a heavy strain on resources and severely handicaps efforts to develop the economies of the poorer nations. Not only is the population of the poor nations rising fast, it is shifting to the cities at an even more rapid rate.[3] The urban growth has produced wretched ghettos and shanty towns in the developing world, more squalid than any slum in the industrial countries. City governments are virtually powerless to cope with the swelling tide of humanity, and sanity and social services are almost non-existent. As living conditions in the ghettos deteriorate, environmental problems rise.

Environmental decay, endemic disease and social disorder are bred in the overcrowding and misery of the slums. But air and water pollution, which are also increasing, come from the industries and technological advances. Industrialization, increased use of fossil fuels, and a sharp rise in the number of cars on the road are responsible. Mexico City has been singled out as having the highest carbon monoxide level in the entire world, exceeding even that of Los Angeles. Mexico City is

ringed by 5,000 factories, which, experts say, account for 20 percent of the pollution. Another 20 percent comes from open burning of garbage. But the bulk of the city's smog—60 percent of it—comes from the million cars, trucks and buses that jam the streeets.

Economic Viability vs. Ecology. "Up to now, poor nations usually turned deaf when rich nations discussed ecological dangers. In developing countries there has been little demand for a cleaner environment," Irwin Goodwin wrote in *The Washington Post,* Aug. 8, 1971. A study by the Organization of American States noted that, "given the amply justified emphasis of policy upon raising living standards in Latin America, environmental protection tends to be viewed largely as irrelevant, and even as a hindrance to development."

Such a view has been quite commonly held throughout the developing world. An Indian government official was quoted as saying: "The wealthy worry about car fumes. We worry about starvation." Ceylon's ambassador to the U.N., Hamilton Shirley Amerasinghe, has stated that "developing countries have of late been warned of the price that has to be paid in the form of environmental pollution for industrial development."

All developing countries are aware of the risks (he continued) but...their economists, and planners must not and will not allow themselves to be distracted from the imperatives of economic development and growth by the illusory dream of an atmosphere free of smoke or a landscape innocent of chimney stacks.[4]

In Africa, an official of the Senegalese government, speaking of water pollution, has said, "The problem is indeed a serious one...we are reaching the point where even drinking water supplies are threatened." The official, Babacar Diop, then observed: "Solving this problem requires international measures. But that is not at all the same as to say that such measures can be considered a sort of compensation or a justification for transferring a part of the aid now given third-world countries to the fight against pollution.... I believe that it is abosolutely necessary to fight pollution, but at the same time, pollution may bring with it certain 'advantages.' "

Curiously, rich countries may also face economy-ecology dilemmas. In the United States, Democratic Party Chairman Lawrence F. O'Brien asked in a recent speech:

What priority does air pollution have to a mother of the core city whose baby has been bitten by a rat? What priority does a polluted lake have to a family whose main recreation area is a littered alley?

If we cannot solve the problems of poverty and squalor and racial bigotry that have created our slums, it will do us no good to solve the problems of water and air pollution and contamination that are despoiling our countryside.

The clear challenge ahead will be to reconcile the urgent need to raise living standards among the two-thirds of the world's people who are desperately poor and to prevent the environmental degradation that will eventually impoverish the entire earth.

Pesticide Popularity in Third World. The reconciliation is likely to prove difficult, not only because of the demand in the underdeveloped world for more industry,

---

3 Annual population growth is currently estimated at 2.9 percent for Latin America, 2.7 percent for Africa and 2.3 percent for Asia, well above the 2.0 world average and Western European (0.6) and U.S. (2.0) marks.

4 Quoted by M. Taghi Farvar, *et. al.,* "The Pollution of Asia," *Environment* (magazine of the Scientists' Institute for Public Information, St. Louis), October 1971, p. 10.

but also because the application of modern technology to agriculture carries with it the threat of environmental damage. A fierce argument is now raging over the use of DDT and other pesticides. DDT (dichloro-diphenyl-trichloroethane) is one of a family of chlorinated hydrocarbons which, along with the newer polychlorinated biphenyls, are used extensively to destroy crop-killing and disease-carrying insects.

Extensive studies have shown that DDT is harmful to a broad spectrum of animal life, killing some species and damaging the liver, central nervous system and reproductive capacity of others. It has been blamed for massive fish kills, and for the inability of some fish-eating birds to develop shells sufficiently strong to protect their eggs—and offspring. Some medical research has indicated that the compound has harmful effects on humans. Rats fed a steady diet of DDT have developed cancer, suggesting—but not proving—that humans might be susceptible also.

DDT is an extraordinarily stable compound which tends to become more and more concentrated the farther along the food chain it moves. DDT has been found in the fat of Antarctic seals and penguins, in the ice of Alaskan glaciers, and in the milk of nursing mothers all over the world. A Swedish toxicologist, Dr. Goran Lofroth of Stockholm University, has reported that nursing infants in Sweden consume twice the daily "safe" limit of DDT set by the World Health Organization.

As an insecticide, DDT has been found wanting by many ecologists. Insects tend to develop immunity to it, making necessary the application of ever-larger amounts and the continual development of newer and stronger pesticides. At the same time, DDT and the other pesticides may harm the natural enemies of the insect pests—birds, for example. For all these reasons, several developed countries, including the United States, have placed controls on the marketing and use of several pesticides and seem to be moving toward an outright ban on them.

The federal government has restricted domestic uses of DDT since November 1969 and the Environmental Protection Agency is expected to complete court-ordered hearings by January 1971 on whether to ban all uses in the United States. The agency estimated that 35 percent of the former uses of the pesticide are now forbidden. The uses that are still permitted are mainly agricultural. No restrictions have been placed on exports of American-manufactured DDT. According to agency officials, Montrose Chemical, the principal U.S. maker, produced 123 million pounds of the pesticide in 1970 and exported 82 million pounds of it.

Pesticides, especially DDT, have strong defenders in the developing world. Dr. Norman Borlaug, father of the green revolution, and developer of the "miracle wheat" strains now in use in many parts of the developing world, recently attacked "irresponsible environmentalists" for their opposition to the use of DDT and other chemical pesticides and fertilizers. "No chemical," Borlaug said, "has ever done as much as DDT to improve the health, economic and social benefits of the people of the developing nations."

Borlaug's view is backed by the U.N. Food and Agriculture Organization, the single largest user of DDT in the world. The FAO opposes any ban on DDT because it has found no acceptable substitute for controlling the spread of malaria, yellow fever, elephantiasis, sleeping sickness and cholera. The organization also emphasizes the use of pesticides in protecting crops against the ravages of insect plagues, such as locusts, cotton worms and corn borers. *Ceres*, the FAO magazine, has argued that "indiscriminate attacks on pesticides should be resisted by developing nations."

Modern technology has introduced into agriculture a host of other substances which, like the pesticides, can cause ecological damage. Among these are mercury compounds (used as fungicides), lead (used in automotive fuel), and phosphates and nitrates (used in fertilizers). Recently the Food and Drug Administration issued warnings against diethyl-stilbesterol (DES), a synthetic estrogen use to fatten cattle, which, it has been shown, may cause cancer in humans and animals.

Aswan Dam Example

Developing countries throughout the world typically need roads, power grids and oil pipelines for a viable economy. But all of them exact some price in environmental damage, and there is inevitably a trade-off between the economic benefits and the ecological disadvantages. Perhaps the cruelest choices come in deciding to build dams. They control floods and provide irrigation water to raise farm yields. And they generate electric power. Unhappily, as a recent United Nations Development Program Food and Agriculture Organization report demonstrated, "dams can raise more problems than they solve."

The classic case is the new high dam at Aswan, Egypt. Throughout history the lower Nile Valley has been periodically inundated by floods. The high dam now prevents flooding. As a result, the rich river silt no longer fertilizes the delta lands, and commercial fertilizer must be used. Flood-borne nutrients no longer reach the sea, and the fish catch in the eastern Mediterranean is declining drastically. Paradoxically, the silt is now building up beyond the high dam, and will eventually render it useless. Controlled irrigation from the new dam is salinating the soil bit by bit, making periodic flushing—an expensive process—necessary. Additionally, parasite-carrying snails are multiplying in the irrigation channels, and schistosomiasis, or biharzia, a debilitating tropical disease, is spreading rapidly.

In a number of ways, the developed countries are a source of the ecological difficulties of the underdeveloped world. The United States, Japan and Western Europe supply the world with its automotive vehicles, its mills, factories and chemical plants. They drill the oil wells, build the refineries and supply the technology available to the developing nations. In the United States, new air pollution laws are so strict that copper smelting operations are being sharply reduced. *Vision*, a Spanish-language magazine which circulates throughout Latin America, notes that "in almost the entire nation it is virtually impossible to build a copper smelter." As a result, smelting operations are being moved to other countries; thus the United States, a big user of copper, is transferring a pollution problem abroad.

Gunnar Myrdal, the Swedish economist, has predicted a "people's movement in developed countries to end pollution and all the harmful effects of technology on the environment." But, Myrdal observes, "for Americans to be concerned enough to do something about the detrimental changing of local ecology by development projects in poorer countries, that will take time."

Perhaps the most important factor of all is the subtle export of attitudes from the developed countries to the less-developed world. The poorer countries have a strong desire and an unquestioned right to seek to raise their standard of living. To a certain extent, they try to do so by utilizing the technology that is made available to them; some environmental damage is accepted as a fair price for the effort. In the process, many political leaders and technologists appear to have adopted the traditional western view that a constantly rising level of consumption is necessary to economic health.

Many ecologists believe, however, that development in the poorer countries cannot and will not follow the pattern of the industrial nations. The constraints are physical; the capacity of the earth is limited. "Just think," someone has suggested, "what would happen to the automobile if 700 million Chinese started driving big automobiles!"

Ironically, many leaders of the developing world have become afflicted with what is termed "growthmania" at a time when even the developed countries are becoming aware that fundamental changes in their own consumption patterns are inevitable. Paul W. McCracken, President Nixon's chief economic adviser, has stated: "simply producing more...if it means putting more smoke in the atmosphere...is not an adequate goal." A leading economist, Kenneth Boulding, has begun to develop a non-growth-oriented economic theory under the title "The Economics of Spaceship Earth." Boulding argues that within the confines of the globe, there are no unlimited reservoirs for extraction or pollution, and that consumption and reproduction must therefore be minimized.

One problem that all industrial countries—and many less-developed countries as well—face in common is the skyrocketing demand for electric power. Electric power needs in the United States are doubling every decade. Every step up in generating capacity—whether through steam generator plants, nuclear power stations, or hydroelectric dams—brings on some environmental disruption. And should the developed countries increasingly turn—as is expected—to nuclear power, the problem of waste disposal will become an international worry.

International Action

Environmental problems are as real in communist as in capitalist countries. The pollution of Lake Baikal in Soviet Siberia has been amply documented. In a recent issue, the *Proceedings* of the Association of American Geographers identified some 30 other examples of serious industrial and agricultural fouling of Soviet inland waters. Earlier in the year, the Soviet government reported a break in one of the country's biggest oil pipelines, located near the Ural River, which empties into the Caspian Sea. Smog and sewage disposal problems plague Soviet cities. In the Eastern European satellite countries, similar environmental problems abound: forests are dying, and industrial soot covers the cities. It is reported that Budapest, Hungary, is capable of treating only one-half of its sewage. The rest contaminates the Danube River.

Ray Vickers of *The Wall Street Journal* reported from Rome, Nov. 26, 1971, the Italian Communist Party had adopted the theme that capitalism causes pollution whereas only communism can provide the political framework for a clean environment. "This seems to be the official environmental party line emanating from Moscow today," Vickers added. "It's being worked into Red propaganda in Britain, France and elsewhere so consistently that there is a Soviet smell to the whole claim." When an Eastern European communist country points its finger at capitalist polluters, "it indeed is a case of the pot calling the kettle black...."

Pollution, however, is finally becoming an issue within the USSR (he continued)...as it is in the capitalist world. More and more newspapers carry feature stories about ecological damage, and conservationists are raising their voices against indiscriminate production without regard for the land, sea and air.

At the ministry of health headquarters in Moscow, a half dozen officials met not long ago with a reporter to outline some of the steps not being taken to combat ecological damage and to protect the environment.

The situation of Japan, Asia's only thoroughly industrial state, is not very different from that of the developed western nations. Since the end of World War II, Japan has come charging pell-mell into the front ranks of the world's industrial powers, and has paid a fearful price in environmental degradation. To some visitors, Tokyo is the most crowded and most polluted city on earth. An observer has written:

In Japan, pollution—whether you pronounce it with two l's or two r's—is a very dirty word. Because, for man and beast alike, there simply is no escape from it. It is in the air you breathe. It is in the rice and fish you eat. It fouls the beaches where you try to swim. It fosters some of the most baffling diseases in medical history. It pounds at people's eardrums around the clock, accelerating the flow of adrenalin and infringing on their territoriality. [5]

A persistent blanket of smog shrouds Japan's sacred mountain, Fuji. Within the city limits of Tokyo, factories discharge 1.7 million tons of waste gases a year; two million motor vehicles spew out 700,000 tons of carbon monoxide. Fifty-five percent of the city's sewage is dumped untreated into the sea. Significantly, the so-called minamata disease—now identified as mercury poisoning from tainted shellfish—was first detected in Japan. Another exotic affliction, Itai-Itai—a word that is translated as "ouch-ouch," since the victim aches all over—was traced to rice contaminated by cadium from the exhaust gases and waste waters of zinc refineries.

The catalog of problems is as endless as it is repetitious. In Italy, seven out of every ten miles of the nation's waterways are polluted, and most of the larger lakes are dead. In Latin America, the big industrial centers such as Sao Paulo in Brazil and Buenos Aires in Argentina have turned their rivers into black and fetid industrial sewers. Even China, the sleeping giant, is awakening to environmental problems. Western newsmen who have been admitted to China in recent months reported seeing or being told of anti-pollution activities.

Economic Barriers to Control of Pollution. A number of other countries have begun to control pollution. Britain has established a cabinet-level post of Minister of the Environment, and given its holder, 37-year-old

5 Darrell Houston, "Remember When You Could See Mount Fuji?," *Alicia Patterson Fund Newsletter,* Jan. 13, 1971.

Peter Walker, formidable powers to intervene in the planning of transportation, housing, land-use and regulation of rivers and coastal waters. One result of rising British interest in a better environment is a 70 percent reduction in air pollution in London, and the return of trout and pike in the lower reaches of the once heavily contaminated Thames River.

For the past half a decade, Paris has been trying to cleanse its air. As an experiment, the city government has set up two 16-foot-high towers around a railway station, Gare de Lyon, with air filtering devices to remove dust and pollutants. In Santiago, Chile, the new Institute of Occupational Health and Air Pollution Research has been set up to gather basic information on the city's mounting pollution. The institute's work is supported by the World Health Organization and the U.N. Development Programme. Japan has hesitantly started its first anti-pollution efforts with the creation of an environmental agency whose task is mainly educational. The Japanese have sought anti-pollution advice from such diverse persons as Russell Train, chairman of President Nixon's Council on Environmental Quality, and Ralph Nader.

Considerable technology for limiting the contamination of air, water and soil has been available for many years. It is just beginning to be applied on any significant scale. And so far, the application of technology is strictly at the local, state or national level; no advances have been made on the international level. In the United States, clear-air and clean-water legislation are prompting industry to make major investment in clean-up techniques. Many states have instituted tax incentives to encourage industrial-pollution abatement. The Atomic Energy Commission, under its new chairman, James R. Schlesinger, has emphasized environmental matters—an area in which the commission had long been accused of showing gross insensitivity. In recent months, the federal government has begun to seek indictments against officers of companies that are consistent polluters.

The chief obstacles to the widespread adoption of anti-pollution technology are economic. Barry Commoner has estimated the cost of halting pollution in the United States and repairing essential parts of the ecosystem at about $40-billion a year for the next 25 years—a total of one trillion dollars. Even such an enormous outlay would not bring the environment all the way back to where it was before the great technological leap after 1945.

Worldwide, the costs would be astronomical. The Organization for Economic Cooperation and Development has estimated that it would take an annual outlay equal to 2 percent of the gross national product of the industrial countries just to ensure that environmental deterioration is gradual rather than rapid. In the United States alone that would amount to $20-billion. Holding the line against pollution, they say, would cost about 4 percent, and repairing past damage while preventing future problems could cost three to four times that much. At present, no nation is likely to make a commitment on so grand a scale. Even if a nation had the resources to do so, it "must bear in mind...the consequences of putting its industries and its economy at a competitive disadvantage, should other nations not follow suit." [6]

Ecologists thus stress the need for an international approach. They cite the decline in levels of radioactive fallout in recent years as evidence that international agreements do have value. They point to the possibilities

Stockholm Conference Highlights

Among the major results of the United Nations Conference on the Human Environment held June 5-16, 1972, in Stockholm, Sweden, were:

• Adoption of the Declaration on the Human Environment containing new principles to guide future international action on environmental issues, including the principle that states are responsible for damages to the environment of other states or international areas.

• Recommendation of a permanent high-level UN environmental unit to coordinate activities, headed by conference secretary-general Maurice Strong of Canada.

• Creation of a five-year, $100-million UN environmental fund for pollution control and other activities, with a 40 percent U.S. share.

• Establishment of a global "Earthwatch" program to monitor environmental trends including air and water pollution, land use and human health.

• Implementation of a worldwide environmental information service to help countries exchange knowledge and data.

• Creation of "genetic pools" to collect and preserve the planet's animal, plant, insect and microorganism resources.

• Agreement on an ambassadorial meeting in London in October 1972 to initiate an ocean-dumping treaty pending final consideration at the UN law of the sea conference in 1973.

• Urging of a shift from chemical control of agriculture pests to a more integrated approach emphasizing biological controls instead of pesticides.

inherent in space technology for creating a worldwide environmental protection system. Under the earth resources satellite program, the National Aeronautics and Space Administration will soon launch Erts-A, an orbiting satellite with infra-red remote sensing devices capable of detecting pollutants from a height of 492 miles.

Environmental programs have already been initiated by a number of regional and international organizations. The World Bank in 1970 appointed an environmental adviser to review all Bank projects for their ecological implications. The Organization of Economic Cooperation and Development, embracing the United States, Canada, Japan and 19 western European nations, has agreed to draft common pollution standards and to work toward a system of enforcement. Eight nations of the East and West—the United States, the Soviet Union, East Germany, West Germany, Britain, France, Italy and Poland—agreed in October 1971 to set up an international research center to investigate common problems arising from the spread of modern technology. The center, to be known as the International Institute of Applied Systems Analysis, would study such critical factors as population growth, food production, raw material depletion and all kinds of pollution.

---

6 Michael Harwood, "We Are Killing the Sea Around Us," *The New York Times Magazine*, Oct. 24, 1971, p. 91.

COSTS OF CLEANING UP ENVIRONMENT COUNTED IN BILLIONS

The emergence of environmental pollution as everybody's issue may be a victory for those farsighted scientists and conservationists whose warnings of impending crisis went unheeded for so many years. But winning popular support for an all-out attack on pollution is but the bare beginning of a solution. A big question is how to go about doing the job. And here the experts often do not agree. An even bigger question is how much people are willing to pay to restore their damaged earth, air, and waterways and to prevent further depredations. Pay means not only money, which will run into many billions of dollars, but possibly the sacrifice of conveniences and luxuries so familiar as to seem necessities to most Americans.

To date, pleas for a cutback of consumption in the interests of environmental protection have won few converts. It is true that some housewives take their grocery bags and egg boxes back to the supermarket for re-use, and here and there conservation zealots ride bicycles instead of drive cars. But these symbolic gestures do not make a perceptible dent in the pollution problem. The load, in fact, has been growing. Air pollution alone has increased over the past four years from an annual outpouring of 142 million tons of pollutants to more than 200 million. Solid wastes cast off by U.S. municipalities and industries now add up to 360 million tons a year; the total is estimated at 3.5 billion if wastes from agriculture, mining and fossil fuel production are included.

Obviously the solution, at this stage at least, is not being sought in sacrifice. When it is cold, householders will turn up the heat regardless of noxious emissions from power plants; and few couples today deny themselves a baby for the sake of population control. Elaborate packaging and throwaway cans have become luxuries not easily given up. Americans typically look to experts rather than abstinence. Technology made the mess, the prevailing view proclaims, so let technology clean it up. The catch is that clean-up technology must be at an acceptable price. The engineering problems, therefore, are closely tied to the economics of pollution control.

Criticism of Slow Pace

Is sufficient technology available at the present time to maintain a reasonably clean environment without lowering present levels of consumption? The question hardly lends itself to a direct answer. Considerable technology for limiting the contamination of air, water and soil has been available for many years and more was added after the government moved decisively into the anti-pollution field.[1] The government spurs technological advance in pollution control in two ways: (1) by providing funds for research and development and (2) by regulatory action that compels polluters to develop more effective environment-protection systems.

One hindrance to an accurate assessment of the state of pollution-control technology is that the pollution problem does not stand still. Not only does the population grow, industry adds to the burden of wastes with new ingredients and combinations that result from changes in processes, development of new products and new consumption patterns of the people. What worked to keep air and water clean yesterday may not be sufficient today.

Though pollution-control technology has made appreciable advances in recent years, it is not hard to find experts who deplore its present state. "Primitive" would suit better than "sophisticated" to describe pollution-control technology now, according to the editor of the American Chemical Society's monthly journal. "It's no secret that pollution control has the least skilled work force available," he wrote. "Pollution-control technology has evolved at a snail's pace."[2]

"Cleaning up this country's air and water will be a much tougher, slower, and costlier job than politicians and environmentalists sometimes make it sound," Gene Bylinsky of *Fortune* magazine wrote. "Without advances in technology the big cleanup can only plod along at best. And there are serious lags in new pollution control technology, as well as in the readiness of business, government and the public to encourage, apply and pay for technological improvements."

Not only is technology laggard but basic scientific knowledge is limited. Scientists need to know more about the character of existing and potential contamination and of specific effects of pollutants in their multitude of forms and combinations. This knowledge lays the foundation on which technology builds. "Existing systems for measuring and monitoring environmental quality are still inadequate," President Nixon said Aug. 10, 1970, in a message to Congress accompanying the first report of the Council on Environmental Quality. These systems are needed to provide data for determining what measures are needed to reduce pollution and to assess the effectiveness of those used. "We need to know far more about the effects of specific pollutants, about ecological relationships and about human behavior in relation to environmental factors," the President said.

Existing data on levels of particulate matter in the urban atmosphere, a scientist told his colleagues at a recent seminar, indicated that they knew the exact chemical composition of "less than 40 percent of the dirt

---

1 Major federal programs in environmental protection date from the Water Pollution Control Act of 1948 and the Air Pollution Control Act of 1955. These were greatly expanded by new congressional mandates during the 1960s. Legislation in 1970 extended government activity still further.

2 D. H. Michael Bowen, "Build a Better Mousetrap" (editorial), *Environmental Science and Technology*, November 1970, p. 877.

in the air of our cities."[3] There were so many factors to be considered—size of the particles, climate, presence of different bacterial and viral organisms, interactions of the various pollutants. The damage to health or well-being of a local environment from gross contamination may be readily assessed. But the long-term effects of lesser levels of contamination are still something of a mystery. "Determining the adverse effects of exposure to very low levels of pollutants over long periods remains an urgent but difficult task," the National Air Pollution Control Administration reported. "Gaps in the arsenal of biological and medical research tools pose still other difficulties."[4]

With knowledge so limited it is no wonder that scientists differ in their over-all outlook on the problem of environmental protection. "Harmful effects on the environment or on other organisms are often assumed, without evidence, to imply biological damage in man," the director of the International Agency for Research in Cancer observed. "In fact there is a surprising dearth of factual data on these relationships."[5] He said limited data did not support the "simplistic" view that any chemical modification of the environment was necessarily bad for man. There are still scientists who protest the phasing out of DDT as an unrealistic rejection of a useful pesticide. Differences among experts as to tolerable levels of radioactivity are well-known.

Water Contamination

During the past decade, the water pollution problem has become increasingly severe. Since 1952, about $15-billion has been spent in the United States in building 7,500 municipal sewage treatment plants and other water-treatment facilities. But some 1,400 U.S. communities and hundreds of industrial plants still drop untreated waste into the waterways. Only 140 million of the country's more than 200 million people are served by any kind of sewer system. "Over 1,000 communities outgrow their treatment systems every year," the Federal Water Quality Administration, an agency in the Department of the Interior, reported in *Clean Water for the 1970s: A Status Report.*

"Fortunately, there is the technological knowledge to deal effectively with municipal wastes," the agency added. "This technology has not been applied to the extent needed to prevent pollution." Stubborn technical problems remain nevertheless. Industrial wastes challenge clean-water technology because of the variety and novelty of alien substances. "Many of the new chemicals are a challenge to detect, much less control," the agency reported. Agricultural pollution of the waterways taxes existing measures for water protection because it combines animal and vegetation wastes in a variety of combinations. Pollutants in the return flow of irrigation waters are particularly difficult and expensive to control.

The Council on Environmental Quality contends that abatement technology is generally available for reducing pollution from industrial sources. Nevertheless, it has pointed to many gaps in basic knowledge pertaining to water-quality control. A full understanding of the connection between pollutants and eutrophication is lacking. Eutrophication is the process by which an excess of nutrients in a body of water produces an undue growth of algae. Algae consume oxygen, resulting in fish-kill. Eutrophication takes place naturally in lakes but over a very long time. The nutrient load discharged into the water by man greatly speeds up the process.

Phosphates in fertilizer and household detergents have been held responsible for most of this despoliation. But recently some experts have begun to say that while phosphates are involved, other elements—nitrogen, heat, carbon—also contribute to eutrophication. Eutrophication has taken place in lakes that had minimal amounts of phosphates.

Sulfur Dioxide and Air Pollution

Techniques for dealing with many air pollution problems arising from stationary sources—electric generating plants, space heating systems, industrial operations and incinerators—are generally satisfactory, according to the National Air Pollution Control Administration. But adequate technology is lacking for "the most significant of these problems."

There is a widening gap between the rising trend of sulfur dioxide emissions and the nation's technological capability for bringing the problem under control, partly because the total national investment in research and development on the problem has not been sufficient to support all the potentially fruitful work that could have been undertaken in the past few years. Of particular importance is the need for practical techniques applicable to electric generating plants....

Even with rapid application of the control techniques now under development...it is unlikely that sulfur dioxide emissions in 1980 will be reduced even to the 1968 level. The rapid growth of the electric utility industry (from 300,000 megawatts in 1969 to an anticipated 600,000 megawatts by 1980) and slower-than-predicted growth of nuclear electric generating capacity are compounding the problem.[6]

Businessmen engaged in anti-pollution work tend to be optimistic about the eventual conquest of pollution. Karel A. Weits, president of the Industrial Gas Cleaning Institute, told the Muskie subcommittee in March 1970: "We believe our industry has the necessary skills and facilities to develop equipment to meet many unsolved problems once they are defined as problems." Equipment was available to reduce particulate emissions from industrial sources to acceptable levels, he said, though industry would have to speed up production of equipment to handle gaseous pollutants. Where profit is the motivation, he added, industry can move ahead fast—faster than government—to find the technical solutions.

If legislation provided sufficient economic incentive, Aaron J. Teller, head of Teller Environmental Systems, Inc., told the subcommittee, all emissions of sulfur dioxide—the major pollutant gas discharged by electric power plants—could be eliminated from this source within five years. "The technology is here," he said. "We are now

3 Glenn L. Paulson (secretary of New York Scientists' Committee for Public Information), "A Piece of the Action," *Air Pollution* (A Scientists' Institute for Public Information Workbook, 1970), p. 19.

4 *Progress in the Prevention and Control of Air Pollution* (third report of the secretary of health, education and welfare to Congress), March 1970, p. 3.

5 John Higginson, "International Research: Its Role in Environmental Biology," *Science*, Nov. 27, 1970, p. 935. The cancer research agency which Higginson directs is based in Lyon, France.

6 *Progress in the Prevention and Control of Air Pollution* (third report of the secretary of health, education and welfare), March 1970, p. 26.

in our second and third generation systems." From his experience in working with both government and industry, he found that "where processes are to be developed to be exploited and sold, you will find the major advances will occur in industry."

Protest of Auto Industry

Makers of products that cause pollution, either as industrial waste during production or as waste cast off after consumer use, tend to be less than optimistic about the swift attainment of goals demanded by environmentalists. Automobile manufacturers, for example, fought against emission standards provided in the Clean Air Act of 1970 on the ground that they lacked the technology to meet the standards. This measure, which the President signed on Dec. 31, 1971, requires a 90 percent reduction in major automobile pollutants—by Jan. 1, 1975, for hydrocarbons and carbon monoxide and by Jan. 1, 1976, for nitrogen oxides. Automobile manufacturers will be allowed a one-year extension of each deadline if they can demonstrate that they tried hard but failed to meet the standards in the allotted time. They could apply for extensions by Jan. 1, 1972, for hydrocarbons-carbon monoxide, and by Jan. 1, 1973, for nitrogen oxides.

Automobile officials insisted they could not meet the deadlines. "Unless the science and technology of emission control move ahead much faster than we believe is possible," L. A. Iacocca, then executive vice-president (later president) of Ford Motor Co., said on Sept. 9, 1970, "we will not be able to meet the standards prescribed by the bill." Even if they were technically feasible, he said, it would take at least two years after establishing an emission standard to perfect the technology and make necessary changes in vehicle design and in manufacturing plants.

Officials of General Motors and Chrysler took similar positions. They cited the difficulty of finding materials capable of withstanding the high temperatures required of exhaust-control devices. Another problem was the incompatability of new systems with many gasoline compounds currently in use. The oil industry has been under pressure to hasten changes in fuel composition to help the automobile industry meet rising pollution-control standards. President Nixon early in 1970 requested Congress to levy a special tax on leaded gasoline to discourage pollution from this source; on Oct. 26 he ordered that federal vehicles use low-lead fuel whenever possible and urged governors to take similar action with state-owned vechicles. The House Ways and Means Committee decided on Nov. 23 to postpone consideration of the tax proposal until 1971.

Industry takes the position that any regulation that discourages or forbids the use of a particular ingredient in a product inhibits the ability to develop more effective pollution abatement and stifles innovative approaches. Environmentalists contend, however, that without specific governmental restrictions industry will take its time developing the necessary techniques.

Industries that contribute to pollution are beginning to complain of confusion in the government's rush to regulate them. The *Wall Street Journal* on Dec. 23, 1970, described the situation as "a Pandora's box of changing and conflicting law, bureaucratic snarls and technical impossibilities." Industry officials say there are too many regulating agencies, standards shift too quickly, and there is "technical chaos" due to disagreement on the nature of pollution, the degree of danger it presents, how it should be measured and differences as to goals. Some confusion may subside now that various federal anti-pollution activities have been consolidated in the new Environmental Protection Agency. The new agency, the product of an executive branch reorganization plan approved by Congress in 1970, formerly came into being Dec. 2 with William D. Ruckelshaus, a former assistant attorney general, as its director.

Advances in Environmental Protection

Technology, the application of science to practical tasks, is a two-edged sword. "It concentrates on immediate effects and often ignores long-range environmental impact. Yet, at the same time, its inventions promise to reverse the trend toward environmental degradation."[7] The development of technology to diminish pollution has moved ahead with government regulation. Historically, the tendency has been to permit pollution until it becomes intolerable. At that point, government action is taken to restrain polluters, who then hasten to develop a more efficient method of compliance than is already available to them.

Government Action. Outbreaks of communicable diseases in the 19th century led to government action that resulted in early improvements of municipal sewage disposal systems. Filtering devices developed at the Lawrence (Mass.) Experiment Station, established in the wake of regulatory action taken by Massachusetts in the 1880s, are still useful in treating municipal wastes. Obstruction of shipping led to enactment of the first federal cleanwater law, adopted in 1886, which compelled polluters to find other means of disposing of refuse than dumping it in New York Harbor. The Rivers and Harbors Act of 1899 extended the prohibition on dumping to other navigable waters.

One section of the 1899 law declares that "it shall be unlawful to throw, discharge or deposit...any refuse matter of any kind or description whatever" other than municipal sewage "into navigable water of the United States" or place it nearby or in tributaries where it could wash into navigable waters. Another section of the law does sanction discharges into waterways, but only if they are specifically permitted by the U.S. Corps of Engineers.

The 1899 law, rarely enforced for 71 years, became the basis for an executive order President Nixon issued Dec. 12, 1970, requiring industries to obtain federal permits before they discharged waste materials into the nation's waterways. Permits would henceforth be issued by the U.S. Corps of Engineers only after state and interstate agencies certified that industrial discharges met existing water quality standards. Existing industrial plants were given until July 1, 1971, to obtain permits. New plants must have them when they begin operations. The Corps of Engineers has estimated that 40,000 factories discharge fluid wastes into navigable waters and thus would be affected by the executive order. Russell E. Train, chairman of the Council on Environ-

7 Harvey Lieber, "Water Pollution," *Current History*, July 1970, p. 29.

mental Quality, called the order "the single most impor- tant step to improvement of water quality that this country has taken."

Fear aroused by illness and death from severe local episodes of smog [8] led to enactment in 1955 of the first comprehensive federal law for air pollution control, which was followed by improvements in abatement technology. Crisis, followed by government regulation, still puts spur to anti-pollution advance. The government's new concern over the harmful presence in commercial fish of mercury, a known poison that has been discharged into waterways since the beginning of the industrial revolu- tion, has sparked a race to find a way of neutralizing mercury residues in lake and river bottoms. Among sug- gested techniques, none of them perfect, are covering the sediment with inert clay, dredging to remove tainted sediment or adding other products to dissipate the mercury.

Testing of Microbes. New or long-neglected prob- lems in environmental pollution control continually seem to rise to critical levels. Oil spills from sea-going tankers and the dumping of ship bilge are not new occurrences but the rising tide of coastal pollution has fostered a demand for quick remedies. Accidents in offshore oil drilling have dramatized the need for better systems of prevention. The open seas, viewed from time immemorial as a safe dumping ground, now are being seen in a new light. Oceanic pollution is emerging as a new problem for the experts to solve.

The rush is on to find effective ways of dealing with oil slicks. Past efforts to cleanse concentrations of oil spillage with chemicals have backfired, augmenting the damage. Much hope rests on the use of concentrations of micro-organisms, which do the job in nature but at a much slower pace than suits man. Bioteknika Interna- tional Inc., of Alexandria, Va., claims to have found the answer in a mixture of 20 different micro-organisms. They break down the oil, changing its molecular structure and rendering it harmless. The company said that tests it conducted on a Potomac estuary showed that the microbe packet can clean 100 square feet of thick black oil in four days. The microbes will be marketed in dried, frozen form.

Microbes may be put to work on the phosphate-eutro- phication problem too. Biospherics Inc., a Washington concern, announced it had devised a process that induces bacteria to consume not only organic wastes in sewage— a normal process—but to extract phosphate as well. After the bacteria settle to the bottom of the sewage (the sludge), they are removed to a separate basin where they are induced, by denying them oxygen, to emit the phos- phate. The concentrated solution of phosphate is then treated to separate it from the flow of sewage and the bacteria are returned to repeat the process on incoming sewage. This process is said to be readily adaptable to existing treatment plants.

Major detergent makers have been speeding up a search for a phosphate substitute. The best found to date from a cleansing standpoint is NTA (nitrilo triacetic acid). But questions of human safety have been raised and manufacturers are reluctant to continue its use until the government completes studies on its effect on environ- ment and human health. Dr. Samuel S. Epstein, chief of the Laboratories of Environmental Toxicology and Carcinogenesis at the Children's Cancer Research Foundation Inc., in Boston, has warned that laboratory studies have shown that NTA is taken up cumulatively by the bones of test animals, that high doses of NTA apparently caused chromosome breakage in cultured human cells, and that a breakdown product of NTA might combine under certain conditions with nitrite to form nitrosamines, which are highly carcinogenic at even very low doses.

Purifying Water Supplies. Though basic methods of treating sewage have changed little over the past quarter-century, the growing burden of municipal wastes has fostered refinements and additions. The basic methods are (1) screening sewage waters to remove large solids and the settling of smaller solids in a sedimentation tank (primary treatment) and (2) bacterial action to remove organic matter, filtering and chlorination (second- ary treatment). Tertiary treatment removes more of the undesirable chemicals in municipal sewage, but it is very costly, involving construction of additional plants at a time when many communities have insufficient pri- mary and secondary treatment facilities. Among the more advanced processes are:

• Use of lime or alum to force suspended solids to clump, speeding up separation of solids and liquids and thus increasing the capacity of existing systems;

• Ridding water of persistent organic matter by passing the effluent over a bed of activated carbon to which the organic matter adheres;

• Forcing unwanted salts from water by passing the effluent through an electrodialysis cell.

"Properly designed and applied...(these methods) will be able to supply any quantity of water for any re-use. But none of these processes will stand alone. They must be used in a series or a parallel plan." [9] Because of the expense, much of the inventive energy in this field is directed toward developing devices or procedures that can be grafted at relatively small expense on existing water treatment systems. "Ultimately, entirely new systems will no doubt replace the modern facilities of today," the Federal Water Pollution Control Administra- tion has predicted. In the future may be such revolu- tionary techniques as the use of reverse osmosis to take pure water out of waste, rather than take pollutants out of the water.

Measuring Air Pollution. Establishment of air qual- ity criteria has set the pace for technology. Technical docu- ments setting forth criteria for carbon monoxide, par- ticulate matter, sulfur oxides, hydrocarbons and photo- chemical oxidants have already been issued by the Na- tional Air Pollution Control Administration. Criteria for other substances will follow. To conduct the studies needed for establishing criteria and for monitoring the atmosphere for compliance has required the development of sophisticated instruments. These devices check both on the general condition of the atmosphere in an area and on particular emissions.

A prototype instrument capable of identifying and measuring malodorous sulfur compounds in the parts-per- billion range has been constructed. An electro-chemical

---

8 The London "killer smog" of 1952 contributed to the death of 4,000 persons. Perhaps the worst occurrence in the United States was at Donora, Pa., in December 1948. In the period of a few days, 14,000 residents of Donora and nearby communities were taken sick and 18 deaths were attributed to the smog.

9 Federal Water Pollution Control Administration, *A Primer on Waste Water Treatment* (1969), p. 14.

sensor for sampling sulfur dioxide in exhaust stacks is being tested. Research promises to provide for the first time a satisfactory device for measuring nitric oxide and nitrogen dioxide. "Diffusion models," which stimulate the movement of pollutants in the air, are being used to guide predictions of pollutant concentrations likely to occur under various weather conditions and emission rates. A "climatological model" may enable planners to forecast the extent to which the future growth of a community, or the application of control measures, could be expected to alter average pollution concentrations. A national air bank and a system for storage and retrieval of air data obtained from the nationwide federal-state-local air sampling network have been established. The National Air Pollution Control Administration is working on standardization of analytical techniques so that data from one community can be readily compared with that of another.

Two approaches are being taken to handle the troublesome problem of sulfur oxide pollution from fuel combustion: (1) to apply devices that remove sulfur from stack gas before it escapes into the air and (2) to develop low-sulfur fuels. Fuels may be naturally low in sulfur or they may be treated to reduce sulfur content. Techniques have been developed to remove sulfur from a low-grade imported fuel oil and a number of companies have been building desulfurization plants. The supply of low-sulphur oil, however, remains low. Efforts to improve coal-cleaning processes for more efficient removal of sulfur are also under way.

The most practical measures developed for application to electric generating plants are new processes utilizing limestone. In one process, limestone is injected into the boiler where it causes sulfurous particles to form. These particles can then be removed from stack gas by electrostatic precipitators. An even more effective limestone process would use scrubbers to remove sulfurous material before it reached the stack. Testing of the first (dry limestone) process was to be completed by mid-1971, when testing of the second (wet limestone) will be initiated.

Long-term gains may come from studies to achieve more efficient combustion so that less waste is thrown off. The United States and Britain have agreed to share technical information on "fluidized bed combustion," a process which holds considerable hope for stack gas reduction. In addition, the government has reviewed the testing of a number of inexpensive, commercially manufactured devices to improve combustion in oil-fired furnaces and it has singled out a flame-retention device. It is said to reduce pollutant emission without impairing the furnace's operating efficiency.

Motor Vehicle Emissions. The Public Health Service estimates that up to two-thirds of all pollutants released into the air in America come from the gasoline engines that propel the country's 105 million cars, trucks and buses. Pollution-control technology for motor vehicles, as first applied in the early 1960s to meet California state standards, dealt largely with reducing hydrocarbon emissions from the crankcase by means of a ventilating system that recycled gases to the engine intake. Crankcase "blow-by" gases are believed to account for up to 25 percent of all hydrocarbons emitted from automobile engines. Anti-pollution controls were later applied to the exhaust system to reduce its outpouring of both hydrocarbons and carbon monoxide.

To meet federal standards for hydrocarbons and carbon monoxide, beginning with 1968 models, auto makers made changes in the fuel system, redesigning combustion chambers and adjusting fuel-air ratios to achieve maximum burning of pollutants and minimize evaporation losses. One new system involves recirculation and reburning of exhaust gases to reduce wastes. A more advanced approach under development involves use of a catalytic device through which exhaust gases would pass. The catalyst would convert pollutants to harmless derivatives—carbon monoxide and hydrocarbons to carbon dioxide and water, nitrogen oxides to nitrogen and other byproducts.

The automobile industry claims that a car 65 to 80 percent "cleaner" than pre-regulation models has already been attained. The following standards were reported to Congress in March 1970 by the Department of Health, Education and Welfare:

Automobile Emission Standards

	1968 national standards	1970 national standards	1971 national standards
	% reduction since 1963	% reduction since 1963	% reduction since 1963
Hydrocarbon emissions	66.9	73.5	85.6
Carbon monoxide emissions	55.6	70.9	70.9

However, the Federal Air Pollution Control Administration, which has authority to establish national standards, expressed concern that "air pollution control systems installed in mass-produced vehicles often lose some of their effectiveness more rapidly than prototype systems do." Another concern was that increases in motor car use would offset gains from limited emission controls. Foreign cars brought into the United States by private persons would be immune to agency standards, but not those brought in for sale.

The air might be cleaner if the government required older cars to be equipped with devices now available for $10 to $20. "If the engine is in decent shape," Iacocca said, "(Ford's) system will reduce emissions by 30 to 50 percent." The air-cleaning gadgets have not been big sellers and there is much skepticism about their effectiveness, especially in the absence of good engine maintenance. Hope rests more with the sophisticated systems to be built into future models.

Some experts believe auto pollution will linger as long as the internal combustion engine remains, no matter how many devices and refinements are added. Auto manufacturers have not shown much enthusiasm for such alternatives as electric cars, steam engines and gas turbines. However, General Motors startled the automotive world in November 1970 by announcing that it had agreed to pay $50-million over the next five years for a worldwide license to manufacture a new type of German-made engine known as the Wankel. The purpose of the purchase, General Motors said, was to conduct "intensive research and development studies of the Wankel rotary combustion engine to determine whether it is suitable

Air Quality Costs, 1971-75*

(in thousands of dollars)

1	Chicago	801,300
2	New York	338,300
3	Pittsburgh	287,900
4	Detroit	263,700
5	St. Louis	257,500
6	Cleveland	209,600
7	Philadelphia	199,300
8	Steubenville, Ohio/Weirton/ Wheeling, W. Va.	166,600
9	Cincinnati	162,800
10	Buffalo	129,300
11	Louisville	114,800
12	Milwaukee/Kenosha/Racine, Wis.	109,600
13	Washington	98,900
14	Birmingham	94,800
15	Baltimore	84,200
16	Denver	67,100
17	Minneapolis/St. Paul	57,800
18	Indianapolis	46,000
19	Youngstown/Warren, Ohio	46,000
20	Boston	45,800
21	Toledo	45,500
22	Harford	43,700
23	Allentown/Bethlehem/Easton, Pa.	42,800
24	Saginaw/Bay City, Mich.	42,400
25	Dayton	42,200
26	Los Angeles	42,200
27	Grand Rapids/Muskegon/Muskegon Heights, Mich.	41,000
28	Houston/Galveston/Texas City	38,500
29	Atlanta	35,300
30	Scranton/Wilkes-Barre, Pa.	30,900
31	Kansas City, Mo.	29,200
32	Tampa	27,800
33	Charleston, W. Va.	26,200
34	Peoria, Ill.	25,000
35	Portland, Ore.	23,100

*Figures include expected cost of controlling emissions from industry, government facilities, and private households, according to conditions prevailing in 1967.

Source: Department of Health, Education and Welfare report to Congress, *The Cost of Clean Air*, March 1970, pp. 58-79.

for GM...applications." The Wankel is not only much smaller and lighter but is expected to be much more adaptable to emission-reduction equipment than the standard piston engine.

Costs of Pollution Technology

The rising demand for more effective measures to protect the environment has stimulated considerable growth in the pollution control business. "Almost overnight the market for anti-pollution equipment has exploded into a five-billion-dollar-a-year business," *U.S. News & World Report* stated Aug. 31, 1970, "That includes new devices, bricks and mortar, and engineering and contract-services. Plant operating and labor costs add hundreds of millions more."

The 1970 annual directory of air pollution firms, published in the November issue of *Environmental*

Science & Technology, showed a 70 percent growth in the number of new companies dealing in pollution control. Many of them were said to offer "novel, sophisticated and frequently exciting concepts in technology." Sales were low, however, and some companies have confided that if they do not receive orders soon, they will be out of business. The magazine attributed the unexpectedly slow sales to high prices. Expectations of a good future for this industry, however, are indicated by the decision of Dun & Bradstreet Inc. to undertake a survey of U.S. plants, beginning in January 1971, to determine the best markets for pollution-control devices in the years ahead.

Estimates of what it will cost to put and keep the environment in good order are imprecise and variable, but all agree that it will be enormously high. When President Nixon proposed in his 1970 State of the Union message that the country spend $10-billion through 1974 for municipal waste-treatment plants, leading Democrats described his plan as inadequate. Sen. Edmund S. Muskie (D Maine) said $25-billion was required "if we were to catch up on the backlog of untreated municipal wastes alone" and perhaps $50-billion if industrial wastes were added. Stewart L. Udall, former secretary of the interior, said a comprehensive program to control water pollution would cost $30-billion in the four years ahead.

Marshall I. Goldman, a professor of economics at Wellesley College, has estimated that $130-180-billion will be required to construct needed facilities to control both air and water pollution and $12-17 billion will be required yearly to operate them. However, he notes that "technological breakthroughs could reduce costs significantly."[10] *U.S. News & World Report* foresaw $71-billion of new spending over the next five years to clean up the nation's air, land and water.

Alan K. Browne, senior vice-president of the Bank of America in San Francisco, found a composite of various estimates indicated that a total of $80-85-billion needed to be spent over the next five years for pollution control, including rapid transit developments, or $300-billion by the year 2000. Whatever the actual figure, Browne wrote in *The New York Times*, Oct. 11, 1970: "We do know for certain...that the cost will be enormous and that control cannot be met alone by nickel-and-dime taxes or nonreturnable bottles...(or) imposts on industrial polluters."

Who will pay the piper? The man in the street knows that he will, whether in the form of higher taxes or higher prices. But he now appears more willing to pay for pollution cleanup than he did in the past. A nationwide poll conducted by Louis Harris and Associates in April 1970 indicated that 54 percent of the people were willing to pay $15 a year more in taxes to finance federal programs of pollution control. The same polling organization reported in November 1970 that Americans felt "the most serious problem" facing their communities was pollution. Of those interviewed, 34 percent cited pollution as the foremost problem, whereas 25 percent cited crime and 14 percent cited drugs.

Environmentalists point out that ultimately the cost of controlling pollution will be offset by savings that accrue from cleaner surroundings. No one is quite sure how to measure the pollution toll. It is costing Americans $35-billion in ill health alone, by the reckoning of Dr.

10 Marshall I. Goldman, "The Costs of Fighting Pollution," *Current History,* August 1970, p. 79.

Paul Kotin, director of the National Institute of Environmental Science. *U.S. News & World Report* calculated that clean air could save the American economy $11-billion a year—the difference between an estimated $13.5-billion damage from air pollution and $2.6-billion spent to control it.

Anti-Pollution Pricing. Economists say pollution-control technology lagged because the price system was not structured to take into account the cost of pollution. There was no incentive for manufacturers to spend more money on developing and installing pollution-control devices; to do so would merely add to the cost of production without providing for an increase in return. The editor of *Environmental Science and Technology,* D. H. Michael Bowen, has pointed out an inevitable consequence of this situation; the striking contrast between the magnificent technology of new industrial plants and the technologically backward sewage system that serves to dispose of their waste products.

Interest is rising in finding some way of putting a price tag on pollution that could be applied somewhere in the marketing system to reflect its actual cost. And actual cost is coming to mean more than specific monetary losses from pollution, such as medical expenses, cleaning bills, repair or replacement of damaged materials, and so on. It also means "social costs" on which no monetary valuation can be put. Social costs are the sundry discomforts and offenses to the senses that individuals suffer as well as the disruptions of social order that are associated with a debased environment. President Nixon reflected the current interest in applying this concept to the economics of environmental protection when he mentioned in his Aug. 10 message to Congress, "the failure of our economy to provide full accounting for the social costs of environmental pollution."

The costs, both social and monetary, could be offset by taxing or penalizing polluters. This practice would induce private individuals to refrain from practices that pollute, such as burning leaves and driving cars with poorly maintained engines. It would also motivate industry to find a way to cut down on pollution at minimal cost. Interest in cost-cutting is apparent in trade-journal advertisements of manufacturers of pollution-control devices. The best-selling devices, according to a recent trade survey, were those that promised low-cost operation as well as pollution control. General Motors' interest in the Wankel engine is attributed, in part, to the hope that, because of simpler structure, it will be less expensive to produce than the piston engine, thus offsetting the cost of pollution control.

Under the Tax Reform Act of 1969, an individual or corporation taxpayer is allowed to amortize the cost of a certified pollution-control facility over a period of five years. The facility must be certified by both state and federal agencies. Several states also provide tax relief for industrial companies to help them absorb the initial costs of pollution abatement. *(List p. 76)*

This relief is generally in three forms: (1) allowing the purchaser to accelerate the depreciation write-off value over a period of one to five years for purposes of income or franchise taxes, (2) exempting the purchase of pollution-abatement equipment from sales and use taxes, and (3) exempting pollution-abatement installations from property taxes.

Ultimately, experts say, entirely new systems for maintaining a clean water supply may be necessary. Starting afresh would be feasible in new planned communities but not in older cities where "new technologies cannot be tried...because they are incompatible with existing systems and obsolete legal, labor and taxation codes."[11] Much of the new technology is directed toward compatibility with existing systems, obsolete or not. Often the selling point is that the new device will make unnecessary the construction of an additional major facility. Controlling pollution at its sources is often recommended too; this means simply not throwing so much contaminating stuff into the air or water. A major change in the basic industrial process itself may be necessary to achieve this goal.

Low Economic Return on Salvaged Waste Matter. Where technology of the future can be most helpful, both from the environment-protection and the cost-saving standpoint, is by developing feasible means of capturing valued elements in wastes and processing them for re-use. To some extent this is already done but not nearly enough to meet its potential. It has been estimated that 45 percent of the iron and steel, 42 percent of the copper, 25 percent of zinc, 21 percent of paper, and 12 percent of rubber is recovered and re-used in American production.

The reason there has not been more re-use of cast-off materials is that it has not been profitable for garnerers of waste. Industry has usually preferred to get fresh materials rather than go to the trouble and expense of reclamation. The costs of collection, separation, cleansing, transportation, and reclamation will probably continue to be a barrier to re-use until an economic incentive can be applied somewhere in the marketing system.

Explaining some of the hurdles that lie between the city dump and the industrial stockpile, Robert R. Grinstead wrote in the December 1970 issue of *Environment*: "Two changes in our official attitudes seem called for... First, we need to treat waste material industries on at least an equal basis with virgin material industries. In fact, until the technology of recycling matures, we may have to go further and favor it for a time, using such devices as subsidies...and a reduction or elimination of existing depletion allowances, favored tax positions, and lower freight rates...." Grinstead added that if the material producer can somehow be given at least part of the responsibility for the disposal problem, a powerful brake on extravagance would exist.

Many possibilities for greater re-use are being explored. Sanitary landfill, probably the best-known practical use of solid wastes, is being extended to create recreational areas, modest hills for landscaping and ski slopes, and is even being considered as a foundation for airports on what is now shallow water close to shore. Another possibility is use of heat from incineration of community wastes as energy for the generation of electric power. The diversion of sewage sludge, with its many nutrients, to fertilize farmland is another usage that could be greatly extended, though it presents such problems as harmful chemicals and transportation costs. The Federal Water Quality Administration has committed $2-million for a

---

11 Athelstan Spilhaus, "The Experimental City," *America's Changing Environment* (1970, Roger Revelle and Hans H. Landsberg, editors), p. 222.

States With Tax Law Incentives For Pollution Abatement

Alabama. Exemptions from property, sales, use, income and franchise taxes granted for pollution abatement facilities.*

Arizona. A deduction for income and franchise taxes is granted with respect to the amortization of the facilities.

Arkansas. Certain exemptions from sales and use taxes.

California. For purposes of personal or corporation incomes taxes, air and water facilities may be amortized for a period of one to five years.

Connecticut. Exemptions from property, sales and use taxes; corporations are allowed a tax credit on income and franchise taxes.

Florida. In computing property taxes, air and water equipment is assessed at no more than salvage value.

Georgia. Exemptions from property sales and use taxes.

Hawaii. Air facilities exempt from real property assessment and from 4 percent excise tax; for income and franchise taxes, five-year amortization permitted for air and water facilities.

Idaho. Exemptions from property taxes.

Illinois. Exemptions from sales, service occupations and use taxes.

Indiana. Exemptions from property taxes, and from sales and use taxes unless facilities are constructed so as to be part of realty.

Kentucky. Exemptions from sales and use taxes.

Maine. Delineated facilities exempt from sales and use taxes; property tax exemptions for all disposal systems that produce no salable product.

Maryland. Partial exemptions from sales and use taxes.

Massachusetts. Exemptions from property and sales and use taxes; deduction granted under income or franchise tax for water pollution equipment only.

Michigan. Exemptions from property and sales and use taxes.

Minnesota. Property tax exemptions; income or franchise tax credit.

Missouri. Exemptions from sales and use taxes.

Montana. Exemptions from property taxes for air pollution control facilities only.

New Hampshire. Exemptions from property taxes.

New Jersey. Exemptions from property, sales and use taxes.

New York. Exemptions from property, sales and use taxes; a deduction from income or franchise taxes allowed for pollution control expenditures. (Exemptions apply also to local sales taxes upstate but not in New York City.)

North Carolina. Partial exemptions from property taxes; persons and corporations may claim state income tax deductions.

Ohio. Exemptions from personal property, sales and use, and franchise taxes.

Oklahoma. Exemptions from sales and use taxes; income tax credit granted.

Oregon. Taxpayer may choose either property tax exemption or income tax credit.

Pennsylvania. Exemptions from sales and use taxes.

Rhode Island. Exemptions from property, sales and use taxes; an income or franchise tax deduction may be claimed.

South Carolina. Exemptions from property, sales and use taxes.

Tennessee. Exemptions from property taxes.

Vermont. Property tax exemptions.

Virginia. An income tax deduction may be claimed.

Washington. Taxpayer may choose exemption from sales-use tax or take a credit against sales-use tax, business and occupation taxes, and public utilities taxes.

West Virginia. Exemptions from sales and use taxes.

Wisconsin. Property tax exemptions; income tax deduction allowed.

Wyoming. Property tax exemptions.

All facilities mentioned refer to both air and water pollution control unless only one or the other is specified.

project to demonstrate that sewage and factory effluent now going into Lake Michigan can be diverted to fertilize barren land in Michigan.

Recycling: Hope for Turning Wastes into Assets. Recycling is the key word in environmental protection now. Recycling involves not merely the piecemeal salvage of this or that waste product, but a totally new approach to the use of resources, which conceives of them as passing through a closed system of use-reuse, so that nothing is essentially wasted though it goes through various stages in its passage through the closed cycle.

The "closed loop" principle is gaining in practical application. Dow Chemical Co., for example, is building 28 new cooling towers at its Midland, Mich., plant with the aim of reusing 50 percent of its cooling water. A new Eastalco Co. aluminum plant at Frederick, Md., will contain a facility for treating contaminated water so that it can be returned to the plant for re-use rather than being dumped into the waterway. The current drive for returning soft drink bottles represents a simple form of recycling. Other reuses of glass in crushed form, for paving materials for example, are being explored.

To make recycling work on a grand scale that would truly safeguard "spaceship earth," it is necessary to view all of nature and all of man's activities affecting nature as parts of a single system. This would put technology into harmony with nature rather than at cross-purposes with it. As Dr. Lee A. DuBridge, former science adviser to President Nixon, recently pointed out, no one really wants to "go back to nature" in a true sense and few would forcibly stop the technology if they could. But technology is not, as some imply, an uncontrollable force; it is up to man to use it for his own good.

ENERGY AND THE ENVIRONMENT BEFORE THE COURTS

For almost a century, Americans have been used to corporations—legal though non-human personalities—going to court to protect their interests. It may not be too long before trees, rivers and mountains can do the same.

Unlikely though it may appear, this could be the outcome of the body of environmental case law developing to answer the question: "Who can speak to defend the environment against the advance of industrial and commercial development?"

Within this evolving body of law was a series of recent decisions concerning the tapping of various sources of energy and the impact of this development on the environment. No major case on this point had made its way to the Supreme Court for argument by early 1973, but lower courts had issued a variety of rulings setting standards for consideration of the environment by persons making these energy decisions. *(Box p. 79)*

Eighty-six years ago the Supreme Court held corporations to be "persons" with the authority—or standing—to bring suit and to be sued.

In the spring of 1972, Justice William O. Douglas suggested that this status be conferred upon inanimate natural objects. Granting trees, meadows and rivers such standing would allow actions threatening them to be challenged before federal courts "in the name of the inanimate object about to be despoiled, defaced, or invaded by roads and bulldozers."

Douglas expanded this suggestion—which he included in a dissenting opinion—noting that ships as well as corporations were considered "legal persons" with this authority.

But before the Supreme Court moves to answer this first question, it must deal with a second basic question in the developing environmental law: "Who has the power to set standards to protect the environment from pollution?"

Early Precedents

The Supreme Court dealt with questions of air and water pollution as early as the first years of this century.

In 1906 the court heard Missouri's complaint that Illinois was dumping Chicago's sewage into the Mississippi River, thus polluting that part of the river which ran through Missouri. The court declined to halt Illinois' action, ruling that Missouri had failed to prove that Illinois was the sole or chief source of the Mississippi's pollution.

But in the opinion, Justice Oliver Wendell Holmes set forth criteria for court action on similar questions: "Great and serious caution" must be exercised, he said, in determining whether such a claim had been proved. Before the Supreme Court intervened, he said, "the case

should be of serious magnitude, clearly and fully proved, and the principle...should be one which the court is prepared deliberately to maintain against all considerations on the other side." *(Missouri v. Illinois and the Sanitary District of Chicago)*

Air Pollution. In 1907 the court did act in just such a case of serious magnitude, issuing an injunction against the Tennessee Copper Co., ordering a halt to the discharge of poisonous gases which drifted across the state's border into Georgia where they destroyed forests, crops and vegetation. Holmes also wrote this opinion.

"The state," he said, "has an interest independent of and behind the titles of its citizens, in all the earth and air within its domain. It has the last word as to whether its mountains shall be stripped of their forests and its inhabitants shall breathe pure air.... When the states by their union made the forcible abatement of outside nuisances impossible to each, they did not thereby agree to submit to whatever might be done." *(Georgia v. Tennessee Copper Co.)*

Water Pollution. In 1921, New York sued to halt the construction of a proposed sewer in New Jersey which, New York claimed, would pollute New York Bay. The court held that the evidence was not sufficient to show that the sewage carried into the bay by the proposed sewer, if treated as the state had agreed, would create a public nuisance through pollution. In its opinion, the court suggested that such problems were likely to be more wisely solved by cooperation between the interested states than by judicial proceedings. *(New York v. New Jersey)*

Ten years later, the court held that New Jersey was entitled to an order halting the dumping of New York City garbage into the ocean. This dumping clearly resulted in the pollution of New Jersey waters and beaches. However, the court did not issue the order immediately—giving the city reasonable time to construct and put into operation additional incinerators to dispose of the garbage which was being dumped in the ocean. *(New Jersey v. New York)*

'Great and Serious Caution'

Renewed concern for the environment in the 1960s and 1970s brought passage of new federal laws to protect nature from man and a marked increase in the number of environmental questions brought before the courts. Most of these were settled in lower courts, but the Supreme Court's docket also began to reflect this concern.

In the 1969-1970 term, the court's docket held only four cases dealing with such issues; all were settled by the court without full arguments. But two years later, the number of such cases on the docket had grown to 15, seven of which won full hearings.

Two of these cases were similar to the earlier pollution controversies reaching the court. Illinois asked for permission to file an original suit before the court against four Wisconsin cities for allegedly polluting Lake Michigan with raw and untreated sewage. (*Illinois v. Milwaukee*) And Vermont brought a case against New York and the International Paper Company for dumping waste products which resulted in the accumulation of sludge deposits in Vermont waters. (*Vermont v. New York*)

Exercising the restraint which Holmes had prescribed, the court in April 1972 sent the Illinois case back to lower federal courts which had, it said, sufficient power to resolve the dispute. And in June it appointed a special master to settle the questions raised in the Vermont case.

Following this same approach, the court also sent back to lower courts for first hearings two other major cases early in the 1970s.

In March 1971 the court sent back to state courts a case which Ohio wished to initiate before the Supreme Court against the Wyandotte and Dow chemical companies for allegedly contaminating Lake Erie with mercury deposits. Justice John Marshall Harlan, in the majority opinion, held that state courts were better equipped than the Supreme Court to resolve the issues in the case—which were of local, not federal, law and of complex technical fact. (*Ohio v. Wyandotte Chemicals Corp.*)

Douglas, who alone dissented from this decision, argued that the court should hear and decide the case which he judged of "transcending public importance." He said that federal law was involved in the pollution of navigable streams and inland waters, which fall within federal jurisdiction. Congress in 1899, he noted, had enacted a law barring discharge of "any refuse matter of any kind...whatever other than that flowing from streets and sewers and passing therefrom in a liquid state" into these navigable waters.

Local Solutions. A year later in April 1972, the court unanimously agreed to send back to federal district court, for first hearing, a case brought by 18 states against the nation's four largest automobile manufacturers for conspiring to delay the development of effective pollution-control devices for cars.

The court noted that legally and practically matters of air pollution must be considered in local contexts, as federal district courts were best able to do. Douglas, in the opinion, wrote that Congress itself had declared the prevention and control of air pollution to be primarily the responsibility of state and local governments. He also noted that different geophysical characteristics significantly affected the way in which different localities could best deal with air pollution. (*State of Washington et. al. v. General Motors Corp. et. al.*)

And in two other environmental cases in the spring of 1972, the court:

• Held that states could not enact any laws stricter than the federal law to regulate the discharge of radioactive waste from nuclear-powered electricity generating plants. Douglas and Justice Potter Stewart dissented. (*Minnesota v. Northern States Power Co.*)

• Held that a federal three-judge panel was correct in refraining from ruling on a challenge to a Michigan law requiring all vessels on the Great Lakes—including those federally licensed and operating in interstate commerce—to equip themselves with sewage storage tanks. The majority held that the state courts should have the first opportunity to interpret the state law, because the state courts might construe the law to resolve the possible federal questions.

Justice Lewis F. Powell Jr. and Chief Justice Warren E. Burger disagreed with the decision, arguing for resolution by the federal court of the dilemma facing the lake vessels—"an immediate choice between the possibility of criminal prosecution or the expenditure of substantial sums of money for anti-pollution devices," which might not be required under another interpretation of the law. (*Lake Carriers' Association v. MacMullan*)

In its 1972-73 term the court agreed to hear arguments on two more questions dealing with federal power to control pollution of air and water:

• Can the government prosecute a company for violating an 1899 law which prohibited dumping refuse into navigable waters without a federal permit for dumping, if no permit program existed until 1970? (*U.S. v. Pennsylvania Industrial Chemical Corp.*)

• Do the Clean Air Amendments of 1970 mean that the Environmental Protection Agency (EPA) must disapprove any state action which would cause any deterioration of air quality? (*Ruckelshaus v. Sierra Club*)

Who Speaks for Nature?

Moving beyond the question of pollution, the court in the early 1970s dealt with several challenges to federal action which would damage natural areas and moved slowly toward an answer to the question of who could speak in defense of nature.

In 1971 the court ruled in favor of citizens who challenged the procedures used by Secretary of Transportation John A. Volpe in deciding to route an interstate highway through a Memphis, Tenn., park. The court sent the case to a federal district court to decide whether Volpe had followed proper procedures in reaching the decision. Early in 1972 the federal court held that Volpe had exceeded his authority and directed him to reconsider that decision. (*Citizens to Preserve Overton Park Inc. v. Volpe*)

And the court held, 4-3, in April 1972—without the participation of Powell or William H. Rehnquist—that the Sierra Club had no standing to challenge federal action allowing a commercial skiing development within a national forest unless the club claimed that it or its individual members would suffer injury from the development. (*Sierra Club v. Morton*)

The *Sierra* decision itself was perhaps less significant than the comments of the individual justices in their opinions, the fullest discussion to date of the question of standing: who can speak in defense of the environment?

Stewart, in the majority opinion, wrote that "aesthetic and environmental well-being, like economic well-being, are important ingredients of the quality of life in our society, and the fact that particular environmental interests are shared by the many rather than the few does not make them less deserving of legal protection through the judicial process." But, he added, any party seeking review of a particular action must claim that he himself is injured by the challenged action.

"The requirement that a party seeking review (of a federal action in the courts) must allege facts showing that he is himself adversely affected does not insulate executive action from judicial review, nor does it prevent any public interest from being protected through the judicial process," wrote Stewart. "It does serve as at least a rough attempt to put the decision as to whether review will be sought in the hands of those who have a direct stake in the outcome. That goal would be undermined were we to construe (the law)...to authorize judicial review at the behest of organizations or individuals who seek to do no more than vindicate their own value preferences through the judicial process. The principle that the Sierra Club would have us establish in this case would do just that."

In dissent, Douglas set forth his suggestion that environmental objects themselves be granted the right to sue for their preservation: "These environmental issues should be tendered by the inanimate object itself. Then there will be assurances that all forms of life which it represents will stand before the court—the pileated woodpecker as well as the coyote and bear, the lemmings as well as the trout in the streams. These inarticulate members of the ecological group cannot speak. But those people who have so frequented the place as to know its values and wonders will be able to speak for the entire ecological community."

This grant of authority was required, Douglas continued, because "most of the inanimate objects that comprise the beauty of America are under the control of a federal or a state agency, but the standards which those agencies are given to follow generally are expressed in terms of the 'public interest.' That phrase...is virtually meaningless.... The federal agencies of which I speak are not venal or corrupt, but they are notoriously under the control of powerful interests."

Douglas' two allies in dissent were Justices William J. Brennan Jr., and—in one of his rare disagreements with the chief justice, who was in the majority—Harry A. Blackmun. Blackmun saw this case as posing "significant aspects of a wide, growing and disturbing problem, that is, the nation's and the world's deteriorating environment....Must our law be so rigid," he complained, "and our procedural concepts so inflexible that we render ourselves helpless when the existing methods and traditional concepts do not fit quite and do not prove to be entirely adequate for new issues?"

Blackmun suggested that the court should:

• Send the case back for hearing in the federal district court on the condition that the Sierra Club amend its case to show individualized harm to its members by the proposed development. If it failed to do so, the case would collapse. But if it did amend the case, the trial court would consider the merits of their complaint.

• Permit "imaginative expansion of our traditional concepts of standing in order to enable an organization such as the Sierra Club...to litigate environmental issues."

And in early 1973 the Supreme Court heard argued another case presenting the question of standing. A group of students, organized as SCRAP (Students Challenging Regulatory Agency Procedures), won a court order blocking imposition of a surcharge on rates for railroad shipments of goods to be recycled. The surcharge had been approved by the Interstate Commerce Commission (ICC) which had issued no statement of its environmental impact; the lower court granted the order requested by the students on the basis that the rate increase had been inadequately evaluated before its approval. The government appealed arguing as one of its points that the student group had

Energy Decisions

In the early 1970s the federal courts began to rule that in many cases a decision to drill oil wells or to build a new nuclear power plant involved an environmental factor.

Atomic Energy. The most success achieved in these early decisions by environmental groups was in the area of nuclear power plants. In 1971 an appeals court halted construction of the nuclear plant at Calvert Cliffs, Md. The court ruled that the Atomic Energy Commission was required by the National Environmental Policy Act of 1970 to consider fully the environmental impact of the plant—including, but going beyond the radiological impact—before proceeding with construction. The court said that "the spectre of a national power crisis" did not justify a "black-out of environmental consideration." *(Calvert Cliffs Coordinating Committee v. AEC)* Later in the year a federal district court halted AEC licensing of a nuclear plant in Illinois on similar grounds. *(Izaak Walton League v. Schlesinger)*

But the AEC didn't lose them all: in 1971 the Supreme Court upheld the ruling of a lower court that states could not set stricter standards than those of the AEC for discharge of radioactive waste. *(Minnesota v. Northern States Power Co.)*

Oil and Gas. Also in 1971 the Supreme Court backed up lower courts' refusal to order a halt to government action allowing the drilling of new oil wells in the Santa Barbara Channel, site of the huge oil spill in 1969. But the government later voluntarily imposed a moratorium on all drilling on federal leases in the channel. The oil companies affected sued the government and won in federal district court; the government appealed the ruling and the moratorium continued in early 1973. *(County of Santa Barbara v. Malley; Gulf Oil v. Morton)*

And early in 1972 a court of appeals had ruled that the National Environmental Policy Act required the Interior Department to issue an environmental impact statement concerning the effect of offshore oil leases in Louisiana. *(Natural Resources Defense Council v. Morton)*

Alaska Pipeline. Environmentalists won court-ordered delays of the construction of the controversial trans-Alaska pipeline. First in 1970 they won an order forbidding the government to issue a permit for construction until a proper environmental impact statement was issued and alternatives were considered. The impact statement was issued in 1972, but in early 1973 a court of appeals ruling again halted any progress on the pipeline. The court of appeals held that the right-of-way requested by the oil companies was too wide to be legal under the Mineral Leasing Act of 1920. *(Later development, p. 22)*

Electricity. In late 1972 the Supreme Court upheld a lower court ruling requiring the Federal Power Commission (FPC) to draft their own environmental impact statement concerning a proposed project and not to substitute for their own statement that of the company applying to build the project. *(Greene County Planning Board v. FPC)* no authority to come in to court to challenge the ICC-approved rate. *(U.S. v. SCRAP)*

Who Will Set the Standards?

Before the court deals with the question of the proper spokesman to defend nature, it will reach—in the 1972-73 term—the question of the proper body to set standards for defense of the environment.

Early in 1972, the court spoke to this question in one area of environmental concern, ruling that states cannot set stricter standards than the federal government to control pollution by radioactive waste from nuclear power plants. *(Minnesota v. Northern States Power Co.)*

Backed by a dozen other coastal states, attorneys for Florida asked the court in late 1972 to rule that the state can impose stricter standards than does federal law concerning the pollution of its navigable waters by oil and other discharges from vessels and port facilities. *(Askew v. American Waterways Operators Inc.)*

Early in 1973 attorneys for the city of Burbank, Calif., asked for a ruling allowing the city to enact an ordinance restricting jet departures during certain hours from an airport within its city limits in order to protect its sleeping citizens from the noise of the take-offs. A court of appeals held that such an ordinance was invalid because it conflicted with a federal regulation. *(City of Burbank v. Lockheed Air Terminal Inc.)*

Central to such controversies are the efforts of business and commercial interests to protect themselves from strict and often expensive requirements that they act to prevent—or to pay for—pollution resulting from their operations. In both the cases to come before the court this term, the business interests have won in the lower courts: in the Florida case it is the shipping industry and the owners and operators of oil terminal facilities, in the Burbank case it is the air terminal, an airline and the Air Transport Association.

Unlimited Liability

Early in 1970, the oil-carrying tanker *Delian Apollon* went aground in Tampa Bay, spilling 21,000 gallons of oil into the bay and creating an oil slick 100 square miles in area.

Spurred by this event and by awareness of the gaps in the federal water pollution law, which imposed only limited responsibility upon polluters to remedy their pollution damage, the state legislature in 1970 enacted a law imposing absolute and unlimited liability for damages upon any vessel or port facility spilling oil or other polluting substance into the navigable waters of the state.

Maritime interests made no effort to comply with the new law, immediately filing suit to halt its enforcement.

In late 1971, a federal court halted enforcement of the state law, agreeing with the maritime interests that:

• To ensure a uniform maritime law, the Constitution gave the federal government exclusive power over maritime commerce, a power violated by the Florida law increasing the liability of maritime vessels.

• State laws such as that enacted by Florida were pre-empted by federal law regarding water pollution and the liability of vessels—limiting the liability of a vessel to the value of ship and cargo.

The state appealed this ruling, arguing:

• The Constitution does not forbid states to act to protect citizens and property from pollution damage. On the contrary, "to the extent that federal law fails...(to do this), the state has a right and a duty to legislate in the area of maritime oil-spill pollution control."

• The federal water pollution law specifically stated that it did not pre-empt state action to control pollution; the state and federal laws are not in conflict; the state law merely takes up where the federal law left off.

"If the state cannot secure a remedy when its citizens have been wronged," said the Florida brief, "the police power of the state is little more than an academic curiosity." The Florida law "makes those who traffic in pollutants responsible for damage to property and the environment which those pollutants cause upon discharge.... To deny the state's competency to do this is to assert that the ultimate burden for oil-spill pollution is properly that of the private citizen or the public treasury rather than those (who)...caused the discharge."

The state law simply enlarged the federal law: the federal law made ships liable only for the clean-up costs borne by government agencies—the state law measured the liability by the actual clean-up costs and by the damage claims of citizens, said the state's brief.

If federalism is anything more than an academic theory, the argument concluded, the Florida law must be upheld. Uniformity in maritime matters under these circumstances is merely a "euphemism for federal hegemony."

In a friend-of-the-court brief, the Justice Department argued that Florida's law was valid—except for provisions requiring ships to carry certain containment gear, a requirement which was an unconstitutional burden on foreign and interstate commerce, it said.

All the other provisions of the law were valid or could be so interpreted, the government brief said. State courts should be given the chance to remove the apparent conflict with federal law by reading the law to make shipowners liable for damages up to the maximum amount allowed by federal law.

Noise Pollution

To prevent the disturbance of its citizens' sleep by the noise from low-flying jets departing during the night from a privately owned and operated airport in Burbank, Calif., the city passed an ordinance barring jet departures between 11 p.m. and 7 a.m. The one airline with a flight affected by the ordinance, the terminal operators and the Air Transport Association won an order halting enforcement of the ordinance on the grounds that: it was pre-empted by federal law regulating air travel, it was superceded by a federal regulation concerning use of certain runways at night to reduce noise, it burdened consumers and it disrupted a uniform system regulating air traffic.

The city appealed. The lower courts' ruling, it said, allows private airport proprietors "to ride roughshod over the rights of owners of property surrounding airports...(and deprives them) of a chance to enjoy life free from constant bombardment by sound waves."

In an unexpected reversal, the government's lawyers, who had argued against Burbank in the lower courts, shifted their position and came to the Supreme Court to argue in support of the city's power to enact the ordinance.

CONGRESSIONAL AWARENESS OF ENERGY CRISIS: 1969-72

Lulled by seemingly abundant supplies of fuel to fill the nation's current power needs, Congress during the first Nixon administration enacted few bills concerning energy. But the years 1969-72 did witness a growing awareness of potentially severe shortages of fuel in the future.

During Nixon's first term, the nation's energy demands grew steadily while output of fossil fuels levelled off or declined. The United States, with 6 percent of the world's population, devoured one third of the globe's energy production in 1972, yet federal authority over energy policy remained fragmented among 64 different departments and agencies.

The nation's energy policies, of minor concern in 1969 and 1970, received increased congressional attention in the following two years.

President Nixon in 1971 highlighted the nation's growing concern over energy resources in the first message of an American President on energy needs. Warning that "we cannot take our energy supply for granted any longer," he proposed accelerated offshore leasing and stepped-up development of an advanced nuclear power plant. The same year both houses attempted to launch investigations of the energy situation, though the effort succeeded in the Senate only. *(Text p. 88)*

Extensive hearings held in Congress in 1972 on all aspects of the energy supply were marked by warnings that unless energy policies were revised and coordinated, the nation in the future would be unable to meet its fuel needs. The unusually bitter winter of 1972-73 brought those concerns to a peak. Shortages of fuel oil and natural gas—which forced some midwestern companies to shut down while others were compelled find alternative fuel supplies—brought an abrupt recognition of the tenuous balance between the nation's power supply and its economic stability.

Legislative Action

Nuclear Power. In the field of energy policy, Congress became most deeply involved in the furor over construction of nuclear power plants, brought to a virtual standstill in 1971 by environmentalists. In 1972 Congress enacted legislation facilitating the licensing of nuclear reactors but refused to free the licensing process of all environmental considerations. *(p. 82)*

Petroleum Policy. Congress also scrutinized the oil policies implemented during the Nixon years. The President's decision in 1970 to retain the oil import quota system provoked a storm of protest from members concerned with petroleum scarcities and high prices, though his action was well-received by the petroleum in-

Federal Regulations: Pre-1969

Although Congress during the Nixon years made few moves to expand federal control over fuel supplies and prices, the government already exerted considerable influence on the nation's petroleum, natural gas and nuclear power.

Since 1959 the oil import quota system had limited the amount of foreign oil brought into the United States, allegedly to protect the national security. The Federal Power Commission set the price of gas sold in the interstate market under the mandate extended by the Natural Gas Act of 1938. License applications for all nuclear power plants were approved by the Atomic Energy Commission.

Federal authority itself was circumscribed by a far-reaching law, the National Environmental Protection Act, enacted in 1969. The act—which required all federal agencies to consider the impact on the environment of all proposed projects—forced the government to consider the environmental consequences of offshore oil and gas leasing, the trans-Alaskan pipeline and nuclear power plants.

dustry and members representing states in which oil was produced. The administration's efforts to boost domestic oil supplies by increasing offshore leasing and building a pipeline across Alaska to carry its oil to the "lower 48" states were assailed by members of Congress who feared the adverse impact on the environment of those moves. *(Alaskan pipeline, p. 16; petroleum policy p. 83)*

Natural Gas. The most controversial question concerning the nation's gas reserves during this period concerned effort to approve a merger between El Paso Natural Gas Co. and a natural gas supplier. Bills to authorize the merger were lodged in committee at the end of 1972 pending a Supreme Court decision on El Paso's appeal to keep its acquisition. Congress did, however, extend for two years the deadline by which states were to adopt gas pipeline safety legislation. *(El Paso pipeline p. 23; natural gas policy p. 87)*

Other Sources. Increased attention was focused on undeveloped sources of energy which promised to meet the nation's future fuel needs. Funds for the fast breeder nuclear reactor—hailed by Nixon as the nation's "best hope" for economical fuel in the next decade—were boosted in 1971 and 1972. Congress enacted a bill in 1970 to encourage development of geothermal resources and monitored the formation of a similar oil shale leasing program. *(New energy sources p. 54)*

Chronology of Legislation, 1969-72

(NOTE: The following chronology is organized by subject matter. When action occurred in different years, it is reported entirely within the story about the bill and not in different places in the chronology.)

Nuclear Power

Shrinking domestic supplies of fossil fuels and the nation's booming demand for electric power produced great pressures during the Nixon years to harness nuclear power, which accounted for less than one percent of the nation's power in 1972.

Congress considered several measures—and in 1972 enacted a bill—to expedite the construction of nuclear power plants, which had been brought to a virtual standstill by environmentalists in 1971.

In a related action, Congress cleared a bill requiring the Atomic Energy Commission (AEC), to view nuclear power plants as profit-making commercial operations subject to antitrust laws.

POWER PLANT LICENSING

Disturbed by power brownouts and blackouts caused in part by delays in construction of nuclear power plants, Congress during the Nixon years considered several bills to expedite power plant licensing procedures.

Environmentalists opposing nuclear power plant construction focused their efforts on the requirements of the National Environmental Policy Act of 1969 (NEPA—PL 91-190). That act directed all federal agencies to prepare and weigh seriously in its considerations a detailed description of the impact on the environment of any proposed project. *(1969 Almanac p. 525)*

Carrying their objections to the federal courts, conservationists succeeded in blocking construction of several power plants. In a landmark decision, handed down in July 1971, the U.S. Circuit Court of Appeals for the District of Columbia in *Calvert Cliffs Coordinating Committee v. AEC,* halted construction of the Calvert Cliffs, Md., nuclear plant on the grounds that the AEC had not fully complied with PL 91-190.

In December 1971, in *Izaak Walton League v. Schlesinger* (James R. Schlesinger, chairman of the AEC), the same court granted an injunction against licensing of the Quad Cities nuclear plant near Cordova, Ill., on similar grounds *(Energy decisions p. 79)*

These court interpretations of NEPA spurred congressional efforts to free power plant license applications from the environmental considerations imposed by the act.

Licensing Criteria. Congress in December 1970 cleared a bill (HR 18679—PL 91-560) requiring the AEC to regard nuclear power plants as profit-making commercial ventures subject to licensing in accordance with the competitive criteria of the antitrust laws. A controversial provision which effectively would have stripped from the Environmental Protection Agency (EPA) its newly acquired authority to set radiation standards was deleted prior to final passage of the bill.

As cleared by Congress, PL 91-560 eliminated from the Atomic Energy Act of 1954 the provision which required the AEC to find a "practical value" before licensing a plant for commercial or industrial purposes. During hearings on a similar measure held by the Joint Committee on Atomic Energy in November 1969, Sen. George D. Aiken (D Vt.) had charged that a small group of utility companies were seeking a monopoly in the field of nuclear power plants. Aiken said that under existing practices the AEC licensed nuclear power plants under a "medical therapy" provision of the law which permitted them to avoid being found in violation of antitrust laws.

A provision of HR 18679—approved by the House but removed in the Senate—would have required the federal agency overseeing radiation standards to commission studies of the standards from the National Council on Radiation Protection and Measurements and the National Academy of Sciences.

Authority to set radiation protection standards had been transferred to EPA from the AEC and the Federal Radiation Council when EPA was established in December 1970. The AEC frequently had been attacked by environmentalists for being more concerned with the promotion of atomic energy than with the promulgation of stringent radiation standards. Both the council and the academy were known to be close to the AEC position on those matters.

Interim Licensing. Responding to warnings of future power blackouts and brownouts, Congress May 17, 1972, cleared for the President a bill (HR 14655—PL 92-307) authorizing the AEC to issue temporary operating licenses for certain nuclear power plants whose operation was necessary to ensure an adequate power supply. About 13 power plants were affected by the bill.

A provision for public hearings with "expedited procedures" on applications for temporary licenses was included in the bill. The AEC and the power industry opposed the provision, contending that speedy licensing could not be achieved unless the hearing requirement was waived.

PL 92-307 amended the Atomic Energy Act of 1954 (PL 83-703) by adding a new section authorizing the issuance of interim operating licenses until Oct. 30, 1973, for reactors whose applications for a full operating license had been contested. The bill specified that all applications filed before Sept. 1, 1971, must meet the NEPA requirements. (A related bill allowing the AEC to issue temporary licenses before having filed the environmental statements required under NEPA passed the House but died at the end of the session when the Senate took no action.)

NEPA Waiver. A major effort to free nuclear power plant licensing procedures from the environmental considerations imposed under PL 91-190 failed in 1972 when the Senate took no action on a House-passed measure to permit licensing of nuclear power plants prior to completion of environmental impact statements by the AEC.

The House approved the bill (HR 13752) in April but the measure was bottled up in a Senate committee at the session's end.

Many House environmentalists warned that HR 13752 marked the first step in weakening the strict provisions of the 1969 act. The bill would have amended

NEPA to authorize temporary licensing of nuclear power plants whose license applications were filed before Sept. 1, 1971, and construction permit applications were filed before Jan. 1, 1970. The interim licenses were to expire no later than Oct. 30, 1973.

AEC Chairman Schlesinger had questioned what he called the "rigid proceduralization" of the NEPA requirements in testimony in March at Senate hearings. The act's "sweeping scope, broadly stated social goals and meager legislative history combine to leave both the agencies and the courts with a formidable task of devising a workable implementation regime," he said.

ENVIRONMENTAL EFFECTS

Attempts by environmentalists to delay construction of nuclear power plants were berated by the AEC chairman during hearings conducted by the Joint Committee on Atomic Energy in October 1969.

AEC Chairman Glenn T. Seaborg charged some foes of nuclear power with engaging in "unsubstantiated fear-mongering" and said that "today's outcries about the environment will be nothing compared to cries of angry citizens who find power failures due to lack of sufficient generating capacity have plunged them into prolonged darkness." The environmental problems associated with nuclear energy were "manageable," he said.

Project Rulison. An underground nuclear explosion—code-named Project Rulison—was conducted in western Colorado in September 1969 to release natural gas located below the surface. Sponsored jointly by the AEC and Austral Oil Co. of Houston, the 40-kiloton nuclear device was detonated to pulverize heavy formations of shale and sand trapping an estimated six to 10 trillion cubic feet of gas. Attempts to block the explosion by court orders failed. The AEC said no radioactivity was released above ground, while the oil company reported in October that damage caused by the blast was minor.

The explosion was the second in the AEC project Plowshare series to develop peaceful uses of atomic power. The first blast, Project Gasbuggy (also to release natural gas), had taken place in New Mexico in December 1967.

A bill setting up a commission to investigate the potential environmental effects of underground uses of nuclear energy was the subject of hearings in November 1969 before a Senate Public Works subcommittee. Academic opinion on the danger of such activities was divided. C. L. Comar, professor of physical biology at Cornell University, told the subcommittee that the benefits to be derived from the peaceful uses of nuclear energy in a controlled situation might outweigh the often-exaggerated risks of radioactive contamination. Lamont C. Cole, professor of ecology at Cornell, said that he regarded many proposed underground nuclear projects as "hazardous to the point of being irresponsible." He emphasized the difficulty of ensuring that no radioactive debris from such an explosion escaped through porous rock or in water.

Petroleum

The major controversies which erupted concerning energy programs during the years 1969-72 concerned the nation's oil policies and efforts to secure an adequate future supply of petroleum, which provided about 45 per cent of the nation's fuel in 1972.

Congress reacted strongly to the Santa Barbara oil spill and the administration's oil import policies, but it enacted little legislation in the area aside from a three-year extension of the oil and gas compact.

Conservationists, consumers and other spokesmen assailed the oil import quota system, which was retained by the President through the end of 1972 despite strong recommendations to the contrary.

Administration attempts to speed up offshore oil drilling to bolster dwindling domestic petroleum supplies were strongly contested by environmentalists. Early in 1969 the massive oil spill at Santa Barbara pointed up the environmental dangers involved in the nation's hunt for oil.

Administration-backed efforts to construct a pipeline across the Alaskan tundra to carry oil to the "lower 48" states also were opposed by environmentalists. At the close of Nixon's first term, construction of the pipeline was blocked pending a federal appeals court decision on whether the Interior Department had considered alternate means of shipping the Alaskan oil when it approved construction of the pipeline earlier in 1972. *(Background, later developments, p. 16-22)*

OIL IMPORT QUOTAS

In the most controversial decision related to energy in his first administration, President Nixon in 1970 deferred any major changes in the oil import quota system and scrapped a report urging its replacement. Both House and Senate subcommittees held extensive hearings on oil import controls following his action.

President Nixon Feb. 20 announced he would retain the controversial quota system until the United States had consulted with foreign governments. At the same time, the White House released a 400-page report by a seven-member Cabinet task force which recommended replacing the quota system with a variable, gradually reduced tariff on oil imports.

Background. During the immediate postwar period, there had been a world shortage of oil. But by the mid-1950s, excess producing capacity developed as new deposits were discovered in the Middle East and Venezuela. Restrictions on oil imports had originated as a means to protect the U.S. domestic oil production from disruptions of world petroleum markets and thereby, according to Eisenhower administration spokesmen, to assure national security. Following administrations retained the quota system.

The system of oil import quotas first was introduced in 1955 in a clause to the Reciprocal Trade Agreements Act (PL 84-86) which authorized the President to impose restrictions on products entering the country in such volume as to impair national security. While voluntary limits on oil imports were begun in 1957, President Eisenhower in 1959 ordered mandatory controls on imports of crude and residual oil. The 1962 Trade Expansion Act (PL 88-794) established a formula regulating oil imports. *(Congress and the Nation Vol. I, p. 203)*

By early 1969, criticism of oil import controls had become widespread. In a Jan. 14 report to the President, the Special Representative for Trade Negotiations recommended a re-examination of the oil import policy to determine whether there was still a need to protect national security through quotas and, if so, whether the administration of the program might be improved.

A critical investigation of the oil industry also was undertaken that year by the Senate Judiciary Subcommittee on Antitrust and Monopoly, chaired by Philip A. Hart (D Mich.). An underlying issue was the pending proposal to create a free-trade zone in Machiasport, Maine, and set up a large refinery to provide New England with low-cost fuel from imported Libyan crude oil.

Nixon Task Force. On Feb. 20, 1969, President Nixon announced that he was assuming responsibility for all decisions relating to oil, and on March 26 he named a Cabinet-level task force to review oil import policy. (President Johnson, to avoid suspicion that he would favor the Texas oil industry, in 1963 had given authority to determine oil quotas to the Secretary of the Interior.)

The Nixon task force was headed by Secretary of Labor George P. Shultz. The other members were Secretary of State William P. Rogers, Defense Secretary Melvin R. Laird, Treasury Secretary David M. Kennedy, Secretary of the Interior Walter J. Hickel (the Interior Department administers the oil quota system), Commerce Secretary Maurice H. Stans and George A. Lincoln, director of the Office of Emergency Preparedness.

The task force was swamped with advice from members of Congress, executive agencies, foreign governments, state governments, and lobby groups. The Justice Department's Antitrust Division wanted to abolish quotas, but the Interior Department recommended keeping them, with modifications to make them fairer and more efficient. The two Departments also took issue with the argument that oil quotas were needed for national security. Assistant Attorney General Richard W. McLaren called the quota system expensive and unnecessary for national security, but Interior Secretary Walter J. Hickel said the national security basis for the quota system was a "reasonable concept."

Task Force Recommendations. In their report Feb. 20, 1970, the majority on the presidential task force recommended phasing out the quota system and replacing it with a system of variable duties on foreign oil imports, effective Jan. 1, 1971. Initially, the tariff for Middle Eastern oil would be set at $1.45 a barrel, with Canadian and Mexican oil entering at 10 cents a barrel and oil from other Western Hemisphere nations entering at $1.25 a barrel. After further review, the tariff schedule would be liberalized in 1972. The initial effect of the proposed tariff system would be a 30-cent reduction, to $3.00 a barrel, in the domestic crude oil price.

Laird and Rogers, while agreeing with the majority recommendation, submitted supplementary views stating that implementation should be postponed pending full consultation with other governments.

Stans and Hickel, joined by Federal Power Commissioner John N. Nassikas (an official observer) filed a separate report arguing for retention of the present system, but proposing an expansion of the quota by more than 100,000 barrels a day annually through 1974.

New Review. In his Feb. 20, 1970, statement, the President had announced that he was establishing an interdepartmental Oil Policy Committee "to consider both interim and long-term adjustments that will increase the effectiveness and enhance the equity of the oil import program."

Nixon said, however, that "major long-term adjustments must necessarily await the outcome of discussions with Canada, Mexico, Venezuela and other allies and affected nations...."

Reaction. Spokesmen for the U.S. oil industry generally praised the President's announcement. The American Petroleum Institute issued a statement terming the President's statement "encouraging" and declaring: "In our opinion the elimination of import controls would seriously weaken this country's ability to meet its energy needs from domestic sources and would have a grave impact on the economy of many areas of the United States."

Sens. Clifford P. Hansen (R Wyo.) and John G. Tower (R Texas)—both from oil-producing states—said they were pleased with the President's decision. Sen. Russell B. Long (D La.), chairman of the Senate Finance Committee, said he would hold hearings on oil import policy.

Criticism of the President's decision came primarily from New England members of Congress, who had led the fight to liberalize the oil quota system. Nine New England Senators Feb. 20 made public a letter to the President demanding an overhaul of oil import policy and calling attention to the high price of fuel oil in New England.

One effect of Nixon's decision to continue the review of oil import policy was to defer once more a decision on granting Occidental Petroleum Co. a quota to import oil into a refinery it planned to construct in the free-trade zone of Machiasport, Maine.

Senate Hearings. In March 1970 a Senate Judiciary Subcommittee on Antitrust and Monopoly, chaired by Philip A. Hart (D Mich.), began hearings on the report of the presidential task force on oil import quotas.

George P. Shultz, secretary of labor and chairman of the task force, endorsed the majority view recommending abolition of the quota system. The oil import quota system "does not reflect national security needs, present or future, and is no longer acceptable," he told the subcommittee. "Besides costing consumers an estimated $5-billion each year, the quotas have caused inefficiencies in the market place." A tariff system as proposed by the task force would protect national security at a much lower cost to the consumer, he said.

Joseph J. Simmons, administrator of the Oil Import Administration within the Interior Department, defended the existing oil quotas. If the country had elected to satisfy its energy needs with cheap foreign oil, the oil-rich Alaskan North Slope would almost certainly have remained unexplored, Simmons asserted. The use of tariffs to replace quotas as a control mechanism was an unworkable suggestion, he concluded.

House Hearings. A second investigation of the oil import controls was conducted in March and April 1970 by the House Interior Subcommittee on Mines and Mining, chaired by Ed Edmondson (D Okla.).

George A. Lincoln, director, Office of Emergency Preparedness, told the subcommittee that changes were needed in the existing system. "I personally believe that a tariff system can be devised which is workable and will safeguard the national security as adequately as a quota system, at less cost to the consumer." Lincoln had been a member of the President's task force and was director of the Oil Policy Committee named by Nixon in February.

(Continued on p. 86)

Congressional Studies of Energy Crisis: 1971-72

Growing concern in Congress over the sufficiency of the nation's energy resources was evidenced by attempts in both houses in 1971 to initiate studies of the nation's resource base and future fuel needs. The following year committees in both houses conducted hearings on the domestic energy supply and several proposals to coordinate responsibility for energy-related decisions on the federal level.

The most exhaustive congressional investigation in recent years of the nation's energy policy was launched by the Senate in May 1971. The task force—which included representatives of the Interior, Commerce, Public Works and Joint Atomic Energy Committees—set up under a resolution (S Res 45) held hearings in 1971 and 1972 on a broad range of issues. Its report was to be published in the fall of 1973.

In the House a related proposal to establish a select committee to investigate energy resources was defeated in 1971. A bill (H Res 155) was rejected by a 128-218 roll-call vote less than a month after Senate approval of S Res 45. Defeat followed a debate in which numerous committee chairmen charged that the proposed unit would interfere with the jurisdiction of several existing committees, particularly the Interstate and Foreign Commerce Committee.

The resolution would have established a seven-member committee to study the availability and ownership of domestic oil, gas, coal and nuclear energy reserves; reasons and possible solutions for the delay in new starts on fossil-fueled power plants, and other issues.

Energy Supplies

Under the mandate granted by S Res 45, the Senate Interior and Insular Affairs Committee held hearings intermittantly between January and August 1972 on the nation's fuel policies.

Administration spokesmen testified in January in support of the President Nixon's proposal to establish an Energy Administration within a Department of Natural Resources. "We lack the qualities of stability, coherence and centered responsibility in our policies addressed to energy matters," Hollis M. Dole, assistant interior secretary, told the committee.

A series of hearings in June focused on potential future sources of energy. Dr. Alfred J. Eggers Jr., assistant director for research applications within the National Science Foundation, termed solar energy the most promising of the unconventional energy sources.

Oil and natural gas exploration and production was examined in August hearings before the committee. Clifford P. Hansen (R Wyo.), a committee member, told his colleagues that "the solution to our energy crisis... is to stimulate domestic (oil) production." Sen. John G. Tower (R Texas) noted that in 13 years or less, the nation will be forced to rely on foreign sources for at least one-half of its petroleum needs. Tom B. Medders Jr., president, Independent Petroleum Association of America, recommended increased tax incentives for domestic oil and gas exploration.

During seven days of hearings in April 1972, the House Interior Committee was told by several witnesses that a continuation of existing policies toward energy issues would likely result in critical shortages of fuel in the future.

"We are facing a fuel and power crisis," Interior Secretary Rogers C.B. Morton told the committee. "Its implications for our economy, our environment...and our foreign policy...are broad and pervasive."

John B. Connally, treasury secretary, ticked off a list of projects to bolster domestic fuel supply which had been blocked or delayed by environmentalists, including increased oil imports and leasings on the outer continental shelf, surface mining of coal and construction of the trans-Alaskan pipeline, east coast refineries, deep-water ports to service supertankers and nuclear power plants. "There have been enough delays. Let us start leasing, exploring, drilling...and using more prudently the resultant clean energy this country needs to keep...our society alive."

Representatives of the coal, oil and natural gas industries supported programs to promote use of their products while conservationists urged that the nation conserve its energy resources.

Hearings focused on the nation's energy reserves were conducted by the House Public Works Committee in August 1972.

Assistant Interior Secretary Dole told the committee that the existing "scarcity will widen as time goes by to include nearly every form and category of energy."

Nuclear power was touted as the answer, over the long term, to the nation's energy shortages. "In the decade of the 1970s nuclear capacity is expected to increase from 2 percent of the total electric generating capacity to 23 percent, to 38 percent by the end of the 1980s and to 50 percent by the year 2000," William O. Doub, commissioner, Atomic Energy Commission, said.

Council on Energy Policy

Various bills to establish a three-person Council on Energy Policy to advise the President and Congress on energy issues were considered in 1972 but none was reported out of committee.

During hearings in August held jointly by the Senate Commerce and Interior Committees, John W. Larson, assistant interior secretary, endorsed the objectives of the bill but said that "President Nixon's proposal for the creation of a Department of Natural Resources will more effectively serve these objectives than the Council on Energy Policy. The proposed (council) would impose yet another bureaucratic layer of government on top of the large number of federal agencies which already exist."

Rep. Hastings Keith (R Mass. 1959-73), sponsor of one of the bills, asserted: "We don't have one, concrete national energy policy. We have instead bits and pieces of policies for each segment of the energy spectrum (which) need to be consolidated."

Barry J. Shillito, assistant secretary of defense for installation and logistics, declared that the oil task force analysis "clearly indicated that a relaxation of import controls over time, coupled with appropriate Western Hemisphere preferences and a security adjustment to prevent undue Eastern Hemisphere imports would... satisfactorily protect security of (oil) supply."

Several spokesmen for the petroleum industry testified on the need to retain the oil import quota system and criticized the presidential task force recommendations on replacing the quota with a tariff system.

1971-72 Developments. As U.S. dependency on foreign sources of oil increased, pressures began to build in 1971 and 1972 to further restrict petroleum imports. Proponents of that view argued that reliance on oil supplied by the politically unstable nations of the Middle East opened the nation to supply uncertainties and a possible embargo by Arab states. In 1972, the United States imported 1,735,256,000 barrels of crude and refined petroleum, 580 million more than in 1969 (1,155,551,000 barrels), according to the Bureau of Mines.

But strict import curbs were regarded as impractical in view of the increasingly scarce domestic oil reserves. The heating oil shortages which plagued the nation during the unusually bitter winter of 1972-73 provoked sharp criticism of the import controls which acted to restrict petroleum supplies.

The administration in late 1972 appeared to support that line of reasoning at least in the short run. The Office of Emergency Preparedness announced Dec. 8, 1972, that it was suspending through May 1973 import curbs on the type of crude oil—No. 2—used primarily for home heating.

SANTA BARBARA OIL SPILL

The adverse environmental effects of offshore oil production were dramatized in January 1969 when an oil well blowout off the California coast poured 235,000 gallons of oil into the Pacific Ocean, forming an 800-square mile slick.

A well off the coast of Santa Barbara—located on a tract leased by the federal government to the Union Oil Co.—burst its seams below the ocean floor during a routine maintenance operation, spewing crude oil from Jan. 28 to Feb. 8 and causing major damage to wildlife, boats and beaches. An estimated 600 birds were affected by the oil, which blackened 30 miles of southern California's beaches. The event mobilized conservationist sentiment as photographs of oil-coated wildfowl and beaches dominated the nation's publications.

Background. Seventy-two leases in the Santa Barbara channel were auctioned to private oil companies by the Department of the Interior in 1966 and 1968, netting $623-million in federal revenue. The Outer Continental Shelf Lands Act of 1953 (PL 81-212) authorized federal control of oil and gas resources on offshore lands, which extend outward underwater from U.S. shorelines as far as 150 miles in some areas. The act authorized the Interior Department to grant leases on a competitive bid system for oil and gas extraction, with lease proceeds and subsequent royalties to go to the general fund of the Treasury. *(Congress and the Nation Vol. I, p. 1036)*

Administration Reaction. Interior Department Secretary Walter J. Hickel suspended all drilling and pumping operations in the channel Feb. 7. Ten days later

he announced new department regulations compelling all firms drilling on offshore federal tracts to be responsible for cleaning up any pollution caused by their operations. Other regulations issued by the department tightened safety rules in an effort to prevent further blowouts and pollution from offshore rigs.

Hickel appeared before a Senate Public Works subcommittee hearing on Feb. 27 to defend his decision announced that day to allow Union Oil Co. to resume drilling in the channel.

Following the recommendations of a presidential task force, Hickel in June authorized resumption of unlimited offshore drilling in the channel by all oil companies having leases in the area. The task force concluded that the only way to prevent further leaks was to pump the field dry. *(Later developments p. 79)*

Senate Bill. A bill to terminate certain leases and suspend others in the Santa Barbara channel was considered by the Senate Interior Committee in May. The administration opposed the bill as unnecessary in light of stricter drilling regulations established by the Interior Department. The committee in July rejected a proposal banning all oil drilling in the channel and took no further action on the related bills.

In the first federal attempt to buy back offshore tracts it had leased, President Nixon in June asked Congress for legislation to establish a federal marine sanctuary in the Santa Barbara Channel. His recommendation would have canceled 20 federal leases in the area of the proposed sanctuary, which was to cover about 198,000 acres. Congress took no action on the administration's proposal.

Long-Term Effects. The most long-lasting result of the Santa Barbara spill was seen in the successful efforts of environmentalists concerned with the potential damage to the environment of offshore drilling to delay certain federal lease sales pending completion of environmental impact statements by the Interior Department.

President Nixon in June 1971 called for accelerated sale of offshore oil leases in the Gulf of Mexico and "other promising areas" in an effort to bolster domestic fuel supplies. A leasing program announced that month by Interior Secretary Rogers C. B. Morton scheduled at least two major oil and gas sales each year through 1975. The leases were to be offered chiefly in the Gulf of Mexico but also in the Gulf of Alaska and—for the first time—on the Atlantic outer continental shelf.

In November 1971 a group of 60 congressmen from eastern states demanded that the department cancel its planned sales off the Atlantic coast.

Three weeks before a major sale scheduled for December 1971, environmentalists filed suit contending that the Interior Department had failed to prepare adequate statements detailing the impact upon the environment of the proposed sales as required by the National Environmental Policy Act of 1969 (NEPA—PL 91-190). A federal district court for the District of Columbia upheld the conservationists' claim and blocked the lease of 366,000 acres off the coast of Louisiana. The court held that the department had not given adequate consideration to other ways to meet the nation's energy needs which posed less of a threat to the environment.

The Interior Department, however, announced in March 1972 that it was considering granting two Louisiana leases later that year after drafting new environmental impact statements. The following month it revealed that the U.S. Geological Survey would conduct "core drilling" on the Atlantic outer continental shelf as part of its "continuing mission to gather basic geological data."

Rep. Norman F. Lent (R N.Y.) criticized the department's Atlantic drilling plans as a "large-scale research effort undertaken at taxpayers' expense, the results of which will be freely available to private industry."

As a result of the district court's December 1971 ruling, no offshore leases were offered by the government until September and December 1972, when 178 tracts were auctioned for a total of $2.2-billion.

During hearings on offshore leasing before the Senate Interior and Insular Affairs Committee in April 1972, petroleum and natural gas industry officials encouraged expanded leasing of lands on the outer continental shelf. John M. Houchin, deputy chairman, Phillips Petroleum Co., noted that only 25 of the 14,000 wells drilled in U.S. waters had created a pollution hazard as a result of a "blowout." The three major oil spills which resulted caused no lasting harm to the environment, he indicated.

OIL AND GAS COMPACT

Congress in 1969 cleared a bill (S J Res 54—PL 91-158) extending for two years—through Sept. 1, 1971—the Interstate Oil and Gas Compact. A further three-year extension—through Sept. 1, 1974—was approved (S J Res 72—PL 92-322) by Congress June 1972. The consent of Congress had expired in the intervening 10 months.

The compact, first approved in 1935, set up a program among the oil producing states to conserve oil and natural gas—the product of a growing public concern in the 1930s that precious reserves of oil and gas were being wasted or destroyed. Under practices flourishing at that time, petroleum was left unused on the ground at well sites and natural gas was burned off at the wellhead. A commission set up under the act fostered the exchange of information concerning conservation practices and related problems among the 29 member states and the petroleum industry.

Natural Gas

The steady growth in the use of natural gas led to concern throughout the first Nixon administration that the nation ultimately would face severe shortages of the popular clean-burning fuel, which supplied approximately 32 percent of the nation's power needs in 1972. Although Congress considered several bills to ensure an adequate supply, no measures were enacted to achieve that goal.

GAS SUPPLY

In September 1969, a Federal Power Commission (FPC) staff report cautioned that a "major new govern-

ment-industry program was needed to ensure the continued growth of natural gas service during the next decade."

Programs to avert a possible shortage of natural gas were the subject of hearings November 1969 by the Senate Interior Subcommittee on Minerals, Materials and Fuels. Hollis M. Dole, assistant interior secretary, told the subcommittee that "a serious supply problem will be fully upon us by 1975 if current trends persist and immediate corrective action is not taken." Dole indicated the administration was increasing gas and oil leasing on the outer continental shelf while awaiting supply boosts expected from completion of the trans-Alaska pipeline and perfection of a technique to extract gas from coal. Industry officials urged the FPC to permit higher gas prices to encourage further exploration and production.

The Senate Commerce Committee in 1972 held hearings on—but did not report—three bills to help alleviate the nation's natural gas supply shortage. Two measures would have amended the Natural Gas Act of 1938 to provide incentives to producers for increasing natural gas reserves. Under the 1938 act, the terms of a producer's contract may be changed by the FPC at any time. The proposed bills would have guaranteed the sanctity of such contracts so that a producer would know what price he would receive and the amount of gas he must deliver. FPC chairman John N. Nassikas told the committee in March that sanctity of contract bills "should induce an increase in gas exploration" while an attorney from Ralph Nader's Public Interest Group, David W. Calfee, opposed the legislation as "an attempt to achieve indirectly the decontrol of natural gas prices."

A third bill considered by the committee would have directed the FPC to make an independent evaluation of proven natural reserves and update their findings annually.

GAS PIPELINE SAFETY

Congress in 1972 enacted a bill (HR 5065—PL 92-401) extending for two years—to Aug. 12, 1973—the deadline for states to enact natural pipeline safety legislation.

The 1,287 individual gas pipeline failures reported to the Transportation Department in 1971 had resulted in 45 deaths, 391 injuries and an estimated $2.6-million in property damage, according to a Senate Commerce Committee report (S Rept 92-829).

As signed into law Aug. 22, Pl 92-401 provided mandatory federal grants-in-aid of up to 50 percent for the costs of establishing state safety programs and enforcing federal interstate pipeline safety standards. Appropriations totaling $11.8-million over three years were authorized by the act. The bill amended the Natural Gas Pipeline Safety Act of 1968 (PL 90-481) which authorized the secretary of transportation to set standards for more than 760,000 miles of transmission, distribution and gathering pipelines in residential and commercial areas.

NIXON'S 1971 PROPOSALS FOR CLEAN ENERGY

Following is the text, as made available by the White House, of President Nixon's June 4 message to Congress outlining his proposals for an adequate supply of clean energy for the future.

TO THE CONGRESS OF THE UNITED STATES:

For most of our history, a plentiful supply of energy is something the American people have taken very much for granted. In the past twenty years alone, we have been able to double our consumption of energy without exhausting the supply. But the assumption that sufficient energy will always be readily available has been brought sharply into question within the last year. The brownouts that have affected some areas of our country, the possible shortages of fuel that were threatened last fall, the sharp increases in certain fuel prices and our growing awareness of the environmental consequences of energy production have all demonstrated that we cannot take our energy supply for granted any longer.

A sufficient supply of clean energy is essential if we are to sustain healthy economic growth and improve the quality of our national life. I am therefore announcing today a broad range of actions to ensure an adequate supply of clean energy for the years ahead. Private industry, of course, will still play the major role in providing our energy, but government can do a great deal to help in meeting this challenge.

My program includes the following elements:

To Facilitate Research and Development for Clean Energy:
• A commitment to complete the successful demonstration of the liquid metal fast breeder reactor by 1980.
• More than twice as much Federal support for sulfur oxide control demonstration projects in Fiscal Year 1972.
• An expanded program to convert coal into a clean gaseous fuel.
• Support for a variety of other energy research projects in fields such as fusion power, magnetohydrodynamic power cycles, and underground electric transmission.

To Make Available the Energy Resources on Federal Lands:
• Acceleration of oil and gas lease sales on the Outer Continental Shelf, along with stringent controls to protect the environment.
• A leasing program to develop our vast oil shale resources, provided that environmental questions can be satisfactorily resolved.
• Development of a geothermal leasing program beginning this fall.

To Assure a Timely Supply of Nuclear Fuels:
• Begin work to modernize and expand our uranium enrichment capacity.

To Use Our Energy More Wisely:
• A New Federal Housing Administration standard requiring additional insulation in new federally insured homes.
• Development and publication of additional information on how consumers can use energy more efficiently.
• Other efforts to encourage energy conservation.

To Balance Environmental and Energy Needs:
• A system of long-range open planning of electric power plant sites and transmission line routes with approval by a State or regional agency before construction.
• An incentive charge to reduce sulfur oxide emissions and to support further research.

To Organize Federal Efforts More Effectively:
• A single structure within the Department of Natural Resources uniting all important energy resource development programs.

The Nature of the Current Problem

A major cause of our recent energy problems has been the sharp increase in demand that began about 1967. For decades, energy consumption had generally grown at a slower rate than the national output of goods and services. But in the last four years it has been growing at a faster pace and forecasts of energy demand a decade from now have been undergoing significant upward revisions.

This accelerated growth in demand results partly from the fact that energy has been relatively inexpensive in this country. During the last decade, the prices of oil, coal, natural gas and electricity have increased at a much slower rate than consumer prices as a whole. Energy has been an attractive bargain in this country—and demand has responded accordingly.

In the years ahead, the needs of a growing economy will further stimulate this demand. And the new emphasis on environmental protection means that the demand for cleaner fuels will be especially acute. The primary cause of air pollution, for example, is the burning of fossil fuels in homes, in cars, in factories and in power plants. If we are to meet our new national air quality standards, it will be essential for us to use stack gas cleaning systems in our large power and other industrial plants and to use cleaner fuels in virtually all of our new residential, commercial and industrial facilities, and in some of our older facilities as well.

Together, these two factors—growing demand for energy and growing emphasis on cleaner fuels—will create an extraordinary pressure on our fuel supplies.

The task of providing sufficient clean energy is made especially difficult by the long lead times required to increase energy supply. To move from geological exploration to oil and gas well production now takes from 3 to 7 years. New coal mines typically require 3 to 5 years to reach the production stage and it takes 5 to 7 years to complete a large steam power plant. The development of the new technology required to minimize environmental damage can further delay the provision of additional energy. If we are to take full advantage of our enormous coal resources, for example, we will need mining systems that do not impair the health and safety of miners or degrade the landscape and combustion systems that do not emit harmful quantities of sulfur oxides, other noxious gases, and particulates into the atmosphere. But such systems may take several years to reach satisfactory performance. That is why our efforts to expand the supply of clean energy in America must immediately be stepped up.

RESEARCH, DEVELOPMENT GOALS FOR CLEAN ENERGY

Our past research in this critical field has produced many promising leads. Now we must move quickly to demonstrate the best of these new concepts on a commercial scale. Industry should play the major role in this area, but government can help by providing technical leadership and by sharing a portion of the risk for costly demonstration plants. The time has now come for government and industry to commit themselves to a joint effort to achieve commercial scale demonstrations in the most crucial and most promising clean energy development areas—the fast breeder reactor sulfur oxide control technology and coal gasification.

Sulfur Oxide Control Technology. A major bottleneck in our clean energy program is the fact that we cannot now burn coal or oil without discharging its sulfur content into the air. We need new technology which will make it possible to remove the sulfur before it is emitted to the air.

Working together, industry and government have developed a variety of approaches to this problem. However, the new air quality standards promulgated under the Clean Air Amendments of 1970 require an even more rapid development of a suitable range of stack gas cleaning techniques for removing sulfur oxides. I have therefore requested funds in my 1972 budget to permit the Environmental Protection Agency to devote an additional $15 million to this area, more than doubling the level of our previous efforts. This expansion means that a total of six different techniques can be demonstrated in partnership with industry during the next three or four years.

Nuclear Breeder Reactor. Our best hope today for meeting the Nation's growing demand for economical clean energy lies with the fast breeder reactor. Because of its highly efficient use of nuclear fuel, the breeder reactor could extend the life of our natural uranium fuel supply from decades to centuries, with far less impact on the environment than the power plants which are operating today.

For several years, the Atomic Energy Commission has placed the highest priority on developing the liquid metal fast breeder. Now this project is ready to move out of the laboratory and into the demonstration phase with a commercial size plant. But there still are major technical and financial obstacles to the construction of a demonstration plant of some 300 to 500 megawatts. I am therefore requesting an additional $27 million in Fiscal Year 1972 for the Atomic Energy Commission's liquid metal fast breeder reactor program—and for related technological and safety programs—so that the necessary engineering groundwork for demonstration plants can soon be laid.

What about the environmental impact of such plants? It is reassuring to know that the releases of radioactivity from current nuclear reactors are well within the national safety standards. Nevertheless, we will make every effort to see that these new breeder reactors emit even less radioactivity to the environment than the commercial light water reactors which are now in use.

I am therefore directing the Atomic Energy Commission to ensure that the new breeder plants be designed in a way which inherently prevents discharge to the environment from the plant's radioactive effluent systems. The Atomic Energy Commission should also take advantage of the increased efficiency of these breeder plants, designing them to minimize waste heat discharges. Thermal pollution from nuclear power plants can be materially reduced in the more efficient breeder reactors.

We have very high hopes that the breeder reactor will soon become a key element in the national fight against air and water pollution. In order further to inform the interested agencies and the public about the opportunities in this area, I have requested the early preparation and review by all appropriate agencies of a draft environmental impact statement for the breeder demonstration plant in accordance with Section 102 of the National Environmental Policy Act. This procedure will ensure compliance with all environmental quality standards before plant construction begins.

In a related area, it is also pertinent to observe that the safety record of civilian power reactors in this country is extraordinary in the history of technological advances. For more than a quarter century—since the first nuclear chain reaction took place—no member of the public has been injured by the failure of a reactor or by an accidental release of radioactivity. I am confident that this record can be maintained. The Atomic Enercy Commission is giving top priority to safety considerations in the basic design of the breeder reactor and this design will also be subject to a thorough review by the independent Advisory Committee on Reactor Safeguards, which will publish the results of its investigation.

I believe it important to the Nation that the commercial demonstration of a breeder reactor be completed by 1980. To help achieve that goal, I am requesting an additional $50 million in Federal funds for the demonstration plant. We expect industry—the utilities and manufacturers—to contribute the major share of the plant's total cost, since they have a large and obvious stake in this new technology. But we also recognize that only if government and industry work closely together can we maximize our progress in this vital field and thus introduce a new era in the production of energy for the people of our land.

Coal Gasification. As we carry on our search for cleaner fuels, we think immediately of the cleanest fossil fuel—natural gas. But our reserves of natural gas are quite limited in comparison with our reserves of coal.

Fortunately, however, it is technically feasible to convert coal into a clean gas which can be transported through pipelines. The Department of the Interior has been working with the natural gas and coal industries on research to advance our coal gasification efforts and a number of possible methods from accomplishing this conversion are under development. A few, in fact, are now in the pilot plant stage.

We are determined to bring greater focus and urgency to this effort. We have therefore initiated a cooperative program with industry to expand the number of pilot plants, making it possible to test new methods more expeditiously so that the appropriate technology can soon be selected for a large-scale demonstration plant.

The Federal expenditure for this cooperative program will be expanded to $20 million a year. Industry has agreed to provide $10 million a year for this effort. In general, we expect that the Government will continue to finance the larger share of pilot plants and that industry will finance the larger share of the demonstration plants. But again, the important point is that both the Government and industry are now strongly committed to move ahead together as promptly as possible to make coal gasification a commercial reality.

Other Research and Development Efforts. The fast breeder reactor sulfur oxide controls and coal gasification represent our highest priority research and development projects in the clean energy field. But they are not our only efforts. Other ongoing projects include:

• Coal Mine Health and Safety Research. In response to a growing concern for the health and safety of the men who mine the Nation's coal and in accordance with the Federal Coal Mine Health and Safety Act of 1969, the Bureau of Mines research effort has been increased from a level of $2 million in Fiscal Year 1969 to $30 million in Fiscal Year 1972.

• Controlled Thermonuclear Fusion Research. For nearly two decades the Government has been funding a sizeable research effort designed to harness the almost limitless energy of nuclear fusion for peaceful purposes. Recent progress suggests that the scientific feasibility of such projects may be demonstrated in the 1970s and we have therefore requested an additional $2 million to supplement the budget in this field for Fiscal Year 1972. We hope that work in this promising area will continue to be expanded as scientific progress justifies large scale programs.

Coal Liquefaction. In addition to its coal gasification work, the Department of the Interior has underway a major pilot plant program directed toward converting coal into cleaner liquid fuels.

• Magnetohydrodynamic Power Cycles. MHD is a new and more efficient method of converting coal and other fossil fuels into electric energy by burning the fuel and passing the combustion products through a magnetic field at very high temperatures. In partnership with the electric power industry, we have been working to develop this new system of electric power generation.

• Underground Electric Transmission. Objections have been growing to the overhead placement of high voltage power lines, especially in areas of scenic beauty or near centers of population. Again in cooperation with industry, the Government is funding a research program to develop new and less expensive techniques for burying high voltage electric transmission lines.

• Nuclear Reactor Safety and Supporting Technology. The general research and development work for today's commercial nuclear reactors was completed several years ago, but we must continue to fund safety-related efforts in order to ensure the continuance of the excellent safety record in this field. An additional $3 million has recently been requested for this purpose to supplement the budget in Fiscal Year 1972.

• Advanced Reactor Concepts. The liquid metal fast breeder is the priority breeder reactor concept under development, but the Atomic Energy Commission is also supporting limited alternate reactor programs involving gas cooled reactors, molten salt reactors and light water breeders.

• Solar Energy. The sun offers an almost unlimited supply of energy if we can learn to use it economically. The National Aeronautics and Space Administration and the National Science Foundation are currently re-examining their efforts in this area and we expect to give greater attention to solar energy in the future.

The key to meeting our twin goals of supplying adequate energy and protecting the environment in the decades ahead will be a balanced and imaginative research and development program. I have therefore asked my Science Adviser, with the cooperation of the Council of Environmental Quality and the interested agencies, to make a detailed assessment of all of the technological opportunities in this area and to recommend additional projects which should receive priority attention.

MAKING AVAILABLE THE ENERGY RESOURCES OF FEDERAL LANDS

Over half of our Nation's remaining oil and gas resources, about 40 percent of our coal and uranium, 80 percent of our oil shale, and some 60 percent of our geothermal energy sources are now located on Federal lands. Programs to make these resources available to meet the growing energy requirements of the Nation are therefore essential if shortages are to be averted. Through appropriate leasing programs, the Government should be able to recover the fair market value of these resources, while requiring developers to comply with requirements that will adequately protect the environment.

To supplement the efforts already underway to develop the fuel resources of the lower 48 States and Alaska, I am announcing today the following new programs:

Leasing on the Outer Continental Shelf—An Accelerated Program. The Outer Continental Shelf has proved to be a prolific source of oil and gas, but it has also been the source of troublesome oil spills in recent years. Our ability to tap the great potential of offshore areas has been seriously hampered by these environmental problems.

The Department of the Interior has significantly strengthened the environmental protection requirements controlling offshore drilling and we will continue to enforce these requirements very strictly. As a prerequisite to Federal lease sales, environmental assessments will be made in accordance with Section 102 of the National Environmental Policy Act of 1969.

Within these clear limits, we will accelerate our efforts to utilize this rich source of fuel. In order to expand productive possibilities as rapidly as possible, the accelerated program should include the sale of new leases not only in the highly productive Gulf of Mexico, but also some other promising areas. I am therefore directing the Secretary of the Interior to increase the offerings of oil and gas leases and to publish a schedule for lease offerings on the Outer Continental Shelf during the next five years, beginning with a general lease sale and a drainage sale this year.

Oil Shale—A Program for Orderly Development. At a time when we are facing possible energy shortages, it is reassuring to know that there exists in the United States an untapped shale oil resource containing some 600 billion barrels in high grade deposits. At current consumption rates, this resource represents 150 years supply. About 80 billion barrels of this shale oil are particularly rich and well situated for early development. This huge resource of very low sulfur oil is located in the Rocky Mountain area, primarily on Federal land.

At present there is no commercial production of shale oil. A mixture of problems—environmental, technical and economic—have combined to thwart past efforts at development.

I believe the time has come to begin the orderly formulation of a shale oil policy—not by any head-long rush toward development but rather by a well considered program in which both environmental protection and the recovery of a fair return to the Government are cardinal principles under which any leasing takes place. I am therefore requesting the Secretary of the Interior to expedite the development of an oil shale leasing program including the preparation of an environmental impact statement. If after

reviewing this statement and comments he finds that environmental concerns can be satisfied, he shall then proceed with the detailed planning. This work would also involve the States of Wyoming, Colorado and Utah and the first test lease would be scheduled for next year.

Geothermal Energy. There is a vast quantity of heat stored in the earth itself. Where this energy source is close to the surface, as it is in the Western States, it can readily be tapped to generate electricity, to heat homes, and to meet other energy requirements. Again, this resource is located primarily on Federal lands.

Legislation enacted in recent months permits the Federal government, for the first time, to prepare for a leasing program in the field of geothermal energy. Classification of the lands involved is already underway in the Department of the Interior. I am requesting the Secretary of the Interior to expedite a final decision on whether the first competitive lease sale should be scheduled for this fall—taking into account, of course, his evaluation of the environmental impact statement.

NATURAL GAS SUPPLY

For the past 25 years, natural gas has supplied much of the increase in the energy supply of the United States. Now this relatively clean form of energy is in even greater demand to help satisfy air quality standards. Our present supply of natural gas is limited, however, and we are beginning to face shortages which could intensify as we move to implement the air quality standards. Additional supplies of gas will therefore be one of our most urgent energy needs in the next few years.

Federal efforts to augment the available supplies of natural gas include:

• Accelerated leasing on Federal lands to speed discovery and development of new natural gas fields.

• Moving ahead with a demonstration project to gasify coal.

• Recent actions by the Federal Power Commission providing greater incentives for industry to increase its search for new sources of natural gas and to commit its discoveries to the interstate market.

• Facilitating imports of both natural and liquefied gas from Canada and from other nations.

• Progress in nuclear stimulation experiments which seek to produce natural gas from tight geologic formations which cannot presently be utilized in ways which are economically and environmentally acceptable.

This administration is keenly aware of the need to take every reasonable action to enlarge the supply of clean gaseous fuels. We intend to take such action and we expect to get good results.

IMPORTS FROM CANADA

Over the years, the United States and Canada have steadily increased their trade in energy. The United States exports some coal to Canada, but the major items of trade are oil and gas which are surplus to Canadian needs but which find a ready market in the United States.

The time has come to develop further this mutually advantageous trading relationship. The United States is therefore prepared to move promptly to permit Canadian crude oil to enter this country, free of any quantitative restraints, upon agreement as to measures needed to prevent citizens of both our countries from being subjected to oil shortages, or threats of shortages. We are ready to proceed with negotiations and we look to an early conclusion.

TIMELY SUPPLIES OF NUCLEAR FUELS

The Nation's nuclear fuel supply is in a state of transition. Military needs are now relatively small but civilian needs are growing rapidly and will be our dominant need for nuclear fuel in the future. With the exception of uranium enrichment, the nuclear energy industry is now in private hands.

I expect that private enterprise will eventually assume the responsibility for uranium enrichment as well, but in the meantime the Government must carry out its responsibility to ensure that our enrichment capacity expands at a rate consistent with expected demands.

There is currently no shortage of enriched uranium or enriching capacity. In fact, the Atomic Energy Commission has substantial stocks of enriched uranium which have already been produced for later use. However, plant expansions are required so that we can meet the growing demands for nuclear fuel in the late 1970s—both in the United States and in other nations for which this country is not the principal supplier.

The most economical means presently available for expanding our capacity in this field appears to be the modernization of existing gaseous diffusion plants at Oak Ridge, Tennessee; Portsmouth, Ohio; and Paducah, Kentucky—through a Cascade Improvement Program. This program will take a number of years to complete and we therefore believe that it is prudent to initiate the program at this time rather than run the risk of shortages at a later date. I am therefore releasing $16 million to start the Cascade Improvement Program in Fiscal Year 1972. The pace of the improvement program will be tailored to fit the demands for enriched uranium in the United States and in other countries.

USING OUR ENERGY MORE WISELY

We need new sources of energy in this country, but we also need to use existing energy as efficiently as possible. I believe we can achieve the ends we desire—homes warm in winter and cool in summer, rapid transportation, plentiful energy for industrial production and home appliances—and still place less of a strain on our overtaxed resources.

Historically, we have converted fuels into electricity and have used other sources of energy with ever increasing efficiency. Recent data suggest, however, that this trend may be reversing—thus adding to the drain on available resources. We must get back on the road of increasing efficiency—both at the point of production and at the point of consumption, where the consumer himself can do a great deal to achieve considerable savings in his energy bills.

We believe that part of the answer lies in pricing energy on the basis of its full costs to society. One reason we use energy so lavishly today is that the price of energy does not include all of the social costs of producing it. The costs incurred in protecting the environment and the health and safety of workers, for example, are part of the real cost of producing energy—but they are not now all included in the price of the product. If they were added to that price, we could expect that some of the waste in the use of energy would be eliminated. At the same time, by expanding clean fuel supplies, we will be working to keep the overall cost of energy as low as possible.

It is also important that the individual consumer be fully aware of what his energy will cost if he buys a particular home or appliance. The efficiency of home heating or cooling systems and of other energy intensive equipment are determined by builders and manufacturers who may be concerned more with the initial cost of the equipment than with the operating costs which will come afterward. For example, better thermal insulation in a home or office building may save the consumer large sums in the long run—and conserve energy as well—but for the builder it merely represents an added expense.

To help meet one manifestation of this problem, I am directing the Secretary of Housing and Urban Development to issue revised standards for insulation applied in new federally insured homes. The new Federal Housing Administration standards will require sufficient insulation to reduce the maximum permissible heat loss by about one-third for a typical 1200 square foot home—and by even more for larger homes. It is estimated that the fuel savings which will result each year from the application of these new standards will, in an average climate, equal the cost of the additional insulation required.

While the Federal Government can take some actions to conserve energy through such regulations, the consumer who seeks the most for his energy dollar in the marketplace is the one who

---

1973 Energy Message

The White House announced on Feb. 23, 1973, that President Nixon would send Congress a special message on energy in several weeks. The text, expected sooner, had been delayed because of the complexity of the subject and because the large number of government agencies involved had not been able to agree on recommendations to the President. *(Box p. 3)*

The President Feb. 15 sent Congress a message on natural resources. Following are excerpts from that message concerning energy:

One of the highest priorities of my Administration during the coming year will be a concern for energy supplies—a concern underscored this winter by occasional fuel shortages. We must face up to a stark fact in America: we are now consuming more energy than we produce.

A year and a half ago I sent to the Congress the first Presidential message ever devoted to the energy question. I shall soon submit a new and far more comprehensive energy message containing wide-ranging initiatives to ensure necessary supplies of energy at acceptable economic and environmental costs. In the meantime, to help meet immediate needs, I have temporarily suspended import quotas on home heating oil east of the Rocky Mountains.

As we work to expand our supplies of energy, we should also recognize that we must balance those efforts with our concern to preserve our environment. In the past, as we have sought new energy sources, we have too often damaged or despoiled our land. Actions to avoid such damage will probably aggravate our energy problems to some extent and may lead to higher prices. But all development and use of energy sources carries environmental risks, and we must find ways to minimize those risks while providing adequate supplies of energy. I am fully confident that we can satisfy both of these imperatives.

---

can have the most profound influence. I am therefore asking my Special Assistant for Consumer Affairs—in cooperation with industry and appropriate Government agencies—to gather and publish additional information in this field to help consumers focus on the operating costs as well as the initial cost of energy intensive equipment.

In addition, I would note that the Joint Board on Fuel Supply and Fuel Transport chaired by the Director of the Office of Emergency Preparedness is developing energy conservation measures for industry, government, and the general public to help reduce energy use in times of particular shortage and during pollution crises.

POWER PLANT SITING

If we are to meet growing demands for electricity in the years ahead, we cannot ignore the need for many new power plants. These plants and their associated transmission lines must be located and built so as to avoid major damage to the environment, but they must also be completed on time so as to avoid power shortages. These demands are difficult to reconcile—and often they are not reconciled well. In my judgment the lesson of the recent power shortages and of the continuing disputes over power plant siting and transmission line routes is that the existing institutions for making decisions in this area are not adequate for the job. In my Special Message to the Congress on the Environment last February, I proposed legislation which would help to alleviate these problems through longer range planning by the utilities and through the establishment of State or regional agencies to license new bulk power facilities prior to their construction.

Hearings are now being held by the Interstate and Foreign Commerce Committee of the House of Representatives concerning these proposals and other measures which would provide an open planning and decision-making capacity for dealing with these matters. Under the administration bill, long-range expansion plans would be presented by the utilities ten years before construction was scheduled to begin, individual alternative power plant sites would be identified five years ahead, and detailed design and location of specific plants and transmission lines would be considered two years in advance of construction. Public hearings would be held far enough ahead of construction so that they could influence the siting decision, helping to avoid environmental problems without causing undue construction delays. I urge the Congress to take prompt and favorable action on this important legislative proposal. At the same time steps will be taken to ensure that Federal licenses and permits are handled as expeditiously as possible.

THE ROLE OF THE SULFUR OXIDES EMISSIONS CHARGE

In my environmental message last February I also proposed the establishment of a sulfur oxides emissions charge. The emissions charge would have the effect of building the cost of sulfur oxide pollution into the price of energy. It would also provide a strong economic incentive for achieving the necessary performance to meet sulfur oxide standards.

The funds generated by the emissions charge would be used by the Federal Government to expand its programs to improve environmental quality, with special emphasis on the development of adequate supplies of clean energy.

GOVERNMENT REORGANIZATION—AN ENERGY ADMINISTRATION

But new programs alone will not be enough. We must also consider how we can make these programs do what we intend them to do. One important way of fostering effective performance is to place responsibility for energy questions in a single agency which can execute and modify policies in a comprehensive and unified manner.

The Nation has been without an integrated energy policy in the past. One reason for this situation is that energy responsibilities are fragmented among several agencies. Often authority is divided according to types and uses of energy. Coal, for example, is handled in one place, nuclear energy in another—but responsibility for considering the impact of one on the other is not assigned to any single authority. Nor is there any single agency responsible for developing new energy sources such as solar energy or new conversion systems such as the fuel cell. New concerns—such as conserving our fossil fuels for non-fuel uses—cannot receive the thorough and thoughtful attention they deserve under present arrangements.

The reason for all these deficiencies is that each existing program was set up to meet a specific problem of the past. As a result, our present structure is not equipped to handle the relationships between these problems and the emergence of new concerns.

The need to remedy these problems becomes more pressing every day. For example, the energy industries presently account for some 20 percent of our investment in new plant and equipment. This means that inefficiencies resulting from uncoordinated government programs can be very costly to our economy. It is also true that energy sources are becoming increasingly interchangeable. Coal can be converted to gas, for example, and even to synthetic crude oil. If the Government is to perform adequately in the energy field, then it must act through an agency which has sufficient strength and breadth of responsibility.

Accordingly, I have proposed that all of our important Federal energy resource development programs be consolidated within the new Department of Natural Resources.

The single energy authority which would thus be created would be better able to clarify, express, and execute Federal energy policy than any unit in our present structure. The estab-

lishment of this new entity would provide a focal point where energy policy in the executive branch could be harmonized and rationalized.

One of the major advantages of consolidating energy responsibilities would be the broader scope and greater balance this would give to research and development work in the energy field. The Atomic Energy Commission, for instance, has been successful in its mission of advancing civilian nuclear power, but this field is now intimately interrelated with coal, oil and gas, and Federal electric power programs with which the Atomic Energy Commission now has very little to do. We believe that the planning and funding of civilian nuclear energy activities should now be consolidated with other energy efforts in an agency charged with the mission of insuring that the total energy resources of the nation are effectively utilized. The Atomic Energy Commission would still remain intact, in order to execute the nuclear programs and any related energy research which may be appropriate as part of the overall energy program of the Department of Natural Resources.

Until such time as this new Department comes into being, I will continue to look to the Energy Subcommittee of the Domestic Council for leadership in analyzing and coordinating overall energy policy questions for the executive branch.

Conclusion

The program I have set forth today provides the basic ingredients for a new effort to meet our clean energy needs in the years ahead.

The success of this effort will require the cooperation of the Congress and of the State and local governments. It will also depend on the willingness of industry to meet its responsibilities in serving customers and in making necessary capital investments to meet anticipated growth. Consumers, too, will have a key role to play as they learn to conserve energy and as they come to understand that the cost of environmental protection must, to a major extent, be reflected in consumer prices.

I am confident that the various elements of our society will be able to work together to meet our clean energy needs. And I am confident that we can therefore continue to know the blessings of both a high-energy civilization and a beautiful and healthy environment.

(Nuclear Power continued from p. 53)
David J. Rose, director of long-range planning at Oak Ridge, wrote recently that no fusion experiment had exhibited "scientific feasibility." Yet, he added, "I will bet a modest amount of even money on success of the Tokamak in the next few years.... My own guess is that fusion power will be available in appreciable quantity by 2000." [11] Rose noted that more optimistic persons believe fusion power will be available by 1990 while "pessimists propose never."

T. J. Thompson, a member of the AEC, cautioned recently that the fusion reactor will not be hazard-free. While it will not involve a "critical mass" as nuclear power plants do, "it will not do away with the need to be careful of radioactivity and the need to store radioactive waste products."

Thompson suggested that scientists direct all their energies to a demonstration of the feasibility of controlled fusion, "even at the expense of some other desirable but non-vital elements of the program." This indeed appears to be the next step in the evolution of fusion power.

---

[11] David J. Rose, "Controlled Nuclear Fusion: Status and Outlook," *Science*, May 21, 1971, pp. 797-808.